MANAGING SUCCESSFUL LEARNING

A Practical Guide for Teachers and Trainers

ROBYN PETERSON

For Mum

First published in 1992

Kogan Page Limited
120 Pentonville Road
London N1 9JN

British Library Cataloguing in Publication Data

A CIP record for this book is available from the British Library.

ISBN 0 7494 0547 3

Typeset by the author on a Macintosh system
Printed and bound in Great Britain by Biddles Ltd,
Guildford and Kings Lynn

Contents

Preface

The contents of this book reflect years of practical experience in delivering training and education programmes in a variety of locations and organizations. I hope they may also reflect good academic standards within the field of learning theory.

In many ways I've tried to bridge the gap between the academic and the practical in writing this book. So I hope it will be of value to teachers in academic settings as well as instructors in business and industry.

Many people have offered their suggestions and valuable ideas over the years. Unfortunately, I can only recognize a few of them here. In particular I received good advice and challenging thoughts from Sylvia Balfour, Gord Bonner, Doug Clark, Richard Guerrier, Patrick Suessmuth, Tony Cunningham, Alfred LeGresley, Holland Peterson and Bill Cumberland. Special thanks are due also to Bill Reddin for his encouraging recognition of this work. And I must also mention the solid emotional support given by Gwendolyn Dainty and Helena Glawdan.

As always, errors in writing style or content must be my responsibility. I only hope that you will find few or none.

Dolores Black at Kogan Page has provided friendly and attentive support throughout the process of turning manuscript into published text. Her suggestions and advice have been invaluable. Likewise, the suggestions and comments made by Robert Jones at Kogan Page proved most productive.

My wish is that you will find this a productive resource and practical reference for meeting the many different instructional challenges that are out there. May you encourage much good learning.

Robyn Peterson
November, 1991

Introduction

The central theme of this book is helping instructors deal with learners in all their diversity to achieve quality results through instructing.

From the start you deal with the meaning and implications of instructing. Then you go through specific guidelines to use in assessing instructional styles. The issues of human motivation, receive solid attention as part of this. Trust comes through as a crucial element here as well.

In the middle of the book you find detailed explanations for planning and delivering excellent instruction. Learner needs, different learning styles, instructional strategies, learning objectives, lesson planning, and positive guidance all receive solid attention and explanation.

You will also find in this book important information and tips for using your voice effectively. Additionally you'll find detailed information and practical instruction for using and responding to questions effectively in your instructional work.

Thirty-four capsule descriptions of different teaching methods appear in Chapter 11. These give you enough information to get you started in using each method, or at least enough to remind you of what each method should entail.

You will also find in this book practical solutions to use in dealing with 'disaster' situations that can actually befall any instructor. The central theme for dealing with these is 'don't panic — think!'

In the final chapter you find an extensive table to use that will help you deal with a wide range of audiovisual media.

In working with this book you should find areas that you will want to come back to from time to time as you deal with new instructional challenges. The extensive index at the back will help you do this. Additionally, the further references listed at the back will provide you with other resources you can consult to help you expand your skills and your instructional creativity.

You're offered here a rich resource to serve you well for years to come. Teaching can be highly rewarding work. The intent of this book is to help you reap the rewards in full.

1 Instructing

You can look at the task of instructing in two lights. View it as a process of simply giving information or orders, or see it as a process for helping people learn. If you're really interested in being an instructor, then your concern must be with helping people learn.

You might also use the word *teaching* here. But this word is loaded with stiff academic connotations in the minds of many. People tend to connect the word *teacher* with primary and secondary schools. You can use the word *instructing*, however, in many different academic settings and in the business world without causing too many misconceptions. We'll use it most of the time here.

Consider the instructing process shown in Figure 1.

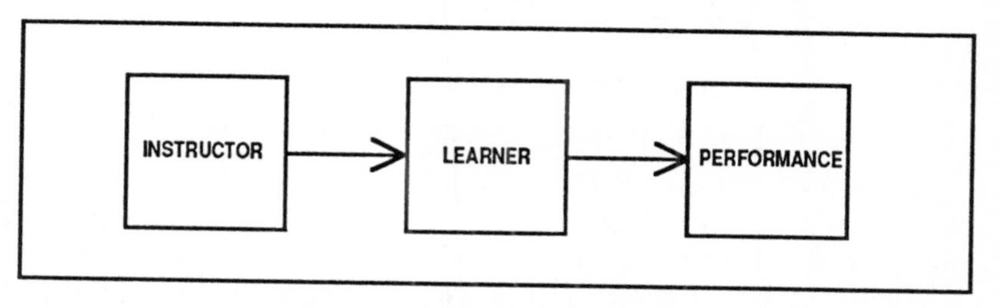

Figure 1 : *Basic Instructional Process*

This diagram is 'open loop', or one way. No provision exists for feedback. It shows the instructor pushing the learner into providing performance. Unfortunately, different people and organizations all too often use this basic design. The assumption appears to be that good learning will automatically take place if the instructor says and does the 'right' things.

The 'right' things often boil down to speaking well, using good illustrations, and 'coming across' well. These things may be desirable, but they do not necessarily equate with good learning. Sometimes they just make for an interesting performance or display.

Good learning almost always occurs only when you have good feedback from and about your learners. You need to know how they are doing and whether or not they are 'on track'. Further, in any kind of longer range instructional process, you need an achievement record of some type for each learner.

Figure 2 shows the instructional process with feedback built in.

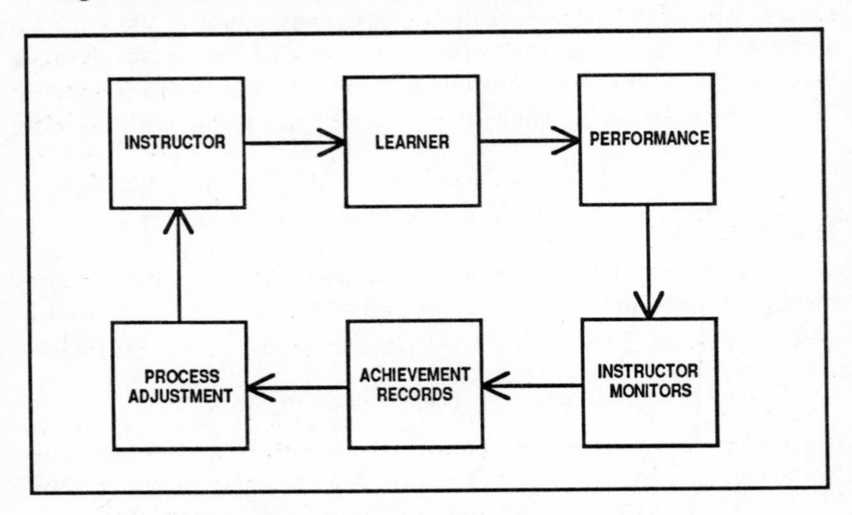

Figure 2: *Complete instructional process*

Now we have a closed loop or two-way process. Notice too that we have a stage for 'instructor monitors' and another for 'process adjustment'. These are important additions.

Whenever you instruct others, you should always plan for and use some form of monitoring. You need to know what is going on in your own lesson. You can achieve this by asking questions, giving performance assignments, or simply being alert for things happening that will tell you how well learning is occurring.

Many managers today are urged to engage in 'management by walking around', or MBWA. As an instructor you can and should also engage in MBWA, only you can think of it as 'monitoring by walking around'.

The 'process adjustment' part of Figure 2 provides for change during the instructional process. It can occur in the context of the lesson or in the context of a complete course. Some instructors can adjust things within minutes based on their monitoring of learners. Experienced instructors often adjust their approaches automatically without having to think about it. A key point here is never to allow any instructional design, no matter how elegant or expensive it may be, to override actual learner performance.

Achievement records in instructing are important, although they are not usually maintained adequately. These records should show clearly what learners have actually done and when. They should focus clearly on the individual learner.

When you're instructing, always consider achievement records for your learners, even if you can only maintain such records mentally. Performance by your learners forms the whole justification for your instructing in the first place. Without adequate learner performance, your instructing could amount to so much noise.

Instructing defined

Instructing should be defined as the process of helping learning to occur. More precisely, you can define it as:

The process of helping learning to occur according to pre-set learning objectives.

In planning for effective learning, your task as an instructor is to provide learning events or experiences that will enable the learner to acquire new skills or knowledge virtually automatically. This is not necessarily easy, but with imagination, care and deftness, you will manage.

If you think back into your own past as a learner, you will probably find that good learning experiences stand out clearly for you because they involved interesting events that somehow brought out new skills from you, or opened up new ideas for you in exciting ways. Your goal as an instructor should be to try to provide similar kinds of events for your own learners.

Using objectives

Objectives are important for instructing. You need a clear idea of what you want your learners to achieve. And you must identify tangible achievements, not fuzzy ones. Good objectives focus on performance. What do you want your learners to do, and when? Further, good learning objectives require standards and conditions: 'Given ... the learner will ...'.

Performance-based objectives do involve some hazards for good instructing. They can lead to an instructional process that is too mechanical and linear. They can cause too much focusing on unimportant behaviours. And they can lead to a certain dehumanizing of instructors and learners.

Keep these hazards in mind when you design and use learning objectives. This way you'll produce objectives that are most likely to produce the results you want.

Letting learners achieve

Providing learning is more of an art than a science, although modern technology does offer you an intriguing array of media to use. The very availability and lure of technology, however, makes it all the more important to emphasize human needs and human characteristics in your instructing.

Modern brain research shows that the human brain does not learn in a neat, orderly way. It is highly eclectic, gathering bits and pieces from all over to make productive new connections. Even under hypnosis the brain can be leaping about considering several different thoughts all at the same time. In essence, the brain makes its own connections in its own ways.

In dealing with your learners, bear in mind the importance of 'allowing them to achieve'. You cannot force them to achieve, but you can provide events and circumstances that will allow them to achieve. And this allowance means having learners achieve in their own ways and, if possible, in their own time.

Learning tends to occur best in a relatively relaxed atmosphere. This sets the stage for flexibility and individual comfort. Your actions as the instructor go far towards establishing and maintaining a relaxed atmosphere.

Once learners are relaxed, you can make sure they have some specific tasks to work on and some tangible goals to reach. Achieving relaxation for learning purposes does not mean simply letting people sit back comfortably. The idea is to achieve a sense of focus and task orientation without making people feel brutally driven.

Involving learners

Practical learner involvement is an important aspect of good instructing. Some say it's the most important. When you get your hands on something your brain quickly acquires vital information to help it fully grasp a learning event. The word 'grasp' itself helps to underline the need for truly getting in touch with learning. Signals zip up to your cortex where they're slotted and considered in light of your previous or associated learning. In this process learning 'takes' and directly influences performance.

When designing learning sessions, always look for ways to involve your learners. And be sure to make this involvement meaningful. With few exceptions, you don't want it to come across as frivolous or superficial. It should connect solidly with the learning objectives involved.

Instructing means learning

Instructing is focused on learning. Without learning, the instructing process is so much noise. An instructor can talk, perform, and use many different technical aids, and still not be instructing if learning is not taking place. This point is easy to say, but it can take some work to put into practice.

Because human beings are so good at learning in a wide variety of situations, poor quality instructing can survive quite well. The comment, *well they did learn something*, seems to satisfy many managers. But this kind of comment stands in the way of finding out whether the instructing involved is all it should be. Poor instruction that is covered up has serious consequences for quality and productivity.

Often the instructor and the learner may be the same person. Self-instruction is the most prevalent form of instruction. We're really learning creatures. No matter where we are, we're always learning something. You notice this especially with children. They're like learning sponges, soaking up learning eagerly and effortlessly to the limits of their brain capacities.

Given the prevalence of self-instruction, you can say that we've all got lots of instructional experience. The trick is to tap into this experience willingly and wisely.

Adult learning

Because of our built-in capacity to learn automatically, the central dilemma of adult education is 'unlearning'. Depending on their experience and education, adults often have to unlearn what they've learnt already, especially in rapidly changing situations. You might say we need re-programming now and then.

For the instructor the crucial thing here is to be on the lookout for areas where adults may need help in unlearning things. Allowance must be made for this before expecting them to learn new things.

At times you can look for bridges between the old and the new. In learning to use a microcomputer, for instance, the keyboard can serve as a learning bridge. People often are familiar with typewriter keyboards. So they can learn to work with their computers through using this familiar device in a new structure.

The most important thing here is to remember that adults can and do learn very well. But you must respect their experience and existing knowledge. And you must deal with them flexibly on the level of equal working with equal. Given respect and cooperation, adults will gladly help you to be their instructor.

Learning to instruct

As an instructor you have an ethical responsibility to relate as well as you can to the learning needs of each of your learners. You require a high degree of sensitivity to them as human beings. And you have to take care in what you say and do. The dignity, self-worth, and capability of each of your learners demand this sensitivity and care. Instructors who ignore these considerations should not be entrusted with instructing others, even at relatively low levels of instructing.

Good learning helps a person to grow as a human being. The process is natural and positive. As an instructor you play an important role in someone's life. And you may influence others far beyond your own realization.

The task of instructing is not a simple one. You cannot learn it quickly. But you can nurture it and develop it over an extended period of time. Ultimately, this careful growth process will benefit you personally and all of those who work with you as learners.

2 Instructing for Individual Learning

The way you learn is unique. Your style of learning may, in its details, be as unique to you as your fingerprints. You like to take in new information in certain ways. You like to have a given amount of lighting, and have it provided in specific forms. You relate to special colours and shadings of colours. You prefer particular sounds and enjoy listening to certain things. In many ways your style or pattern of learning reflects your individuality in this world.

Each of the learners you instruct is just as unique in learning style as you. Always bear this in mind. A teaching method that works very well for one learner may be disastrous for another.

Experience will lead learners to expect certain things to occur in their learning. This expectation affects the success or failure of a training or education programme, often profoundly. If your learners decide you're not doing the kinds of things they believe an instructor should do, they may refuse to learn from your lessons. They might not realize they're reacting this way, as it could occur non-consciously. Even so, your learners could really believe that your failure to apply the 'rituals' they've come to expect from an instructor means you have nothing of value to teach them.

Mass learning

By and large most school systems tend to ignore learner uniqueness, though they might talk about it, or pay it wonderful lip service. The imperatives of so-called educational efficiency dictate the use of methods and structures designed to promote mass learning.

Mass learning is a hit or miss affair. The approaches used may meet the needs of most learners some of the time. They may even meet the needs of a minority of learners all of the time. But they certainly don't come close to meeting the needs of all learners all the time.

Under mass learning conditions teachers usually are so structured or limited that they cannot give sufficient individual attention to their learners. Sometimes this leads to learners turning to each other for advice and support. But some learners will become so discouraged that they will drop out of the system entirely.

Learners from families that encourage learning automatically have the advantage over learners from families that offer meagre support. The more massive and impersonal the education system, the more family resources make a difference.

Learning disability

In many cases the singularity of your learning style is rendered more unique by the possibility of some form of learning impairment. Some authorities estimate that 40 percent of the students in any given school suffer from some sort of learning disability. Hearing problems, sight problems, emotional problems, physical disabilities, and so on, can interfere strongly with someone's ability to learn.

Training and the education model

Business and industry too often imitate the mass learning practices of the formal education system in their training activities. But their results have not been as uneven as those attained by the schools. This occurs because learners in company training programmes are employees. They've been selected because they possess common needs. So they have a better grasp of their learning goals, and are more likely to push for success.

Our learning styles

Learners differ in the way they use their senses. Many people are highly visual. They relate to pictures and images. Pleasing colours and designs appeal to them. They want, literally, to get the picture.

Other people relate strongly to sound. They like to hear things. Music, well-turned phrases, interesting rhythms, freedom from disruptive noises, and so on, appeal to them. They will lend their ears to you.

Some people like touching things. They make strong use of their kinaesthetic sense. They push, prod, stroke, manipulate, and generally get their hands on what they're learning. They like to have something highly tangible to work with. They want to get the feel of whatever is going on.

Numbers of people relate well to taste. They distinguish readily between sweet and sour, bitter or salty. They may not want to eat what they learn, but they understand feelings of sourness, or the idea that events could leave a bitter taste in their mouths. They might also use an expression such as, 'I just ate it up', to indicate strong interest in something.

Some people are highly sensitive to smells. Certain smells have automatic associations for them. Bad smells or overwhelming smells could actually block them from effective learning. As part of our ancient brain heritage smells go instantly from the nose to the olfactory area of the brain. This area is located immediately above the nose. The brain mediates and transforms all of our other primary senses. But smells go straight in without interference. So we can react to smells swiftly. And we react to smells without always realizing we're doing so.

Other people are primarily intellectualizers. They relate to abstract words and concepts. They like to play around with ideas. Pure thought for them is most appealing. As learners they may seem remote from things, almost ethereal. You may see their eyes glaze over as they drift off into the distance on flights of thought.

Many people are active explorers in their learning. They like to wander around and poke into things. They don't like to deal with things second-hand. They want to see for themselves. Explorers can become restless in learning situations if they're forced to remain still or to remain in a confined area. This may be one of the reasons why boys can experience a lot of trouble in conventional schools. The male brain often seems to check things out directly rather than relying on descriptions from others. The female brain more often appears to check things out based on information received from others.

The whole area of sex differences opens up another large area of learning differences. Sex differences in learning have not been clearly established. Our knowledge at the moment involves apparent tendencies, and many of these could arise from environmental rather than biological factors. It's still an interesting area for exploration and discovery. Perhaps it always will be.

Some people are information acceptors. They can be quite happy to learn about things from listening to others, from reading books, or from watching video programmes. They may well prefer to receive a lot of information about a new skill or a new item of equipment before actually working with it.

Some people are holistic in their learning. They see whole structures based on fragments of information. Sometimes, of course, the whole structure they think they see may be faulty. Nevertheless, they do like to have a general idea right from the start of where things will take them in a given learning situation.

Other people are segmenters or incrementalists. They're content to bite on one chunk of learning at a time, confident that a succession of chunks will gradually reveal a pattern. They believe each segment adds to their learning in some way.

Some people are rational in their learning approach. They want to know the logic of each step or event in their learning. Why is it important? They become impatient if activities or information seem vague or unconnected. They place high value on clearly demonstrated information or skills.

Other characteristics of different learning styles exist. Enough have been set out here to illustrate the phenomenon. Numbers of standardized tests exist to provide more definite means of helping reveal our individual styles. Simpler tests can, however, give you a preliminary feel for your own areas of learning preference.

To give yourself a preliminary assessment, respond to Questionnaire 1. Details of how to score yourself using this questionnaire follow.

Questionnaire 1: YOUR LEARNING PATTERN PROFILE

Please examine each of the following statements and then identify the degree to which each of the statements accurately describes your own preferred way of engaging in learning. Use a rank order method, assigning a 1 to your most preferred pattern, a 2 for your next preferred pattern, a 3 for your next, and finally a 4 for your least preferred learning pattern.

A. You're quite happy to take information as it comes in any learning situation. In the longer run you're sure that it eventually will all come together for you. In fact, you believe that the information itself really provides the only reasonable structure for you to work with. The thinking involved in your learning should be relatively free wheeling. You like to have the opportunity to allow your mind to fit things together on its own, often with sudden flashes of thought. ☐

B. When you are learning something you like to have all the required information organized within a total framework. And this framework should give you a good idea of where all the information will lead from the outset. While learning you like to have a clear and rational path for your thinking to follow. Straightforward guidelines or easy formulas that you can readily use are very useful to your learning. You like to feel that you're always making progress, and that the teaching you're receiving is logical. ☐

C. In your opinion all the information you receive in a learning situation eventually falls into place somehow. You're not too concerned with the 'big picture', or an overall idea of where everything will lead. You're confident that the information will make sense sooner or later. In order to help you handle the information effectively, your thinking should be guided by clear-cut patterns or models. Logical links should exist to guide your thoughts properly from one point to the next. ☐

D. You should have at least an outline idea of how all the information you receive will eventually fit together at the start of a learning situation. In a sense, you like the idea of a 'mental map' that you can use for placing items of information into appropriate slots in a general learning structure as the teaching process continues. The thinking involved in your learning should be fairly free wheeling. You enjoy finding things suddenly coming together in your mind through intuitive insights or sudden flashes of understanding. ☐

Basic learning patterns

The ***Segmenter/Rational*** (No. 1) types are very concerned with the logic of things. They are likely to be 'no nonsense' type of people. The Segmenter/Rational types also take in information in sequential chunks, on the assumption that these chunks will gradually lead to a whole product. These learners prize instruction that seems well organized.

The ***Holistic/Rational*** (No. 2) types of learners like things to be logical, but they also prefer to have at least a rough idea of where things are going from the outset. These learners like well-laid-out time schedules for learning activities. They may well pose the question, 'What are we doing this for?'

The ***Segmenter/Intuitive*** (No. 3) types of learners deal with things comfortably in chunks. And they will happily develop insights and personal learnings from each chunk of learning that takes place. These learners may, at times, have to be torn away from a given part of a learning programme in order to go on to the next part.

The ***Holistic/Intuitive*** (No. 4) types of learners want whole concepts to deal with, even if these concepts are only sketchy ones. And these types of learners delight in experiencing flashes of insight or understanding about whole processes. Unless you are careful, you may find they can readily jump to wrong conclusions. They might then move swiftly with something, thinking they have learned it, only to run head on into major difficulties. You have to be prepared for this, and stand ready to move in quickly to provide immediate clarification or critical chunks of needed information.

Most of us have elements of all four of these styles in our approaches, although we will favour one or two over the others. A few of us are restricted to just one of these four styles. And very few people can move into any one of the four virtually at will.

The keys to The Learning Pattern Profile

Each of the four statements in Questionnaire 1 corresponds to one of the basic learning patterns we've just gone over. Here are the patterns:

Statement A — Segmenter/Intuitive
Statement B — Holistic/Rational
Statement C — Segmenter/Rational
Statement D — Holistic/Intuitive

By using the numbers shown in the Learning Style Window (Figure 3), you can write down the pattern for yourself and any other person who completes the Learning Pattern Profile. The pattern shown in our box, for instance, would come out as 3 – 2 – 1 – 4. The numbers in themselves indicate no priorities. They simply let you use a convenient shorthand for setting out the patterns. The first two numbers in the pattern are particularly important. These show the dominant styles at work.

In assessing an entire group or class of learners, you would write down the learning pattern for each person. Keep these as a record somewhere, and think through what they're telling you about the right instructing styles to use.

Who are you teaching?

By reviewing the way you filled out the Learning Pattern Profile, you gain some valuable insight into your own learning preferences. In setting out to teach people, knowing your own learning preferences is important, because these preferences will influence the way you teach. Without thinking about it, you could easily want to teach people as though they were all learners with similar ways of doing things to your own.

When assessing the reactions of learners to the different methods you use or the different lessons you teach, keep in mind the four key learning patterns. This will enable you to pick up on the clues that people inevitably give off.

In some cases, if you've used the Learning Pattern Profile with a group of learners, you may wish to share the results with them. This will help to validate the results by encouraging people to confirm their patterns. It will also help people to realize that their own personal styles are not the only ones you as the instructor should be addressing.

Sizing up your learners quickly

People tend to combine two or more style traits in their basic learning patterns, and the Learning Style Window (Figure 3) provides a convenient means of identifying these pairs according to their distribution in a given group.

If you don't have the time to perform a full-scale assessment of the different learning patterns in a given learning group, use the Learning Window to help you conduct a quick and easy survey. It won't be as accurate as using the questionnaires or other learning trait instruments, but it will give you a rough indication of the different types of people you're dealing with.

	Segmenter	**Holistic**
Rational	**1**	**2**
Intuitive	**3**	**4**

Figure 3: *The learning style window*

In conducting the quick and easy method, listen carefully for the kinds of concerns that people express, particularly near the beginning of a learning session. As you hear samples of one of the four different types speaking up, put a tick into the appropriate quadrant of the window. Do this until you've checked off each person in your group. You will end up with a usable means of deciding how best to vary your instructing style to match the learning styles of your class.

Primary sense modes

Once you have an idea of the basic learning patterns you're dealing with, you should try to obtain some idea of the primary sense modes your learners appear to be using in their learning activities. Careful listening or monitoring of your learners will help here.

What you're looking for are verbal and non-verbal clues from the responses and actions of your learners. Does someone tend to use terms such as, 'I see what you mean?' Or does someone else often say something like, 'That sounds good?' You may notice someone else say, 'I like to get the feel of things', while yet another person may say, 'I like the rationale for this technique'.

In these four sample comments you have visual, auditory, kinaesthetic, and intellectual types of statements. The use of a particular kind of statement says something about the primary sense preference of the person using it. Over a long enough period of time, you can develop a fairly solid identification of this sense preference pattern in any individual. This is one of the key aspects of a field of study called 'neurolinguistic programming', or NLP for short.

Another questionnaire can give you some insights into your own sense preferences or the preferences of the learners you're working with. Before reading on here, you may wish to go ahead to fill out Questionnaire 2. Then you can come back to obtain some interpretations.

This questionnaire is based on what are called 'representational systems' in NLP. Four key systems are involved here: ***visual, kinaesthetic, auditory*** and ***intellectual*** (sometimes called digital). NLP involves an additional representational system to these four. This is 'olfactory/gustatory', dealing with our senses of taste and smell. This system does not generally form a major part of anyone's representational system, but it does have importance. In a sense you might consider it an additional sense flourish. So be on the lookout for learning situations that are likely to smell right and taste right!

By examining the responses of individual learners in your group, you gain a much better understanding of their representational tendencies. This, in turn, will give you valuable guidance in the kinds of activities to emphasize or not emphasize in your teaching approach. This questionnaire will also enable you to check out your own representational tendencies, giving you something to build on to your knowledge about your own learning pattern.

Questionnaire 2: YOUR INFORMATION STYLE

Please respond to the following questions according to your own preferred way of taking in information.

		Yes	No
1.	When someone gives me directions for finding a particular location, I'm quite comfortable with receiving a spoken description to guide me.	❐	❐
2.	If I have to assemble something (e.g. a bookcase), I prefer to have diagrams as opposed to trying to follow written directions.	❐	❐
3.	When I'm given a description of a new technique or idea, I have a tendency to generalize the technique or idea into the basic concepts that seem to apply.	❐	❐
4.	I find it very useful actually to become physically involved in manipulating a machine, tool, or object related to something I'm learning.	❐	❐
5.	In order fully to understand something, I have to know its rationale, and be able to relate to the arguments in its favour.	❐	❐
6.	Unless I can actually have some sort of 'hands on' experience with something, I have a great deal of difficulty in really understanding it.	❐	❐
7.	I need to hear careful explanations of things before I can start to develop a good understanding of them.	❐	❐
8.	To me a picture really is worth a thousand words. If I can receive good visual descriptions, I usually gain a clear understanding of what I'm trying to learn.	❐	❐
9.	I need to feel in touch with things in a tangible way before I really can understand them. Physical contact is very important to my understanding.	❐	❐

10. I'm a good listener. Describe something to me with the spoken word, and I generally understand it quite well. ❐ ❐
11. I like to see what I'm trying to understand. Once I have a good look at something, it comes across to me very well. ❐ ❐
12. Give me the conceptual base for the subject you want me to comprehend. Once I have this, understanding comes easily to me. ❐ ❐

This questionnaire does not force your choices, so someone could theoretically end up responding 'yes' to all questions. That's fine, she or he would be indicating equal comfort with any one of the representational systems.

Here is the breakdown of the representation systems used in Questionnaire 2:

Visual	2, 8, 11
Kinaesthetic	4, 6, 9
Auditory	1, 7, 10
Intellectual	3, 5, 12

Training for active learning

Before we go on, fill out Questionnaire 3. It will give you some more interesting information about yourself.

Questionnaire 3: WHAT'S YOUR LEARNING MODE?

Please respond to the following questions according to your own feelings about how you like to learn. (SA strongly agree, MA moderately agree, MD moderately disagree, and SD strongly disagree.)

		SA	MA	MD	SD
1.	The instructor must carefully lay out the path for me to follow in my learning.	❐	❐	❐	❐
2.	An instructor must always know the 'right' answers to questions or problems that may arise about the subject he or she is teaching.	❐	❐	❐	❐

3. I need to have a sense of accomplishment in my learning. ❐ ❐ ❐ ❐
4. I always want to know exactly where I'm going next in my learning. Learning surprises must be at a minimum ❐ ❐ ❐ ❐
5. When I discuss things with my instructor, I feel strongly that the discussion must take place at the level of an adult talking to another adult. ❐ ❐ ❐ ❐
6. I believe firmly that I must often be trusted to take responsibility for my own learning through individual assignments or tasks. ❐ ❐ ❐ ❐
7. Most learners can't make useful suggestions about the way given subjects might best be presented for their own learning. ❐ ❐ ❐ ❐
8. My achievement of learning is always the instructor's responsibility, not mine. ❐ ❐ ❐ ❐
9. There's always one best way for an instructor to teach any particular subject. ❐ ❐ ❐ ❐
10. I need to have the instructor present continually to give me help or directions as needed whenever I'm trying to learn something. ❐ ❐ ❐ ❐
11. I like the idea of having to work things through on my own from time to time in a learning situation. ❐ ❐ ❐ ❐
12. Sometimes I really like to learn new things just for the sake of learning them. This can give me a good sense of personal growth. ❐ ❐ ❐ ❐

Active learners take the initiative in helping themselves to learn in many different situations. They don't wait for instructors to come along and show them how to do things. They work on figuring things out on their own. For them teachers or trainers are helpers or consultants in their learning, not autocratic authority figures.

The pedagogic approach

The formal education system developed the authoritarian or 'pedagogic' approach to teaching. The learners they aimed at were mostly children. Malcolm Knowles, one of North America's top experts on adult learning, points out that the word 'pedagogy' comes from ancient Greek. It literally means the guidance or tutoring of boys ('paid' meaning 'boy' and 'agogus' meaning 'guide' or 'tutor').

Knowles developed the term 'andragogy' as a suitable word for describing the teaching of adults. So you can call training for active learning andragogy if you wish.

Authoritarian learning

Once people have been programmed to be good dependent learners in a pedagogic system, they may come to identify only authoritarian types of instructors as good ones. ('They really know their stuff', could be the typical comments made by learners describing such instructors.) In some ways this may be a little like a hostage tending to identify with his or her captors.

In this context it's interesting to note that many experts on learning in the Japanese education system are calling for Japan to become far less authoritarian in its approach to learning. The rigid pressures are such that too many young students are driven to suicide.

Training adults

While a pedagogic approach might seem reasonable for children (and this is by no means proved), it must be questioned seriously as an approach for the teaching of adults. With their deep experience of life and work, adults are equipped to question authority effectively and productively. When prevented from doing so, their motivation suffers.

Unfortunately, when it comes to adult training in business and industry, the pedagogic approach seems to hold sway. Yet, with its stress on authoritarian, instructor-dependent methods, it often gets in the way of real learning.

Scientific management and learning

Alvin Toffler, author of *The Third Wave*, uses the term 'Second Wave' to describe the traditional kind of industrialism that has been with us since the end of the nineteenth century. This 'smoke stack' form of industrialism stresses heavy manufacturing and assembly line methods. Set procedures and set ways of doing things are very important here.

At the end of the nineteenth century Frederick Taylor introduced the concept of 'scientific management' (sometimes called the 'Taylor System') in a major way. This form of management basically fitted human performance to the needs of machines and assembly lines. Time and method studies or work simplification techniques were important tools. These ignored the individual humanity of employees in order to incorporate them as flesh and blood cogs in the workings of mass industry.

The basic approach to training in business and industry was influenced markedly by scientific management and the needs of mass, mindless industry. For this reason it's not at all surprising to find that the authoritarian model of training has had such an influence on all types of training activities. Many people now equate this model with 'efficiency' in training.

The academic education system too has been shaped strongly in this century by the notions of scientific management applied to educational programmes of all types. These notions led to class rotations, different teachers for different subjects, short and specific learning sessions, paper evaluations, and an emphasis on the numbers of learners (products) passed through the educational system. You might call this the 'body count' approach to teaching.

A body count approach can produce numbers that may delight some minds, especially the more bureaucratic ones. But it falls well short of the mark for instilling excellence. And it probably now is doing our society an economic disservice.

Alvin Toffler uses the term 'Third Wave' to describe the kind of post-industrial society we increasingly seem to have. Our economy is now an information economy. Mass information transmission and knowledge workers are dominant themes. In this type of world change, flexibility, creativity, and openness are musts. If they're not brought to the fore in academic learning and business training, loss of markets, mass lay-offs, and economic decline become inevitable.

Active training

This approach to training or teaching puts its focus on individual learners as fully human beings. It provides a healthy degree of independence for learners set within a structure of personal learning achievement based on solid learning objectives. This more democratic form of teaching brings out strong individual effort in most learners. In some cases, however, learners may need to be acclimatized to this type of training. This may be the case especially if their previous learning experiences occurred in authoritarian learning environments.

Training that promotes active learning leads to learners who are:

- self-assured
- open to change
- flexible
- motivated
- creative
- responsible
- competent

Active learners become active problem solvers and employees with initiative. Exactly the kind of employees more and more organizations need to meet the competitive demands of the nineties.

Comparing passive learning to active

The following table of learning descriptions shows the distinction between learning situations that promote active learning and those that impose passive learning or the pedagogic approach.

Passive learning	Active learning
• emphasizes authority figures and authoritative references	• emphasizes development by learners of their true capabilities
• uses a high degree of structure	• relatively unstructured
• discourages individual assertiveness	• expressions of individual opinion are encouraged
• uses aggressive competition as an achievement measure	• focuses on performance requirements set outside the learning situation

- ...rmation in ...mpartmental-
- information is treated in an open and 'flowing' way
- ... is 'provided' by ...tor(s) or the system
- planning involves everyone
- ...es on covering content, not ultimate performance
- content is treated as a resource, not as an end in itself
- authority figures make regular judgments about learner capabilities
- performance feedback is highly valued so that learners can judge themselves
- instructional methods tend to be 'one way'
- two-way methods are the norm, with learners very much involved in decisions about how they're taught

Permissiveness

Many people fret that active learning really constitutes permissiveness. This has especially been true in discussions about public education. In dealing with adults, however, we're really talking about providing individual opportunities, an issue of central importance to all adults.

Permissiveness in itself is not bad. It only becomes a problem when learners lack a sense of direction and have no idea of what they can or should achieve. The real problem here is lack of leadership.

What people rightly condemn in poor learning situations is aimless activity or sheer chaos masquerading as learning experiences. Some people may describe these types of learning situations as examples of 'open learning', but they're really examples of abandonment.

Discipline in learning

Productive learning requires discipline. But this is self-discipline, not discipline imposed from outside, especially if that outside discipline is arbitrary.

In the workplace, learning discipline arises from the requirements of particular tasks or jobs. Standards, objectives, and goals are vital.

Does the authoritarian mode have a place?

Despite the virtues of active approaches, situations might still exist that require at least some dependence on the part of learners. Major elements of risk or cost could dictate this. There may well be times when it could be foolhardy simply to let learners 'run free'. Sometimes learners just have to know or practise certain things before they can start exercising their own creativity.

The authoritarian mode does have a place. But it's a place that should be visited with care and only to meet highly specific needs that this mode can best address.

Reviewing Questionnaire 3

Now's a good time to take a closer look at the questionnaire, 'What's Your Learning Mode?'. The following questions from this questionnaire show a ***passive*** orientation to learning:

1, 2, 4, 7, 8, 9, & 10

The following questions show an ***active*** orientation:

3, 5, 6, 11, & 12

The passive questions outnumber the active ones. This should not skew your results, as the four-choice format within each question provides the necessary balance for achieving internal validation of the questionnaire.

When scoring the results for this questionnaire, assign points according to the following table:

		SA	MA	MD	SD
Question	1	1	2	3	4
Question	2	1	2	3	4
Question	3	4	3	2	1
Question	4	1	2	3	4
Question	5	4	3	2	1
Question	6	4	3	2	1
Question	7	1	2	3	4
Question	8	1	2	3	4
Question	9	1	2	3	4
Question	10	1	2	3	4
Question	11	4	3	2	1
Question	12	4	3	2	1

The scores on this questionnaire can theoretically range from a low of 12 to a high of 48. In practice you will find that scores generally range from a low of 25 to a maximum of 46. Figure 4 gives you a more graphic means of display for your own score or for the scores of other people.

Someone scoring at the 12 level, ***Closed,*** would be scoring at a pathological level. In fact, someone this dependent or passive would not be able to respond to the questionnaire!

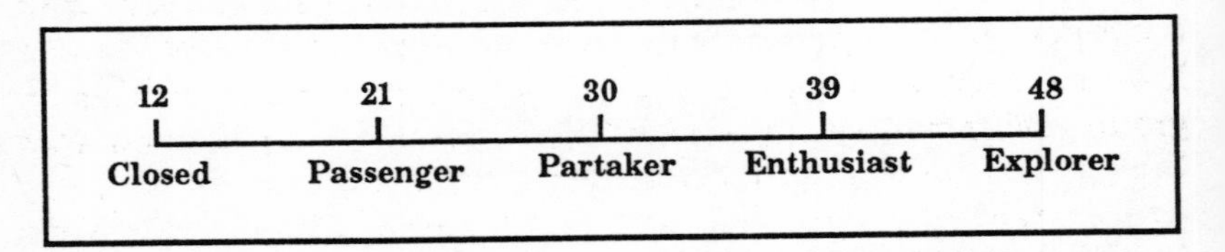

Figure 4: *The learning mode scale*

Some people may score near the 21 mark, putting them at the ***Passenger*** level. You should have definite concern for them, because they would be likely to drift during a lesson, and would need prodding and constant supervision to remain active.

Many people score just under the 30 mark. So the ***Partaker*** position is quite popular. These people are essentially passive in their learning modes, but they can be coaxed into becoming more active. This applies especially if they come to understand that active learning really does work, and it can be fun.

A lot of people score in the low 30s. Very often you'll find that the average score of an entire class ends up in this range. The same thing applies to the median score (the score with as many scores above it as are below it). When you have groups of learners like this, you can open things up quite well, provided you take some pains to help them see the benefits of the active learning process from the start.

Numbers of people score above 35 on the Learning Mode Scale. They've moved into the ***Enthusiast*** range. They're willing to tackle things on their own, and to exercise a healthy amount of initiative. Usually they'll be quite willing to work cooperatively with you in the conduct of the lesson, although they may wish to question some of the things you propose to do. Just be prepared to help them understand in practical ways why given learning approaches will prove useful.

If a high proportion of learners in your group score above 35, be prepared for some active sessions. And, especially, be prepared to take part in some vigorous discussions. Led properly, such groups can really be invigorating for the competent instructor. This applies particularly when you have a good sample of people scoring in the 40s.

One situation that can be frustrating for you is to have a split between a significant number of people scoring above 35, and a significant number scoring at or below 26. Your best bet here is to try to set up small groups with each group containing a balance of low scorers and high scorers. This way, if you have enough small group assignments, the learners themselves will tend to balance things out with their own behaviours. Unfortunately, you still run a clear risk that one of these two groups will downgrade your teaching in the comments they make on evaluation forms (so called) that might be used at the end of the learning session.

One aspect of all this that you should pay close attention to is the question of true active learning versus sheer activity or self-expression. Bear in mind the difference between informed and uninformed opinions. Some people do like to speak up and work independently, but they may lack competence in what they do. Further, they may not realize that they lack competence. This is the reason why it's so important, if possible, to have and use objective standards of performance for assessing competence levels.

Truly active learners work in self-effective ways while measuring themselves continually against reasonable performance criteria. Anything less than this could simply be wilful self-expression.

Your own learning mode

Most instructors score reasonably high on the Learning Mode Scale. This seems to go hand in hand with their interest in being teachers or trainers in the first place. But it's important to realize that you must never assume that the score of your learners will automatically be the same as or near your own. Usually your own will be higher, certainly than the average or median of your class.

By keeping in mind the idea that you're probably ahead of your learners in your own learning mode, you can help avoid falling into the trap of automatically assuming that the different things you try in your teaching will receive the same degree of acceptance from your learners as they would have if you were the learner.

When you're trying out different methods or techniques, take care to explain them at least a little, and be ready to give your learners the right guidance to ensure they don't miss the concepts. Of course you don't want to go overboard here, and give too much guidance. But look for that balancing point between too much and too little.

Active success

Training for active learning or andragogy is not all that widespread in business and industry, or academe. Decision makers of various types are still quite leery about its merits. But the only way to prove its value is to use it.

Any system that is not used will not work. It's as simple as that.

The beauty of the active approach is that it almost always works and works well, provided it's planned for and directed by people who know what they're doing.

If you're a trainer or have training responsibilities, you owe it to yourself and your organization to work towards active learning programmes. This will lead you to training success. And this, in turn, paves the way for organizational success.

Providing encouragement

Real and meaningful challenges fit well with active learning. Trainers can use these to real advantage. And when learners deal with these challenges effectively, they deserve good, honest praise.

We'll deal more a little later with the uses of positive guidance. For now, just remember that a little praise goes a long way. Always be ready to give it.

Working with your learners

Several different ways of assessing individual differences in your learners have been presented in this chapter. You will find one or all of them useful for helping yourself to deal more effectively with your learners. You will find too that your own approach to instructing will become more flexible and assured.

At all times, when you are assessing the learning approaches of others, try to develop some honesty with yourself about your own learning preferences. The way you learn has a lot of influence on the way you teach. The next few chapters will help you to develop your understanding of others and yourself with a view to helping you develop better as an instructor.

Before going on to those other chapters, it might be wise to take a look at some points that should be kept very much in mind for teaching adults, especially adults operating in actual work settings:

1. Treat adult learners always as your equals.
2. Make use of individual or small group assignments regularly.
3. Recognize the accomplishments of individual learners.
4. Set your instructional style according to the degree of active learning apparent in a learning group.
5. Invite learners to share with you their own ideas about the way instruction should be conducted (but don't appear to be confused while you're doing so).
6. Once learners start to work on a task, try not to interrupt them too often with additional instructions.
7. At all times keep your instructional approach flexible, and be prepared to change what you'd planned to do, even at the last minute.

8. Let your learners know that you put a good measure of trust in them through your own specific and consistent actions.
9. Make sure you clarify your own role in class sessions to a reasonable degree, especially regarding your expectations of the learners.
10. Let learners know at least the general outline of the instructional programme from the start of that programme.
11. Provide rationales for the things that occur as part of a class session, particularly if the learners are likely to consider these things really 'off beat'.
12. Never appear to have 'lost control' of yourself or the instructional session.

These points taken together form a blend of active and passive learning characteristics. They give you a pragmatic structure for dealing with most types of real learning groups. Different groups will vary, of course, in their relative degrees of activity or passivity. Just be prepared to adjust your own instructional style to match.

Even in the more Third Wave types of settings, adult learners expect a certain amount of control and direction from instructors. They expect trainers or teachers to design learning sessions, and then to be available to help to a reasonable degree while those sessions take place.

Final thoughts

Change in the process of learning is welcomed by most adult learners. But they still have a strong desire for predictability in any type of setting. They generally have strong views about what they want to learn and why.

You should always feel free to experiment and innovate, but you should not conduct training 'on' learners. You should always conduct it 'with' them.

Our individual learning views and behaviours are deeply ingrained, and some of them may well not be subject to change. Always they are very important ingredients in the instructing/learning process. They may help or hinder, but they will have an important and tangible impact. You ignore them at your instructional peril.

Instructors who work with their learners as they really are will more than likely achieve good results. You may not achieve them to the degree you wish, but you will achieve such results, certainly in the longer run.

Deal in an informed way with your learners and they will deal effectively with you as their instructor. Realize that you are all participants in a unique and beneficial learning performance. With foresight, insight and concern, you can work effectively with most of the unique learners you're ever likely to encounter.

3 Motivation for Learning

Motivation essentially concerns our own accomplishments. We plan for them, work for them, and then achieve them. Depending on our 'motivational maturity', the accomplishments we work for can be relatively minor, or they can be long term and quite subtle. But you cannot reduce motivation simply to a question of tangible purposes. It also has a dimension of inner sustenance, a sense of personal satisfaction.

The word 'motivation' finds its origins in the Latin word, 'motivus', and this word means 'motion' or 'movement'. When applied to human beings, motivation does connote movement, but it is movement closely linked to what really 'makes us tick', or what really drives us. We want to move in our lives, and we need to move. We need to have a feeling of growth or personal development.

You can see the beginnings of motivation in a baby. It reaches out to touch things, to experience them, and to measure its own impact on them. This process forms a major component of the brain's programming. Babies reach out into their world and receive feedback on their thrusts and probes. All of this activity teaches them many things, and it helps to develop their motivational profiles.

In examining Figure 5, the importance of consequences for human motivational development shows up very clearly. We tend to repeat doing those things that give us good consequences and to refrain from doing those things that yield poor or negative consequences. At the same time, we know that many people continue doing things despite bad consequences. Something deeper is often at work.

Conditioning may lead us to do or not do certain things or to avoid doing certain things. But conditioning processes only take us so far in looking at the shaping of human behaviours. We all have certain predispositions built into our brains at birth. And these predispositions can have marked impacts on the development of our individual motivational patterns.

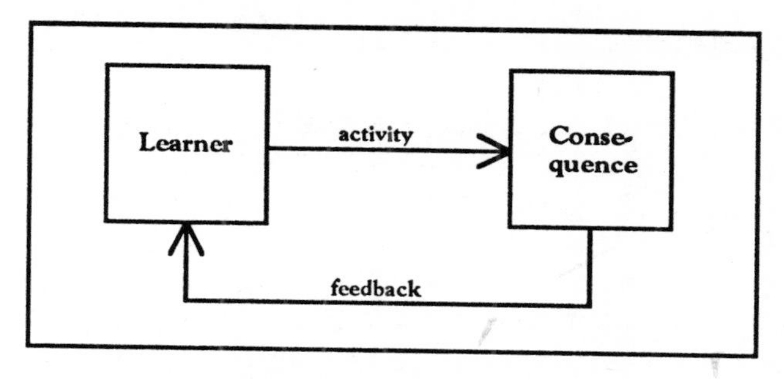

Figure 5: *Basic motivational structuring*

Personal motivation patterns

Every human being has a distinctive motivational pattern. What rewards one person may mean nothing to another, and vice versa. Each one of us searches for meaning in this life. And this search is, to a large extent, a search for what motivates us, or really 'turns us on'.

When it comes to the world of work, motivation can be a very powerful force. Motivated employees produce well and with pride. They need little urging to work. An enterprise filled with motivated employees is a very happy place, and the happiness is infectious.

A very young person might be motivated by the promise of a new toy or some sweets. As he or she becomes older, the rewards might become extra allowances or borrowing the car. As adults we may become motivated by a job promotion, a rise, or a special treat prepared by a wife or husband.

We know that some forms of motivation can be more lasting or significant than others. Momentary rewards might bring immediate pleasures, but they only bring fleeting instances of motivation. A few minutes or hours of motivation may ensue, but momentary motivation has little lasting effect. In fact, many authorities on motivation do not consider fleeting or momentary motivation really to be motivation at all. It may best be described as an immediate or basic reaction. In more long-lasting cases it may represent the power of incentives.

In our society we too often tend to use the word 'motivation' quite loosely. In daily conversation we may make little or no distinction between fleeting motivation and longer-term motivation. And this tendency can cause a good deal of confusion when it comes to trying to improve motivation.

The Motivation Depth Gauge®

A hierarchy helps us examine human motivation more carefully. The Motivation Depth Gauge® shown in Figure 6 provides a hierarchy to help us with this task.

The deeper you look on this gauge, the deeper the form of motivation you're examining.

At the ***reaction level*** we're prompted to do things immediately. A sudden draught might cause us to close a window. A few raindrops might lead us to open an umbrella. A sudden shout can prompt us to turn around. At this level immediate signals or prompters can get us to do things quickly, but their effect is very short term.

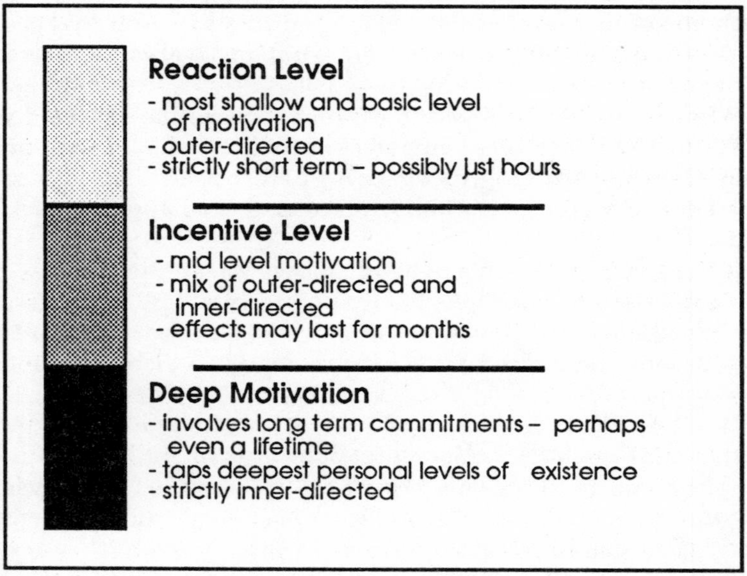

Reaction Level
- most shallow and basic level of motivation
- outer-directed
- strictly short term – possibly just hours

Incentive Level
- mid level motivation
- mix of outer-directed and inner-directed
- effects may last for months

Deep Motivation
- involves long term commitments – perhaps even a lifetime
- taps deepest personal levels of existence
- strictly inner-directed

Figure 6: *The Motivation Depth Gauge®*

The ***incentive level*** at the middle depth on our gauge deals with specific rewards or consequences desired by the person involved. These are the kinds of things you can work towards.

Motivators at this level have an impact for much longer than those at the reaction level. Here you can work towards agreed goals or outcomes. And these can be self-selected.

The deepest level of motivation is simply called ***deep motivation***. This is the most significant form of motivation for the individual human being. It provides you with the strength 'to move mountains'. It involves personal fulfilment and endurance despite hardship. Deep motivation might never cease for a given person. It's the kind of motivation that sustains the real pioneers of a given field of endeavour. We can expect to experience it only rarely.

Motivating learners

From an instructional point of view, you may often wish to motivate your learners. Certainly, motivated learners will learn much more effectively and they will be more pleasurable to teach. But this process of motivation is not straightforward.

You can try to motivate learners at the reaction level. Here you need immediate kinds of rewards. Sometimes these might take the form of positive words or gestures. Or they might take the form of material rewards such as coins, sweets, badges, or other 'tokens'. Some of this kind of motivation looks suspiciously like bribery. And the border line between bribery and reactive motivation is not always easy to identify.

We use bribery to prod people along. It's a means of getting people to do something they probably would not otherwise do. Any deeper form of motivating activity aims at reinforcing or strengthening something a person might really want to do already. The idea of motivation here is to induce him or her to do it better and more enthusiastically. In some cases outright bribery may suffice to start a person performing a given task, which may then allow deeper motivation to be applied. So bribery used this way might well be used as part of an overall motivating strategy.

If you always tried to motivate people at the reaction level, you would face a frustrating task. You would need to keep on hand many different kinds of immediate rewards. Because reactive motivation is so shallow and short term, you would also have difficulty in getting people to sustain their output on longer-lasting projects or assignments.

Inner connections

Because motivational impact is unique to each one of us, especially at the deeper levels of motivation, personal involvement is needed by the person being motivated. He or she must clearly understand the rewards or goals available and how they can be attained. This requires some patience and tact on your part.

Fundamentally, you cannot truly motivate another person. All you can really do is *to help her or him become motivated.* And this distinction is much more than an academic one. It's what actually works in real life.

A key part of the word *involve* is the syllable *in.* To feel genuinely involved in something, you have to feel an inner connection with it. You might not be able clearly to identify the nature of that inner connection, but you know when it's present.

We have all felt inner connections in the past. These are the kinds of events or actions that bring out deep responses within us. They give us a kind of psychic joy. And it's this joy that tells us when a deeper level of motivation is occurring.

Because motivation is an individual phenomenon, the kinds of inner connections that might occur for us in life can be quite varied. I may well experience inner connectedness in a situation that does not affect you one way or the other. So I might become motivated in that situation while you remain unmotivated.

We don't often take stock of the kinds of things that motivate us deeply. Sometimes we just rely on what others tell us. If this happens, we run the risk of people doing things for us that they consider motivating, that don't motivate us at all. And then we might feel guilty about our own lack of motivation!

Just think of the situation that might occur if someone who is not a football fan is given great tickets to a game by someone who is. The recipient is really not motivated. But he or she might worry that the generous gift giver might feel hurt if no enjoyment is shown. So, in some desperation, the receiver of the gift might feign enjoyment.

As an instructor you can help people to recognize better the kinds of events that really connect inwardly with them, and so provide their motivation. You can also reassure them if they become motivated through experiences that differ significantly from those that motivate others.

The more people awaken to their motivational preferences, the more they become able to identify their preferences to other people, including the ones they work for.

Setting the 'motivational contract'

The chances are that adult learners in a typical training programme will have a fairly good idea of the origins of their own motivation, but it will still be incomplete.

Open discussion about motivational needs before the start of any new training programme makes a good investment for all concerned. During this motivational 'contract setting' phase, everyone must come to understand clearly the incentives involved for them. This process will help you as the instructor, and it will help the learners as well. They will have a much better idea of what they can get out of the programme, and what they should look for.

The initial discussion about the motivational aspects of any major learning activity must be as open as possible. You should try to find out the interests of your learners — both work-related and leisure. This will help you to identify the kinds of activities they will find rewarding.

If you wish, you can formalize things more by assigning small groups to discuss key issues in your subject that they would like definitely to address during the programme. This kind of activity can serve several purposes in addition to helping you identify the motivational patterns. It can help to improve the situational comfort right away, help you to verify your subject content, give you some idea of the levels of reception of the people in the groups, and generally allow you to gauge the types of learners you'll be dealing with.

More self-effective or active learners carry with them a lot of their own motivational initiative. They often find deeper levels of motivation from rewards or events that other people might consider small time or shallow. Learners of this type can help a great deal in the planning and implementing of a sound motivational strategy. They can even help in setting and sustaining your own motivation! But you have to be prepared to let them.

Using incentives

Incentive motivation works well for most learning activities. But you have to use it carefully and methodically. And its application requires openness, consistency and uniformity.

Good feedback is vital to successful incentive motivation. People need to know exactly how well they're doing as they work towards planned results and accomplishments. Clear and open learning objectives help to ensure this.

For most practical purposes, motivation at the incentive level will prove more effective in training sessions than the other two levels of motivation. It's more significant to the individual than reaction level motivation, and you can plan its development more readily than is the case with deep motivation.

Deep motivation

The existence of deep motivation must not be ignored, just because it's not easy to work with. It is far too powerful and significant for that.

In the case of longer-term projects or learning activities, deep motivation may gradually emerge from incentive level motivation. Alertness to the signs of deep motivation can help instructors to encourage motivation that starts to deepen in this way. The signs of this kind of deepening show up in the performance someone gives as well as her or his sense of enthusiasm about what must be done.

Unfortunately, in too many cases, when learners start to develop deep motivation their teachers fail to recognize the signals. This can lead such teachers not only to miss the opportunity of using the learning benefits of this most significant form of motivation, but to actually *de-motivate* the person concerned by taking away or somehow spoiling the very thing that had been developing their deeper level of motivation.

When signs of deep motivation occur, do what you can to encourage its emergence. The process can be an exciting one. And it provides motivation to others.

Look for examples of long-lasting excitement, enthusiasm, and apparent inner satisfaction. People will communicate these emotions with all sorts of behaviours. And don't forget to look for these signs in yourself as well.

Deep motivation, when it does occur, overcomes many obstacles. It has formidable staying power and requires little external sustenance once it's operating. You can't do much to make it happen. But you can certainly prepare for the possibility of it happening.

Motivational fulfilment

One level of motivation can emerge from another and shift back again. Motivation is seldom a 'steady state' business. Flexibility is inherent to motivation and to working with the concept of motivation.

The type of event or stimulus that motivates a given person can vary not only because of individual differences, but because of the degree of motivational maturity as well. Take a look at Figure 7 to see the different degrees of motivational fulfilment any human being can experience.

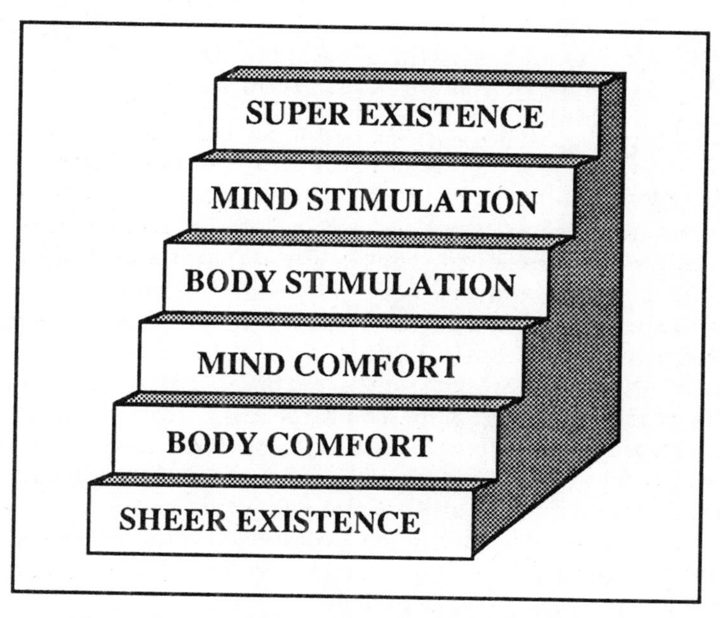

Figure 7: *The steps of motivational fulfilment*

Your own life experiences equip you to relate to the different steps shown here. And we can take a further look at each step in the following descriptions.

Sheer existence

At this step you're in poor shape from a motivational and life standpoint. Food, shelter, warmth, or other kinds of survival needs would provide motivation here. Historically, harsh prison or prison-like institutions have taken advantage of this motivational state to keep prisoners or other types of captives in line through the sheer brutality of imposed conditions.

Given sufficient misfortune, everyone has the potential to end up in this state, at least for a short time. Plane crashes, shipwrecks, natural disasters, and so on all have the potential to throw us down to this step in short order.

Some people exist in the state of sheer existence through flaws, distortions, or problems in their thinking. They are, in effect, 'prisoners of their own minds'.

In normal business or industry situations you're not likely to encounter learners operating at this lowest step, even for a short time. Unfortunately, there are reports of people working in this state in some companies in third world countries.

The kind of work you would get from someone in this state would be unthinking and very mechanical. You would really be dealing with a human robot.

Body comfort

Everyone experiences the body comfort stage of motivation from time to time. There is little that is worse than finding yourself in a situation that produces acute physical discomfort. Here you would share some of the feelings of the person in the sheer existence state. The critical difference is that you can usually do something about it.

Motivation at the body comfort stage can develop from promises of comfortable furniture, good food, and a generally soothing atmosphere. The effects here are basic and short term in their impact. But lack of provisions for body comfort can bring about de-motivation. And de-motivation will disrupt any human group. Just think of the howl that goes up when the cafeteria fails to provide someone's favourite dish.

Motivation needs in the body comfort state can be met with a little thought and some material provisions. By meeting these needs, you can prepare people to go on to higher forms of motivation.

The trap for the motivator here is to think that human motivation needs can be met entirely at the body comfort step. The kinds of things that people can think up for their body comfort are almost endless. And you still have to do something for their minds.

Mind comfort

This arises from an inner sense that everything is all right. In this state people need assurance about the security of their situation. They need to know that no threats or hazards exist, or that such dangers will be properly controlled.

Reassurance about the future is important at this stage too, especially as it relates to someone's likelihood of acquiring a new skill, mastering new knowledge, or retaining a job.

Personal comfort can be very beneficial to people. But it carries with it little sense of action. Learners can become quite comfortable, and then end up doing little or nothing. In a word, they can 'drift'. This is something the effective instructor must remain alert to.

Body stimulation

People need some form of stimulation to get them going, to raise them to a productive level of motivation. Physical and body stimulation can arise simply from some form of physical activity. In a sense, good physical activity provides its own rewards. It tones the body, improves blood circulation, keeps useful muscles from going to flab, and generally keeps you from vegetating.

Good physical exercise promotes better thinking. More oxygen arrives in the brain and the general inflow of sensory stimuli activates our thinking. The net effect is to provide us with more ideas to work with, along with a better ability to deal with them.

People who take part in a regular exercise programme know it produces a good feeling throughout the body. And useful exercise need not occur only as a formal kind of process in set programmes. Walking provides good body stimulation in many different situations. And this is something instructors are always wise to bear in mind.

In the classroom people should have the opportunity to move around from time to time. You can accomplish this with job rotations, the array of tasks someone needs to carry out, and a variety of other arrangements. The main thing is to try to avoid simply parking someone in one spot all day long and expecting him or her to work at a healthy level of motivation.

Mind stimulation

At the next highest step of motivation fulfilment we come to mind stimulation. Motivation arises here from the power of thoughts or ideas. Concepts, projects and problem-solving episodes provide gocd mind stimulation. You're dealing here with the power of human imagination. The better you are at conjuring up and describing in-depth visions of potential outcomes, the better this stage of motivation works. Powerful visions pack a lot of motivational impact.

In many ways motivation in the mind stimulation state has a more profound impact than motivation at the lower steps. It relates to full-scale mental or knowledge work. And because people are so well-equipped mentally, this stage of motivation works in a uniquely effective way.

You can invoke mind stimulation with the effective use of language, particularly if your words help people to see and hear things well in their minds. When people have a good mental fix on prospective accomplishments and understand how these will occur, their motivation becomes very strong.

Super existence

The final step for us to consider is that of super existence. This step is not reached very often. But everyone can experience it at times, if only for a few moments.

It occurs when we feel particularly good about an accomplishment. This feeling includes a sense of deep identity with what we've accomplished, and sense that it really is something special. It's a healthy form of feeling 'high'.

You can experience this feeling if you've just completed a major project, and other people give you praise for your hard work and the unique contribution you've made. You identify with the praise and sense that it is a unique and proud expression of your very essence as a human being.

You do not reach this state automatically when someone else praises you. Nor do you necessarily need to hear from other people at all. What counts is that you have a deep inner sense that you've done things just right, and feel especially good about yourself and life in general.

In the state of super existence you rise above the daily strifes of this world, going 'beyond yourself'. This state gives you a unique degree of inner peace and contentment, a sense of deep personal fulfilment. At this step outside reinforcers or rewards can almost be dispensed with. The person in the super existence stage will be motivationally self-sufficient. You become completely satisfied inside.

Of course no one is likely to remain in this state indefinitely. At some point most people who experience super existence must come back to earth. But they will remember what this highest level of motivation felt like, and will seek to repeat it.

Super existence is so powerful a motivational stage that even a few seconds'worth is important to you. For this reason, you really do need to 'stop and smell the roses' now and then, or recognize that there are things of value that lie beyond the immediate and the practical. Give yourself the chance to enjoy the little pleasures that occur each day. Any one of them might contain a few moments of super existence. And remember to provide your learners with these opportunities as well.

Working on motivational maturity

The concept of different steps or states of motivation should not blind us to the potential of motivation at the lower levels. Just as we saw in examining the Motivation Depth Gauge®, so too with the motivational steps: the lower stages have their place in the total scheme of things. The basic demands imposed by a physical body ensure this. We can all become hungry, thirsty, cold, or frightened.

On any given day we can operate in widely different states of motivational fulfilment. But if we are truly growing as human beings, we won't dwell over-long on the lower levels. And we can come to recognize the higher level features of what we might at first have thought were lower level activities.

When you eat you can simply stuff yourself with food to keep your body going, and this will satisfy you at the body comfort stage. But you could also 'dine'. In this case you would mentally savour the atmosphere, the presentation of the food and drink, the conviviality of your fellow diners, and many other mind stimulation sensations. In this way the process of eating can become the source of a much deeper level of pleasure.

Other kinds of activities involve multiple motivational

possibilities as well. You can ride a bicycle to get from point A to point B, thereby giving your body stimulation. Or you can ride and give your mind stimulation as well. Let yourself feel the wind on your face and hair, delight in the sway and speed of the ride, and otherwise become more completely receptive to all aspects of this activity.

Some people refer to the fuller experiencing of simple activities as developing a sense of *flow*. With some practice, you can learn to flow with any task by allowing yourself to 'get into it'. The key lies in becoming more receptive to the full range of mental stimulation possibilities in the activity concerned.

In some cases the experience of flowing with a task or activity becomes a form of self-hypnosis. And this is fine. Everyone experiences varying forms of hypnosis every day. It's not a strange force imposed from without, but a natural function of the brain you can come to use with more and more confidence and control.

You can work on your motivational fulfilment very successfully. So never let yourself get into a thought pattern that leads you to believe you must rely on forces or people external to yourself. The path to fuller motivation is open to everyone.

Motivation and personal growth

Consider Figure 8. At the start of a given learning experience you may have a perceived goal you're seeking to achieve. Once achieved, you can experience its consequences. These lead logically to some inner reflection which may cause you to re-evaluate your original perception of your goal. You could either come up with another goal, or decide to restructure your views about your original growth. Either one of these possibilities is an example of personal motivational growth.

In achieving motivational fulfilment or maturity learners may have to re-evaluate their goals numbers of times as inner reflection causes them to focus on deeper aspects of motivation. As the instructor you can stand ready to help with this important process. In doing so you're assisting people undergo personal change. So your responsibility here is a fundamental one.

Personal change can occur quickly or gradually. Sometimes people are well aware of their own changes. In other cases friends and associates must point them out. We often evolve or grow as individual human beings without fully being aware of doing so.

The process of achieving motivational maturity is a never-ending one. It's truly intertwined with our lives. So instructors who learn to work with it well can have a life-long impact on their learners.

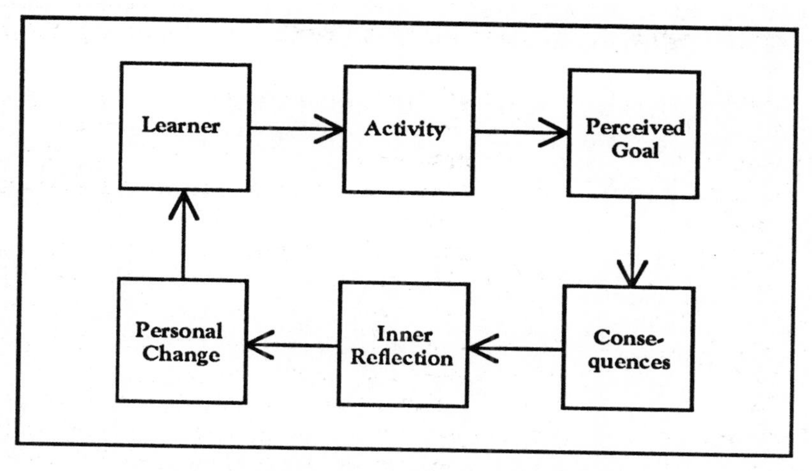

Figure 8: *Motivation and personal growth*

Relating to the Motivation Depth Gauge®

The steps of motivational fulfilment relate very well to the Motivational Depth Gauge®. Take a close look at the preceding diagram to see this relationship.

REACTION LEVEL	–	**sheer existence**
	–	**basic body comfort**
INCENTIVE LEVEL	–	**full body comfort**
	–	**mind comfort**
	–	**body stimulation**
	–	**basic mind stimulation**
DEEP MOTIVATION	–	**full mind stimulation**
	–	**super existence**

Figure 9: *Relating to the depth and level of motivation*

We noted earlier that the incentive level of motivation, for all practical purposes, offers the best scope for general use in motivating learners. So you can really work best with full body comfort, mind comfort, body stimulation, and some mind stimulation activities in conjuring up motivational strategies.

Using motivation in your instructing

Whatever you're teaching, always be on the lookout for ways to reassure people about the events going on around them. This helps to address mind comfort needs. Do this verbally or with specific actions.

You can help meet body stimulation needs by ensuring that people take reasonably frequent breaks from a particular activity, especially if it's a routine or mechanical activity. During these breaks, encourage people to stand up and move around.

In meeting body stimulation needs during lessons look for ways to give learners physical experiences of the subject or objects connected with the subject, particularly if these experiences can provide some degree of real physical stimulation. You will often find that people are grateful to be able to get their hands on things. It deepens their learning, and makes them feel better about it.

Good discussion, challenging questions, or inspiring comments help to bring about mind stimulation. Because people are so language-oriented, the right words often have great motivational power. The trick here is to connect the right words to the right learning activities.

Because the higher levels of motivational fulfilment are more significant for deeper motivation, they can sometimes 'drown out' or push aside apparent needs at lower levels. So effective mind stimulation activities will sometimes divert people from concern about their lower level needs. This is at least part of the reason why 'inspirational speeches' have historically been capable of turning things around in human affairs. The same thing can apply to learning situations.

In considering the activities you can use to help bring about motivation in your learners, keep the word *incentive* very much in mind. In a basic sense always try to answer the question, 'What's in it for the other person?'. Then look for the comfort or stimulation factors that you can realistically supply during the learning sessions.

There is no limit to the number of incentives you could use while instructing. You just have to use your imagination to look for the rewards, activities, or responses people will be likely to relate to well at the incentive level.

Planning personal growth

Adults are all goal-directed beings in most of their activities. Except for the most immediate kinds of goals, these goals are perceived ones. Goals set at the lower level of motivational fulfilment can be quite tangible, so the perceptions involved will be reasonably accurate. Goals at the higher levels, however, involve more mental anticipation. Perceptions at these levels may become quite distorted. As an instructor, you should do whatever you can to help people perceive their goals accurately at the higher stages.

The consequences of goal achievement provide the potential for the use of incentives. As far as possible, you can strive to ensure that the incentives provided to learners will help them become motivated as a result of achieving learning goals. Learning objectives will help in making your motivational activities more precise. Often these objectives can become the goals.

The inner reflection part of the personal growth process involves cognitive and affective (thinking and feeling) reactions within the learner. These reactions impact directly on the way people experience things to deepen learning, to render it more effective and significant. You cannot intervene directly in someone's inner reflection, but you can try to ensure that the learner has good food for thought and good feelings about this food.

Our motivational structure is a complex one. Researchers are only gradually becoming aware of all its ramifications. We certainly do not know enough about it yet to 'prescribe' motivational development completely accurately for different people. But we can usually make shrewd guesses. And these guesses will be all the more shrewd or accurate the better we know the person involved.

If you work with learners over a long period of time, you should make a point of monitoring their personal growth. In some cases you may find it wise to maintain some form of record to allow you to do this most effectively. From careful monitoring of the way people change, you can find out how well your motivational strategy for a given group of learners is working.

Strategies for human motivation in learning situations are

very important. You need to think through clearly not only what you want your learners to learn when and how, but what the motivational aspects should be as well. By paying good attention to the motivational strategy, you can help to ensure that your learning designs really work. And that will prove motivating for you!

While human motivation is not a mechanical stimulus-response activity, any competent instructor can certainly develop it in learners, at least to some extent. The key is to think in ways that relate well to the steps of motivational fulfilment. Then apply the products of your thinking practically in your lessons.

4 Trusting to Learn

One of the ingredients vital to developing a healthy level of motivation is trust. Sometimes we take this quality for granted. Other times we tend to treat it far too lightly. But trust really is an important issue in dealing with your learners. And it's well worth a chapter of its own.

Trust or lack of it is with us every day. We trust bus drivers to transport us to where we're going. We trust lifts not to fall out of control. We trust buildings not to burst into flames or suddenly crumble. And most of us trust the majority of our co-workers to do their jobs.

We distrust too slick sales people, politicians, and a wide variety of people with messages they tell us will turn our lives around — guaranteed! We basically prefer to trust, but sad experience has taught us the value of distrust.

Under the right circumstances trust can work as a very powerful force in human affairs. It can make for honest communications between and among people. It can clear the pathways for profitable cooperation with others, and it can generate a feeling of good will. Too much trust, unfortunately, can blow up in your face at times.

When trust exists in a business setting, it makes for a great deal of true business efficiency. 'My word is my bond' can have real meaning, practicality, and efficacy. When oral agreements can be relied on to have actual effect, the need for lawyers and carefully-worded contracts is quite low. Trust can promote speed, and it can sweep away the clutter of too much paper work.

The traditional means of carrying on business within the City of London proper puts a lot of stress on trust. You take someone's spoken word as sufficient. Large business transactions can take place over the phone. A similar tradition prevails in the international gold market, and in numbers of other business settings.

You cannot, of course, go into these settings cold and expect to be trusted. You have to earn trust through your deeds. But once you've earned trust, you have a precious asset that cannot be purchased at any price.

Measuring trust levels

Questionnaire 4: TRUST?

Please respond to the following statements according to your own reactions to them. (SA strongly agree, MA moderately agree, MD moderately disagree, and SD strongly disagree).

		SA	MA	MD	SD
1.	Most of the time you can trust politicians to keep their promises.	❒	❒	❒	❒
2.	I believe that policemen are usually honest.	❒	❒	❒	❒
3.	You just can't trust other people very much at all.	❒	❒	❒	❒
4.	Usually you can believe what a member of the clergy says to you.	❒	❒	❒	❒
5.	It's a good idea never to believe what a salesperson says to you about the product he or she is trying to sell to you.	❒	❒	❒	❒
6.	Whenever you ask someone to do something for you, it's always a good idea to check afterwards to make sure they've actually done it.	❒	❒	❒	❒
7.	I believe that people will tell you the truth most of the time.	❒	❒	❒	❒
8.	Most people, given a chance, would steal something from their place of work.	❒	❒	❒	❒
9.	As long as you give them a fair chance, most people can be trusted to carry out the promises they make to you.	❒	❒	❒	❒
10.	Almost everything you hear from others in this world needs to be taken with a generous-sized grain of salt.	❒	❒	❒	❒

11.	Whenever money is involved, trust unfortunately, becomes a real luxury.	❐	❐	❐	❐
12.	As long as you treat people honestly and honourably, they will tend to be trustworthy.	❐	❐	❐	❐

In sizing up the types of learners you're dealing with, you should make some decision about the level of trust that they likely can handle. You can do this through observing their behaviours, including their responses to your questions. More passive or dependent types of learners tend to be lower in their trust levels, while active or self-effective types of learners tend to be the opposite.

If you find it convenient, you might wish to use the preceding Questionnaire to take some measure of existing trust levels.

If you haven't done so already, you may wish to take a crack at filling out this questionnaire yourself at this point. We'll be getting into its scoring next.

Learner trust

When you set out to teach people, you are automatically asking them to trust you. You want them to believe you have something worthwhile to teach. You want them to feel some sense of motivation about their learning. And you want them to have faith that the information you provide is worth having.

You can come right out and simply ask learners to trust you, but this usually is not enough. Ask yourself the simple question, 'Why should they?'. Most of the time you have to earn their trust. A recital of credentials can help (although this may sometimes appear defensive, thereby generating distrust). Better if you can demonstrate in some tangible and practical fashion that you really are worth trusting here and now.

What is trust? Essentially it involves a reliance on or belief in the integrity, certainty, and strength of a person or thing. It implies faith. When I put my trust in you I have faith that you will do what I want you to do.

Learners who trust their instructors will prove more cooperative than those who don't. They will accept challenges, tasks, and assignments quite readily. They will look to you for guidance, and generally will heed that guidance.

Trust involves self-fulfilling prophecies. If I trust you, then you will tend to return that trust (the mirror phenomenon). In brief, trust begets trust. As an instructor, you have a very important role to play in setting a high trust atmosphere. By trusting your learners, and showing that you trust them, you increase the chances that they will trust you.

You cannot give trust totally naively, of course. You have to consider the background of your learners. If they have been used to distrustful environments and all the con games such environments produce, they could well run wild in a situation that suddenly gave them a great deal of trust. They would not immediately understand or appreciate the change. It's a similar problem to that of trying to teach passive learners using active methods. Low trust learners have to receive trust in small doses over a longer period of time. They have to learn to become trustworthy.

In a learning environment filled with trust a certain electricity fills the air. Instructors and learners all respect each other. They tend to listen well, and not to question harshly or crudely. In this kind of environment learning really can flourish.

To build trust in others you have to take risks. You have to let people undertake things on their own, even if you are afraid they will not live up to your expectations or hopes for them. If you are willing to do this, you will often be pleasantly surprised.

Scoring the 'Trust?' questionnaire

Some of the questions in this questionnaire reflect a non-trusting frame of mind, while others show a trusting frame of mind. The following are the ***high trust*** statements:

1, 2, 4, 7, 9, & 12

Here are the ***low trust*** statements:

3, 5, 6, 8, 10, & 11

The scores on this questionnaire can range between a low of 12 and a high of 48. You can set them out on the 'Scale of Trust' which follows:

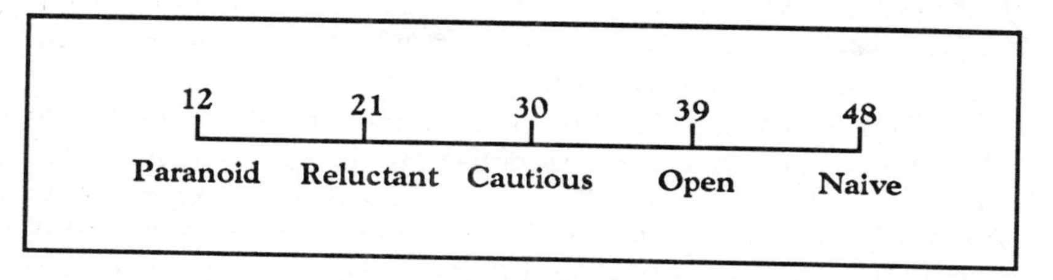

Figure 10: *The scale of trust*

For all the virtues of trust, it is possible to be too trusting, just as it's possible to be too distrustful. Extremes are not healthy.

The terms used on the Scale of Trust may seem a bit loaded. But they do help to show the essential differences between the high and low ratings. They also illustrate the point that scores near 'cautious' are probably the healthiest ones for people to use most of the time in today's world.

To score the responses to this questionnaire, use the following score table:

		SA	MA	MD	SD
Question	**1**	4	3	2	1
Question	**2**	4	3	2	1
Question	**3**	1	2	3	4
Question	**4**	4	3	2	1
Question	**5**	1	2	3	4
Question	**6**	1	2	3	4
Question	**7**	4	3	2	1
Question	**8**	1	2	3	4
Question	**9**	4	3	2	1
Question	**10**	1	2	3	4
Question	**11**	1	2	3	4
Question	**12**	4	3	2	1

In a learning situation you would usually want to achieve a level of trust significantly warmer than 'cautious'. Certainly the 'open' position is ideal. This gives you a clear trust target to work for in your teaching.

Situational trust

The types of people you deal with and the situations in which you deal with them are important considerations for the way you use trust with your learners. In effect, you must engage in 'situational trusting', or gearing your trust approach to the trust levels of your learners just as you would gear your instructional approach to their differing learning modes.

In general you can say that the higher the trust atmosphere, the greater the scope for creativity and productivity. In a high trust environment you can help people to accomplish things they might not previously have believed themselves capable of accomplishing. High trust can help people reach beyond existing levels of performance in substantial and exciting ways, thereby promoting excellence.

In reality not many settings operate in a high trust way. Some collegial groups, human networks, and a few small companies might qualify. Certainly good team-work generally requires a healthy level of trust. Some learning situations can achieve a high level of trust. Generally, however, external factors make it difficult to achieve or sustain.

Trust and productivity

	Distrust	Low Trust	Moderate Trust	High Trust
High Skill	3	4	5	7
Low Skill	1	2	3	4

Figure 11: *The trust/productivity matrix*

Differing levels of skill linked to differing levels of trust will make a difference to productivity. Consider the matrix in Figure 11. The numbers on this matrix do not represent actual units of any kind. They simply show relative weights that might be given to productivity with the cross-related skill and trust levels.

People with low skill levels in a distrustful setting would have a very poor level of productivity. This level would improve with skill development. But if the distrust remains, you might only move from the 1 level to the 3. This represents a significant improvement in productivity, but it could go much higher with more trust. The ultimate level of 7 occurs with a combination of high trust and high skill.

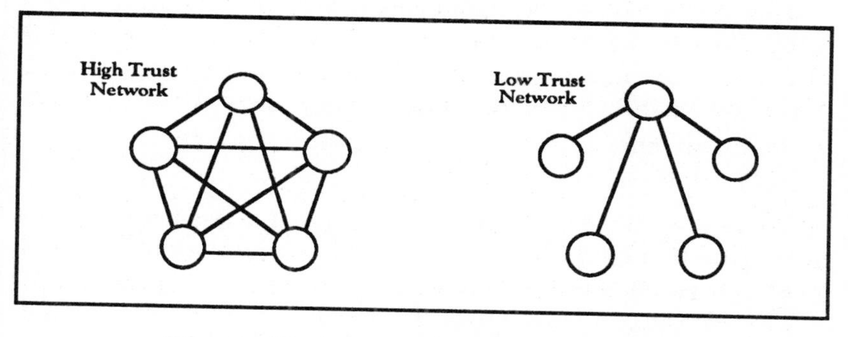

Figure 12: *Low trust/high trust networks*

Communications and trust

As you might expect, communications within higher trust environments are healthier than in lower trust environments. This provides much of the underpinning for improved productivity.

The number of communication links that exist within a human group reflect the level of trust. Many links go hand in hand with high trust. Figure 12 ('Low Trust/High Trust Networks') helps to illustrate this.

In low trust environments a good deal of emphasis is placed on restricting information flow. This illustrates the old adage that 'knowledge is power'. Low trust environments keep things secret, or simply do not disclose information. As a result, they usually end up with strong rumour mills and widespread misinformation.

High trust situations encourage discussion and open participation. Authority can be analysed and questioned. In high trust learning environments, instructors cannot pose as all-knowing experts. They must show themselves to be active and competent knowledge-seekers.

Building trust

The following are some of the steps instructors can take to build trust between themselves and their learners:

1. Provide information fully and freely.
2. Encourage learners to design and work on assignments of their own choice.
3. Give praise generously, when merited.
4. Maintain an attitude and tone of openness.
5. Remain reasonably accessible to people.
6. Ensure that materials, equipment and locations are available for learners to use on their own.
7. Show genuine interest in what people are doing.
8. Exercise patience at all times.

These steps will go far towards building a trusting environment. And this kind of environment will encourage the growth of trust in people's minds and in their actions.

The building of trust environments is no easy matter, especially in cases where distrust has existed previously. In such cases moves towards more trust could be seen as mere manoeuvres designed to exercise control through more subtle means. Generous amounts of time and patience are usually needed to prove that trust is to be applied in a genuine way.

The learning views that people have can also be an important factor. Some learners will view trust-building actions by instructors as not quite proper, or as signs of weakness or doubt. They could view trust environments not as opportunities for learning, but as opportunities for doing nothing.

More dependent or passive types of learners will tend to react against high trust learning situations. They will shy away from taking responsibility for their own learning, and will often walk away from trusting types of instructors.

Active or self-effective learners welcome situations of high trust. They enjoy the chance to prove themselves and to achieve results in their own ways. High trust instructors really help them bring out the best in themselves.

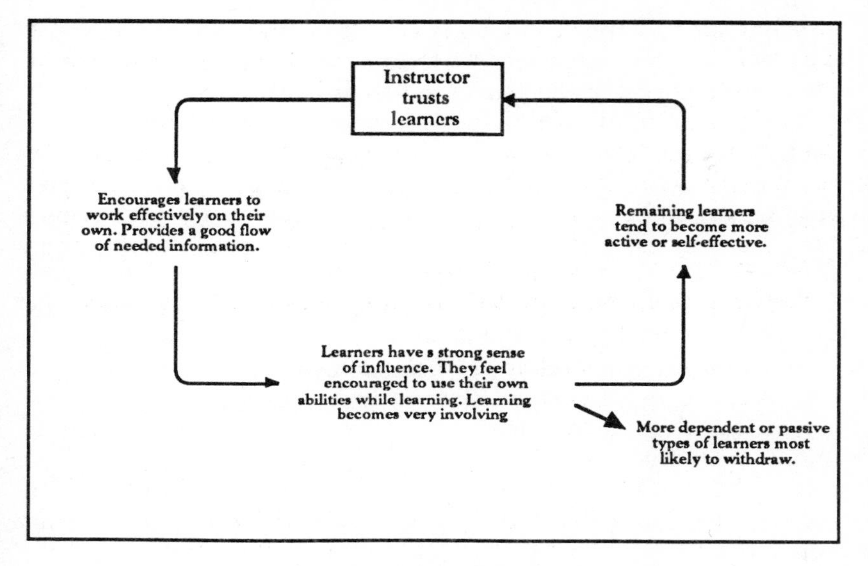

Figure 13: *The instructional trust cycle*

Getting the trust right

High trust learning environments encourage active learners, but they tend to discourage passive learners. So these environments will not necessarily produce successful learning right away.

The mix of active and passive learners in a given class will predict the likelihood of success in using more trusting approaches with them. It's for this reason that the wise instructor needs to size up the learning views of his or her learners effectively, while taking some care in setting up an environment for good learner motivation.

When learners are thrust into courses in large institutions or in business and industry without much regard to their learning backgrounds, the results of those courses will usually be mixed. And when so-called training evaluation forms produce negative results, the problem often lies not with the course or the instructor, but the learning expectations of the learners filling out those forms. So passive learners experiencing a high-trust learning environment may consider the learning situation poor and unorganized, and take their revenge in the remarks they make on the evaluation.

What may further complicate things is that passive learners may rebel or grow impatient with the idea of taking much time at the beginning of a course to sort out their learning preferences.

The upshot of all of this is that instructors must take care in using trust in the learning strategies they design and use. In some cases, you may just have to go with a higher than comfortable degree of distrust, simply because too many of your learners are passive types, and the course will be too short to change them. Ironically, this will produce situations in which instructors who are normally highly trusting may adopt more authoritarian approaches.

If you're in doubt about the trust level of a given group of learners, it generally pays to be cautious with your trust level at the outset. It's much easier later on to go from lower trust to higher trust than it is to go from higher trust to lower. Another way of putting this is to say that people are much happier with restrictions being lifted than they are with restrictions being applied.

Going with the learning flow

While teaching a given group of people pay close attention to how active or passive they are. If they're quick to volunteer for things or take to assignments eagerly, you can generally assume that a higher trust level is in order. If they don't volunteer quickly or tend to question assignments at length, so demonstrating their reluctance to participate actively, take it easy with the trust levels you use. In some cases, you may have to be a little distrustful. Remember, you can't expect to undo years of learning conditioning in a short space of time.

When learners relax and show willingness to take more learning responsibility, you can relax too and allow the trust levels to rise. Trust is a two-way street, so you really have to work with your learning group on this.

In those situations where trust occurs naturally and assuredly, the comfort levels for everyone will rise. Productivity increases, just as the Trust/Productivity Matrix helps to demonstrate. Further, and as a wonderful bonus, instructors in these situations will feel that they are working at their best. Trusting learners help good instructors to become even better.

The powers of trust

Trust is a precious and powerful commodity. It can achieve wonders with human performance, but you cannot apply it blindly. Plan your use of trust carefully. It's too important to apply carelessly or sloppily.

You can introduce trust in small measures over time as people demonstrate their capacity to respond. However it comes into play, trust is a powerful force for learning success. Used correctly, it's bound to produce long-term benefits for the learning process. And that will reflect well on you as an instructor.

5 Styling Your Instructing

We've now taken a look at some important aspects of learners, and we've linked these aspects to the ways in which you should approach teaching. In this chapter we'll delve into this linking of your instructing to your learners in some more specific ways.

First, it might be a good idea for you to complete Questionnaire 5. We'll examine its implications a little further on.

Just as individual learners have their own unique approaches to learning, instructors have their own favoured or characteristic styles. Some instructors find that their styles work quite well for them. Others experiment with different styles. And still others couldn't care less.

Style components

Your style of instructing involves aspects of tone, consideration, dominance, encouragement, involvement, exhortation, belief, determination, patience, sincerity and empathy. Some instructors involve their learners visually, verbally, or physically. Others pour out words and let them fall where they may. Some convey a deep sense of respect for their learners. Others convey contempt. All instructors create some sort of impression in the minds of their learners through their styles.

Your style can set a tone that is pleasant or harsh. You can sound supportive or uncaring. And the tone you set can arise from your voice, your gestures, your facial expressions, your movements, or the kinds of things you ask learners to do. Whenever you teach, you set some form of group atmosphere with your tone. Depending on the type of atmosphere you set, learning may be enhanced or hindered.

Consideration for others can be conveyed to some extent by your tone. People can feel a sense that you care for them. Or they can pick up quickly on whether or not you seem to know they exist. The considerate instructor sees tasks and activities from the point of view of the learners. She or he will strive to say or do things that take learner feelings and capabilities effectively into account.

Questionnaire 5: YOUR INSTRUCTIONAL STYLE PROFILE

Please take a look at the following paragraphs and rank each one of them according to the degree to which you believe that the paragraph describes your own instructional style. (1 = most typical of myself, 2 = next most most typical of myself, 3 = third most typical of myself, and 4 = least typical.) If you haven't instructed before, simply respond to these questions according to the way you think you would instruct:

A. I join fully with my learners in making teaching decisions, including the planning and conduct of lessons, and the content to include. I'm open to learner opinions, attitudes, and ideas. I feel that they are my equals, so they may well contribute as much to the learning process as I. ☐

B. I generally have quite a good idea of what I want to put across to my learners. But it's important for me to find ways of helping them understand the subject in their own terms. You might say that I use a selling approach. I try to gain sound and enthusiastic responses from learners. In essence, I want to convince them to see things the way I see them. ☐

C. I basically know what I want to have people learn. In my view I must ensure that I set out my content in clear, forthright, and well-organized terms. Essentially I tell my learners what they need to understand. It's very important to set forth my own ideas quite definitely. I want my learners to pay close attention to what I say. ☐

D. I like to ensure that my learners basically demonstrate to me what they can do. So I'll set out learning activities for them that prompt them to do things, so that I can carefully monitor their performance. I provide them with timely praise when they perform well. I also provide positive guidance as needed to help learners build effectively on their existing abilities ☐

Some instructors feel a strong need to dominate their classes. This can arise from feelings of insecurity or self-doubt. An urge to dominate might also arise from outbursts of learner hostility, or anticipated learner hostility. The dominating instructor could easily be following the philosophy of, 'Get them before they get you!'

Encouragement in your style can come across to learners in numbers of ways. The most effective and most powerful is personal recognition. When I recognize you as a unique individual, and when I recognize your accomplishments, you feel more involved in things, and you feel some improvement in your sense of motivation. The instructor who can truly encourage learners comes close to becoming the ideal teacher through this one characteristic alone.

Varying degrees of learner involvement can occur with varying instructor styles. In general, the higher the degree of learner involvement, the higher the amount of learning. This assumes, of course, that the learners are being involved in something worthwhile in the first place. Instructors can provide for involvement by inviting it , or they can set things up so that it occurs inevitably. Whatever the means of achieving it, involvement is a highly desirable aspect of an instructor's style.

Exhortation is much favoured by politicians and 'motivational' platform speakers. It urges people to do things for higher purposes. Great deeds, great purposes, and great promises flow freely. And a good exhibition of exhortation can be very moving, very inspiring. It can serve well to get things started, but it cannot sustain learning over a longer period of time. Instructors who possess good exhortation skills can, in effect, sprinkle some spice throughout their teachings.

If an instructor really believes something deep down, this comes through to her or his learners in crystal-clear fashion. People are very good at identifying phonies. But an instructor who conveys a personal sense of belief can prove very persuasive indeed. If you are convinced about something, it increases the chances that you might be able to win me over. If you seem to be just going through the motions, I may well wonder why I should even be bothered about what you have to say.

An instructor's beliefs are conveyed by little things. Words, acts, and reactions accumulated over a period of time reveal a lot to your learners about your beliefs. And what you believe plays an important role in the success of what you teach.

Your style comes through in other ways as well. Do you exhibit determination? Are your points of view set out directly and with some sense of vigour? A sense of direction, definiteness, and emphasis can impress learners very much. They pick up on this and are all the more likely to give credence to what you have to say. Your strength helps learners to build their own strengths.

Patience can be an aspect of your style. Do you rush at things, or do you tend to take it easy? Do you interfere quickly with what people are doing if they appear to be a little slow at learning something? The adage goes, 'patience is a virtue', and when it comes to instructing, this certainly applies.

Sincerity too is important. You can convey honesty, respect, and a touch of dignity in your instructing. This way too, you help to avoid any danger of arrogance creeping into your dealings with learners. Sincerity coupled with accuracy of your content can achieve a great deal of success for your instructing activities.

Empathy can be difficult to apply. It refers to the degree to which you can put yourself in your learner's shoes. With care and observation you can relate closely to their concerns and learning difficulties. You never lose sight of the learners' viewpoints in all your lessons. Through empathy you can help people to open their minds to new things and to make use of this new information quickly and effectively.

Your instructional style has many different facets. Achieving just the right style for a given group of learners in a particular situation is not easy. But an awareness of style and some attempt to adjust it readily will work for you, even if your instructional experience is limited.

Examining your style

Just as you can use a window device for examining your learning style, so too can you use such a device for looking at your instructing style (Figure 14).

In looking at this diagram you can see that four key styles are displayed: *director, persuader, developer* and *associate*. Questionnaire 5 ('Your Instructional Style Profile') that you may have filled out earlier in this chapter relates directly to the grid. Each paragraph in that questionnaire relates to one of the four key styles of instructing. We'll discuss each of these styles further in the next few paragraphs. Before we do, you might like to see if you can now relate the paragraphs in the questionnaire to the correct style on the grid just by using the diagram itself. This way you'll start to develop some insight into your own style profile.

	Passive	**Active**
High Focus on Learner	**3. Developer**	**2. Persuader**
Low Focus on Learner	**4. Associate**	**1. Director**

Figure 14: *The instructional style grid*

Now let's take a look in further detail at these styles.

In looking at the grid you can see that the ***director*** style has a low focus on the learners, but it is active. So the instructor using this style carries the lesson. He or she provides a lecture, gives a one-way demonstration, assigns learners to perform tasks, or otherwise employs an instructing style that takes charge, leaving little room for learner activity. By so doing, the instructor is taking the *learning pressure point* onto his or her own shoulders, rather than putting this pressure on the learners, thereby crowding out potential learner activity.

This style also leaves little room for considering the feelings or reactions of the learners. Given the right conditions of learner and setting preparation, this style can work efficiently. But it is dangerous to use in situations where learner demonstration of skills is important. In training workers to perform dangerous operations, for instance, this style could contribute to danger if used too much.

The ***persuader*** style places a high focus on the learner, while continuing to involve the instructor actively. The pressure point now weighs on both the instructor and the learners. Using this style the instructor hopes to get people actively involved in dealing with the content concerned. This may entail using questioning or leading discussions. Using this style the instructor looks for various ways to sell learners on given concepts, ideas and actions. Learner viewpoints and reactions must be monitored very carefully by the instructor using this style. The central thrust of this style is to persuade the learner to buy in to the lesson and its objectives.

The ***developer*** style follows logically from the persuader style. This style places a high emphasis on the learner, while the instructor's role is downplayed: so the pressure point here remains primarily on the learners. The main activity for the instructor using this style is to monitor learner performance in order to provide timely guidance and encouragement. Recognition of learner achievements is vital with this style. In a sense, you might identify this style as the most productive from the point of view of learning excellence.

Because the developer style gives the instructor a low profile in the learning setting, inexperienced observers may believe that the instructor is not really teaching at all. But this is far from being the case. In fact, the developer style is the best fundamental instructing style.

The ***associate*** style is not fully an instructing style as such. Using this style the instructor becomes an equal among equals, one more learner. This is the full collegial position, and everyone shares the pressure point evenly. This style is well suited to sophisticated and accomplished learners. Astute learners can learn very well from this style. They benefit from associating with an instructor in an open way, thereby learning from the little things she or he does or says. If the learners are carefully selected, this style works most productively.

Considering your style

The four key styles illustrated by the Instructional Style Grid in Figure 14 do not cover all possible style variations by any means. But they do provide a basic guide for planning and monitoring your style. They also help you to determine what other aspects of style you should use and how. The persuader style, for instance, demands a convincing tone, and it works best with a good level of sincerity. The developer style requires a tone that is supportive and sincere. The director style delivered with conviction helps to start people thinking in the right direction.

One important point to keep in mind when deciding on which key style to use is the degree of *competent performance* required by the learners. The higher the degree, the more important it is to use a style that allows for a lot of learner activity. The developer and associate styles do this. In this kind of situation it isn't the instructor's performance of the task to be learned that's vital, it's the learner's. This is a fundamental point, but it's often lost to sight in business and institutional settings. This may arise partly from the fact that training evaluation questionnaires so often concentrate on the instructor's performance and not the learner's, a curious distortion indeed.

Scoring the Instructional Style Profile

Now let's take a look at Questionnaire 5, that you may have filled out a little earlier. Here are the key styles represented by the different statements:

Statement A —	Associate
Statement B —	Persuader
Statement C —	Director
Statement D —	Developer

Now you can examine your responses to find out your own style pattern. Don't just concentrate on your first choice, but look at the overall sense of your four choices. Are you tending to rate putting a high focus on the learners at the top of your priorities? Do you rate being personally active in your style the highest? Do you seem to have a distant link with your learners? Check out all these questions, then think about the kinds of influences you've experienced that could explain your style pattern. Finally, and perhaps most importantly, do you wish to change your pattern? If so, in which direction? More emphasis on your learners? More emphasis on being passive? Relate to your own work situation as much as possible, and decide.

One logical pattern would be to plan on moving from director to persuader to developer to associate in training programmes. This would enable you to downplay your own activity as your learners show signs of being able to carry the learning load or accept the learning pressure point. This way you key your style directly to the modes displayed by the learners.

In their excellent book, *Management of Organizational Behavior,* Paul Hersey and Kenneth H. Blanchard develop their theory of situational leadership in good, basic style. The four styles they identified for leadership purposes include *telling, selling, participating,* and *delegating.* A rough similarity exists between their styles and the styles set out in this chapter for instructing.

The situational aspect of the Hersey/Blanchard approach concerns the linking of a leadership style to a particular level of follower *maturity*. A similar link-up is possible between instructing style and learner competence or receptivity.

Learning receptivity

Human learning does not occur in a neat, easy-to-describe manner. Stimulus-response explanations, for instance, so favoured by behaviourists, are really quite limited for explaining much about learning beyond a relatively primitive level.

Every person has her or his own style of learning, as we've already discussed, and each of us has developed learning brain paths in different ways. No two people are alike in the neural circuitry of their brains. Each one of us can be operating at a level of understanding or preparedness that differs from the levels of the people around us when we enter different types of learning situations.

Present day learning theory and brain research combine to support the idea that human learning probably is a hierarchical activity. We learn things in depth, or we can learn them superficially. We learn most things in stages (but not necessarily the stages developed by Piaget), and these stages have cognitive, affective, and behavioural dimensions.

One concept that helps in understanding the different levels of learning is that of *receptivity*. This refers to the degree to which you are actively aware of the events around you combined with the degree to which you're capable of dealing with them effectively. Receptivity has a connotation of probing or seeking for information in the outside world, rather than simply waiting for it to make itself known to you in an obvious way.

Many things go on around us every day, but we're really consciously aware of only a relatively small number of them. We may pick up on a few at the non-conscious level, but the great majority go right by us. Sights, sounds, patterns, vibrations, smells, feelings and so on, can occur within range of our sensory abilities, and yet we may not actually notice them.

The following everyday examples help to illustrate some aspects of receptivity at work. Have any of these ever happened to you?

1. You're shopping and are trying to find a particular item in the shop, but you just can't. Finally, you ask a shop assistant to help you, and he plucks it from a shelf just in front of your nose.
2. You're driving to a location different from the one you usually drive to on this day of the week, and you suddenly realize you've turned off at the intersection you usually turn off at, instead of going on to the one you meant to turn off at today. This phenomenon can occur also when you're walking or using public transport.
3. Someone says something to you, and you say, 'Pardon me?' Immediately after this you realize what the person said, so you're able to respond before she or he can repeat the comment.
4. You're walking along the street and have just passed someone walking in the opposite direction, when he or she suddenly speaks to you. Immediately you realize it's one of your good friends, but you hadn't apparently recognized him or her earlier.
5. You're in a crowd somewhere, perhaps shopping. All around you is a general din of people talking and shouting. Suddenly, you feel your ears tingle and perk up — you realize someone just used your name.
6. You're walking along a street you've walked along many times before, when suddenly you notice a particularly interesting feature on a building. It seems unique and brand new to you, but judging from the age of the building, you realize you must have walked past it many times before without noticing it.

The examples can go on, but we have enough here to illustrate the point. Many different sights, sounds, patterns, vibrations, smells, feelings, and so on, can occur within range of our sensory abilities, and yet we might not actually notice them at all.

The human brain is an exclusion device, not an inclusion one. Through life experience we have learned various forms of selective blindness, deafness and general sensory numbness to a wide variety of events or signals.

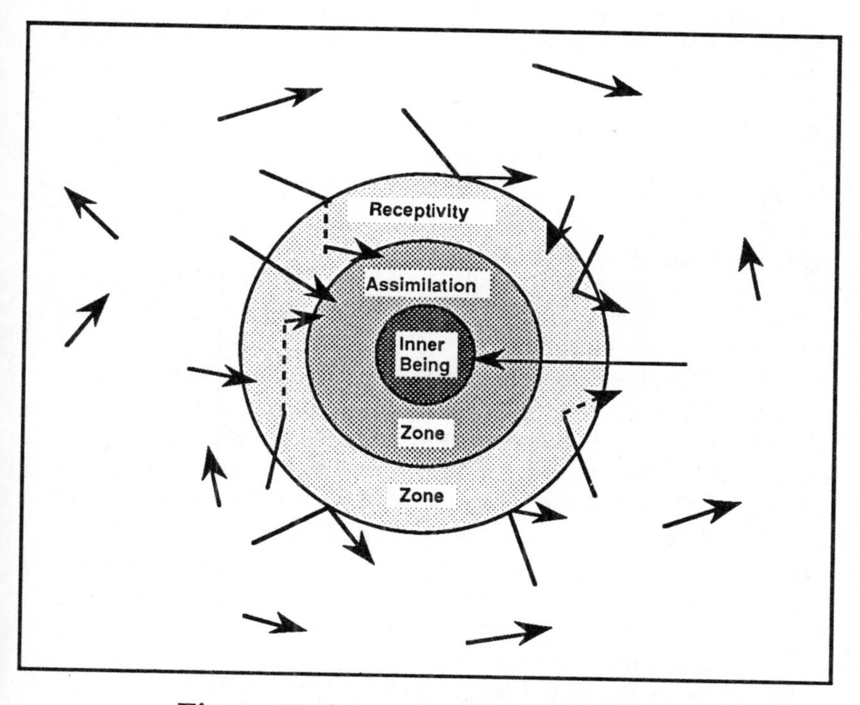

Figure 15: *Our comprehending mind*

When you stop to think about it, this fact makes perfectly good sense. After all, we just couldn't cope in the world if we had to try to deal with absolutely every signal available to us. In effect, we have to build in a priority system which tells us, 'This is an important signal', or 'Pay no attention to this signal'. If these priorities are well founded, then they work for us. But if they're haphazard or disorganized, then they do us no service. In many respects we see here the difference between an educated mind and an uneducated mind. The educated mind knows what matters, while the uneducated mind may well ignore important little bits of information.

People can always learn to tune into new or different signals. You can do it simply by trying. Do you hear the creaking of the boughs of a tree? Can you detect differences in a variety of bird calls? Do you know the sound of unsynchronized aircraft engines? Can your eyes pick out a significant feature on someone's face at a distance? Can your eyes or fingers tell the difference between salt and sugar? Can your nose pick up the smell of ozone or marijuana? The list can go on endlessly, but enough are given here to make the point.

You know that people can be trained to improve their listening skills and their observational skills. They can also be trained to improve their taste sensitivities, their sense of smell and their alertness to different kinds of vibrations. All these skills and more are vital to learning a wide variety of technical skills. With the right training, people can come to realize how much significant information is available to them through just a little sensitivity and attentiveness. People can and must be trained to improve their reception levels for specific areas of knowledge or applied expertise. This is an integral part of good training or teaching.

As people are trained or educated, their general receptivity improves. They come to realize that better attention-giving can yield good results in many different fields of endeavour. This is a major part of the reason why educated people are generally easier to train. Indeed, they are very good at self-training. The one caveat here is that some educated people may have learned what they know in relatively mechanical or rote ways. In such cases, they may not really be educated at all, despite possessing diplomas or degrees from the 'correct' institutions.

People with diplomas but a lack of real education often ruin their own receptivities by seeking to impose criteria they've learned by rote on all they encounter, even though these criteria may be wildly inappropriate for the subject concerned. It can take some time and patience to help such learners 'unlearn' their arbitrary, formula-laden ways. In some cases the time is simply not available, so these people go on to wreak their havoc elsewhere.

Figure 15 helps to illustrate the occurrence and role of receptivity in the normal human mind. You can see that you have to be receptive to a given item or bit of information before there is any hope of it becoming assimilated in the mind or learned. Our mind receptivity levels see to this. If we're not tuned in at that level to a certain type or form of signal, then we simply won't pick it up at all.

Without appropriate receptivity, learning is virtually impossible, unless the points made in a learning situation are so strong or so obvious that they will penetrate even the most unaware of minds.

Regular work activities require that we have receptivity to all sorts of important signals. What does your car's steering wheel feel like if one of your tyres has too little air in it? What is the immediate signal you should look for to tell you that the carriage doors of a train are about to close? What smell are you sniffing for when the waiter pours a small amount of wine into your glass from a newly opened bottle? What tell-tale sounds or vibrations tell the skilled worker of problems in an air-conditioning unit? What kinds of magnetic anomalies tell a geologist that a certain rock formation is worth digging into for possible mineral wealth? Think of all the signals that are important to you in your life and work, and you can comprehend the significance of receptivity in your thinking.

Automode

Bear in mind that receptivity works mainly at a non-conscious level. When we've really learned something, especially if it's a more physical kind of skill, we become essentially non-conscious about it. Some psychologists term this 'becoming mindless' about the skill.

Whether you drive a car, ride a bike, play tennis, or use a keyboard, you possess many skills that you no longer have to think about in a detailed, conscious way. When you drive a car, for instance, most of the manoeuvres of your hands, feet and eyes occur automatically. In effect, you switch on a brain programme for driving, and that programme takes over, leaving your conscious mind free to think about other things, or just to go along for the ride. If something sudden or dangerous pops up, your conscious mind is called upon to handle the anomaly. Once it's handled, the non-conscious brain programme takes over again.

Some refer to non-conscious ways of operating as being on automatic pilot, and this is an apt term. You might also call it *automode.* Interestingly, this mode is analogous to being in a state of hypnosis. We seem to drift in and out of states of hypnosis every day. This helps to explain why we sometimes fail to take in certain things around us.

It is quite possible that we are really only conscious in the fullest sense of the word for about twenty minutes a day. This is not twenty minutes all at once, but little segments of seconds scattered throughout a typical day. Of course different people vary. Some may have more conscious time, others less. But the variance is a matter of minutes. Simply put, you just can't be conscious for all your waking hours. But your waking hours are illuminated from time to time by flashes of consciousness.

Consciousness and learning

Consciousness can interfere with task performance. A skier successfully zooming down a hill will probably wipe out if he or she starts thinking consciously about the necessary body movements. Similar difficulties occur in playing tennis, football, hockey, in typing, operating various kinds of machines, and so forth. Conscious thinking can hurt performance. For this reason, posing the question, 'What are you doing?' at the wrong time can be disruptive, and lead to lesser performance.

Conscious thinking can cause difficulties in learning. Most of our learning occurs in non-conscious ways, simply through solid experience with and exposure to the knowledge or material to be learned. This is part of the reason why more involving methods of instructing work best. They help people to take in a lot of relevant information at non-conscious levels through actually working with the information in a meaningful way. Learner relaxation in the learning situation helps to promote non-conscious information acquisition. Anxiety or stress can induce too much consciousness, which is counter-productive to good learning.

Non-conscious receptivity

Conscious thought processes can cause us to think about issues or points that really aren't relevant to the subject at hand, thus interfering with learning. The mind that hasn't yet learned something can assign inappropriate priorities to different types of signals through sheer ignorance. And this brings us back to the receptivity issue again. Non-conscious receptivity is an important key to good learning.

How can you develop your non-conscious receptivity? The main path lies through sheer experience. You allow yourself to go with things, to assume you'll learn, not to approach learning in a tense, highly critical way, but rather in a relaxed, flowing way. The saying 'go with the flow' with its Zen overtones is a very useful one. By going with the flow of experience we learn. It's as simple as that.

The instructor's role

What's the instructor's role in all of this? The key role for the instructor lies in providing good learning experiences. The instructor is an *arranger of learning experiences*. And the more involving these experiences are for the learners, the better.

Learning mode and receptivity

When learners come into any new learning situation, their reception capabilities for the materials and activities involved will often be questionable. As a result of previous learnings or mislearnings, they may even exhibit a fair amount of 'blindness', 'deafness', or other form of insensitivity to events around them, even though these events might be highly significant for the subject being taught. The good instructor, naturally, can find this most frustrating.

Lack of receptivity based on ignorance of the full ramifications of a subject is understandable. After all, this is part of the reason for being a learner in the first place. What is less understandable in many learning situations is the kind of perverse pride that can come into play when a learner refuses to develop her or his sensitivity to important items of information. This type of learner is usually excessively dependent or passive.

More passive types of learners are less receptive to the things that may surround them. You could put them in a room filled with unique learning experiences and they would tend to ignore these experiences until some authority figure came along to guide them. Passive learners can take a lot of coaxing to open up their receptivities.

Active or self-effective learners are more generally receptive to information. They're prepared to take the initiative in ferreting out important details, and require relatively little guidance from instructors or other authority figures. Truly active learners can be highly successful on their own.

The link between active learning and receptivity is a close one. But the two characteristics are not identical. Active learning requires quality standards. And these standards will usually arise out of some form of learning objective. Receptivity, however, can exist in a more general way. In fact, in some situations a person could be too receptive. To obtain results you must focus your receptivity in a definite way. The active or self-effective learner can do this.

Productive receptivity

When it comes to learning you can think of productive receptivity as opposed to non-productive receptivity. Productive receptivity is relevant to the subject being learned. People who already know a lot about a given subject area will, naturally, be much more sensitive to points of information that are meaningful for it. So they will possess productive receptivity. And it's receptivity of this type that you're interested in for the purpose of arranging learning experiences.

Non-productive receptivity can lead people into all sorts of interesting side channels that could cause them to diffuse their learning energies on wild goose chases. They may well learn a lot, but their learning could involve fairly trivial things. Their form of learning lacks discipline or precision. Learners with this form of receptivity learn many things, but they can miss learning the right things.

Non-productive receptivity, despite its shortcomings, does have its place. Some forms of creativity or problem solving need this kind of wide open readiness to receive even the smallest items of information. Similarly, basic research demands this fullest kind of receptivity.

For our purposes, productive receptivity is the form of receptivity to concentrate on. This is the type of receptivity that applies in the overwhelming majority of instructional situations, especially in the realm of business and industry.

Reception levels

You can use the concept of receptivity in a practical way for doing some analysis of the types of learners you'll be dealing with prior to actually meeting them. The key to this practical use is to think of receptivity being framed using the stages showing in the following box.

These terms give you a quick means of judging the stage of receptivity that applies to given learners, either individually or in groups. In making your judgment calls here, remember to relate the learner's reception level to the subject concerned. The question of *subject competence* is vital in deciding on someone's receptivity.

1. UNAWARE
2. AWARE
3. INVOLVED
4. ACCOMPLISHED

A person operating at the **unaware** level, just as the term suggests, has no awareness or a very vague awareness of the subject concerned. To achieve learning objectives with someone at this level you must employ instructional techniques that help to develop awareness. You can develop this awareness at a non-conscious level through use of the right words, actions, or examples.

At the **aware** level of receptivity the learner has basic information about the subject concerned, and is at the threshold stage of the necessary learning. The learner at this level is well programmed mentally actually to do something in the required learning area. This is the stage at which *cognitive mapping* is important. You want the learner here to develop useful mental guidelines to apply in actual practice. These guidelines should, as far as possible, strongly emphasize clear images that learners can manipulate in their own minds.

Experimental work increasingly shows the importance to human learning of image embedding as part of cognitive mapping. This relates well to Ericksonian hypnosis with its stress on embedded suggestions. Neurolinguistic programming has a similar emphasis in helping people to 'reframe' critical issues in their minds. Super-learning has image embedding at its core (the book *Super-learning* by Sheila Ostrander and Lynn Schroeder delves into this in very readable fashion). The increased use of mental rehearsals in various sports is also closely related.

We seem tantalizingly close to a time when instructing will have to change in some quite dramatic ways to take advantage of our increasing knowledge of the power and effectiveness of the human brain. Some of the current work in developing *expert systems* is truly astonishing. In the meantime, bear in mind that your instructing should make generous use of images. Always be on the lookout for apt metaphors or analogies you can use to help learners tune in mentally to the points you want them to learn, especially when you're dealing with them at the unaware or aware stages of receptivity.

	Active Learning	**Passive Learning**
Conscious Subject Focus	**3. INVOLVED**	**2. AWARE**
Non-conscious Subject focus	**4. ACCOM-PLISHED**	**1. UNAWARE**

Figure 16: *The learner receptivity grid*

At the **involved** level the learner actually is doing something tangible with the tools, instruments, or concepts related to the learning objectives. Some form of actual performance occurs at this level. The learner might not perform at a competent level for a while, so it's important to provide enough time for her or him to practise the skill until the required performance level is reached.

The learning experiences you arrange for learners at the involved level should relate as closely as possible to actual on-the-job performance. Sometimes you'll find it pays to use your imagination and creativity to plan the most effective types of experiences.

Beware at the involved level of what some flying instructors have called the 500-hour syndrome. This is the point in flying training when student pilots may feel they really know how to fly, they've learned it all. This is the same point at which they're most prone to accidents.

Students in other learning situations may experience similar feelings at a certain point in their training. They believe they're ready to take off completely on their own, but they still need some final points of instruction to move them properly into the accomplished level. The instructor in this situation must use patience and help the learner understand that just a little more practice time is needed for true quality work.

In most cases, learners who reach the **accomplished** level have actually graduated from whatever training or teaching programme they had been taking. So their further contact with the instructor would be purely voluntary, by chance, or as a result of on-the-job requirements. Trainees could have learned a given job skill and then worked with their former instructor back on the job. In a university setting, students could have obtained a graduate degree, and then gone on to work with their former professor as associates in some form of further project.

In some cases learners may reach the accomplished level while still taking their training. Learners at this level might well rival you, the instructor, in the skill and knowledge they can apply to the subject concerned. But don't feel intimidated. That's part of the instructor's job.

When people reach the accomplished level well before a course ends, it could be a good thing, or it could show a problem. If you want people to have lots of practice in a supervised situation, you may want them to reach the accomplished level while they are still trainees. If this is not the case, then having a lot of people reaching this level before a course ends may indicate that the course is too long for the level and types of learners involved. Either way, it's something that requires careful attention.

The Learner Receptivity Grid

In many ways the grid in Figure 16 brings it all together. It displays the reception levels of learners. But it also interrelates these to learning modes and the critical question of conscious versus non-conscious learning.

From the diagram you can see that the learner at the unaware level operates at a passive level for the subject concerned and lacks consciousness of the need for a focus on that subject. Some people have referred to this as the state of *non-conscious incompe-*

tence. That is the learner is incompetent in the subject, but isn't yet conscious enough about it to realize this fact.

In using the term 'passive' here some confusion is possible with real learners. At the start of a given course learners might be very active, but they're active on their own agendas. In the case of an industrial training programme, for instance, they might still be actively engaged in thinking about the ins and outs of the latest work crisis. In this kind of case the instructor must command attention in no uncertain way. The director style of instructing is needed in definite, sometimes authoritarian, terms. The military are well used to this in their training. They make no bones about commanding attention at the start of their training sessions, and their attention-getting devices can be quite loud indeed.

School or college instructors may have qualms about commanding attention with their classes. But the principle remains the same. If students are truly at the unaware level, yet are very active in their behaviours directed towards other issues or subjects, the teacher must take charge. Otherwise, he or she runs the very definite risk of becoming a glorified baby sitter.

Notice from our grid how learners can operate at a conscious level of learning at two different reception levels. In the aware level they are, in effect, prepared for entering the involved level. This preparation mode is vital, especially for learning more physical or kinaesthetic kinds of skills. By the same token, it should not be drawn out needlessly. (As some organizations do, for instance, when time tables urge instructors to fill in time before moving on to a more active phase of learning.)

At the final level of receptivity in our grid, notice that the learner has slipped back into a non-conscious state for dealing with the subject concerned. But this is a different type of non-consciousness to what the learner started out with. Now he or she has reached that mindless or automode state we talked about earlier. Like skilled race car drivers they just go ahead and perform, without consciously thinking about it. And this is where that flowing or Zen state can come into play.

When people have truly reached the accomplished level, they should be able to give quality performance with an effortless appearance. This you can see, for instance, in watching the performance of an accomplished violinist. No matter what the field, when people still appear to be straining or working hard in a conscious way, they've not yet reached the accomplished level for that subject area.

Incidentally, people will often complain that they feel tired after a full day of concentrated learning, especially if they're not used to being in a classroom situation. A major part of the reason for this is simply that they're having to use their brains in conscious mode more than usual. Similarly, instructing is draining work, because it imposes a higher quotient of conscious work on the instructor than most people are used to.

Situational instructing

Recall now that we saw earlier in this chapter that the different key instructing styles could be related to learner reception levels to produce situational instructing. Let's make that link now.

In general, the higher the learner's level of reception to the learning concerned, the more passive you can be in your instructing style. More receptive types of learners will tend to instruct themselves to a greater degree, and will see you as more of an assistant to their learning activities than a learning task master.

The instructing/learning continuum shown in Figure 17 allows us to picture the interaction and structure of instructing styles, learning modes, and reception levels. In examining it you can see the progression from unaware to accomplished learner corresponding with the learner becoming more active in the process as the instructor becomes more passive. The whole requires time, and it requires care on the part of the instructor to ensure that he or she, in effect, backs off as learners become more capable.

If you use an instructing style inappropriate to the reception level of your learners, you risk intruding on their learning inappropriately, with consequent risk to the quality of that learning. A director style used with learners at the active level, for instance, would probably cause resentment. It would also be likely to slow up the learning process. Similarly, an associate style used with learners at the unaware level would likely cause confusion as learners experienced a sense of floundering or lack of direction.

The essence of the situational approach is to shift instructing styles accurately and smoothly as learner reception levels change. For this reason you should not concentrate on just one key instructing style. You may find, however, that the persuader and developer styles become your most-used ones. 'Pacing' your style with your learners' reception levels is crucial.

It is quite possible that you'll use all four key styles in most of the lessons you teach. You might even shift from one to another and then back. Preferably, you should be able to shift from the more active to the more passive in a tidy progression. It all depends on where your learners really are in their learning modes and their states of receptivity.

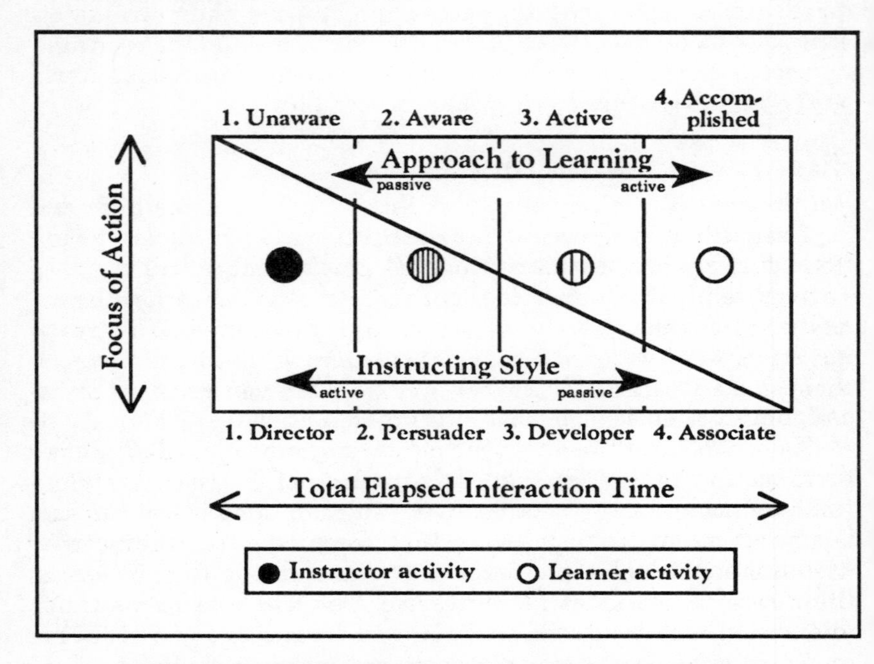

Figure 17: *The instructing/learning continuum*

Almost always you'll want to move your learners from at least one stage to the next (most likely the director to persuader). In most cases, though, you should aim at using at least three instructing styles in a given course or training programme (director – persuader – developer). This way you should be able to send your learners on to their next course or the workplace ready to move into the accomplished level. All of this should be related carefully to well-conceived learning objectives.

It is possible to have combinations of these levels and styles. So a learner could be at the unaware/aware level, more or less a dawning realization point. By the same token an instructor could use a style such as persuader/developer, combining selling with encouragement of learner efforts.

Usually you'll find that learners naturally grow from one reception level to the next, becoming more active all the while. This shifting of levels will probably not occur in a rigid or jerky manner. Rather, it will be a gradual shift, with the exact point of shift being hard to identify. Similarly, your instructional styles should shift carefully and subtly. You don't suddenly announce, 'Well, you're receptive enough now, so I'm going to develop you more!'

Critical confrontation

Sometimes you'll feel tempted to force growth on your learners. You may feel that their receptivity level should have risen, and yet they're still working too passively.

Forcing learner growth can be tricky, because you have to time your changes or transitions from one style to another accurately to avoid confusion or loss of confidence on the part of your learners. This means you have to be sure that learners are truly ready to be shifted. But, as part of your task of arranging learning experiences, this could be vital. With practice, you should be able to develop a better feel for doing this appropriately.

As part of your forcing strategy, you may need, in effect, to use 'critical confrontation'. This means picking a time to simply confront your class with your perceptions about their lack of apparent receptivity increase, despite their apparent readiness for it. In doing this you should pick on specific events or points to illustrate your statements. Then throw the session open for discussion. The results can be dramatic.

Sometimes people just hadn't realized their lack of behaviour change. Sometimes they're genuinely shocked to realize they've continued in a passive way, and may laugh nervously as the realization hits them. Other times, people will say they're just not used to being allowed to grow in a learning session. Their fundamental learning modes may be holding them back. In other cases you may find that learners received information from other people that you hadn't known about that caused them to behave rigidly with you.

In most cases critical confrontation can clear the air and bring about productive changes. In some cases, of course, the opposite can happen. People might simply resent having their shortcomings brought out in the open. They will experience all the human problems of dealing with unpalatable truths about themselves.

Obviously, you don't use critical confrontation lightly or without careful thought. The dangers are too many for that. And one of the dangers is that you will lose the group. In most cases, however, the results will be positive.

If you're thinking of using critical confrontation be aware of two very important points.

First, you must leave yourself with sufficient 'cushion' time for letting the group work through its feelings before the course ends. An absolute minimum of one-third of your total course time or one day, whichever is less, provides you with a good time measure here.

Second, beware of using critical confrontation in an organizational culture that will not be supportive. Many managers have insufficient understanding of the learning process to realize the significance of the critical confrontation process. For them you'd simply come across as a hectoring, aggressive instructor.

Sometimes you may wish to use critical confrontation at the individual level. The earlier the better is the rule here. If you have a learner who just doesn't want to take your course, and wants to use all the available time to sabotage your instructing efforts, confrontation is called for. Of course this should take place as discreetly as possible, and without engaging in name-calling or other aggressive actions. Make sure the learner realizes she or he has a choice to make, then ensure that it's made — 'Either take the course in a productive frame of mind, or depart. It's your choice'. You might also refer to this as 'disinviting' the learner to take part in your programme.

Dealing with individual disruptive learners in a definite way is essential. Otherwise they will simply interfere with effective learning for everyone else. Of course, if some kind of counselling can be arranged, do so, again setting this out as a choice for the person to make.

Critical confrontation works, but you have to use it carefully, just as though you were handling nitroglycerine. Like nitro, it can blow up in unpleasant ways. But, like any good explosive, it can produce dramatic breakthroughs.

Mixed reception levels

The classes you have to deal with may often contain people whose reception levels are individually quite different. If you're dealing with adults in the workplace, this almost goes without saying. The same thing applies, of course, as we've seen earlier, to their learning modes.

In dealing with a mixed group you may have to use a style that's a bit more formal than you'd really prefer to use, simply to keep with you the people at lower levels of reception or in more passive modes of learning. Still, you somehow need to give those people with higher reception levels or more active learning modes some form of recognition. This may involve learning delegation, or it may involve calling on these people from time to time to share their learning and abilities with everyone else.

Working with a mixed group takes more time and effort. Ideally, you should have a group that's more homogeneous in its learning capacities. Here's a role for course planners and those with responsibility for selecting people to take courses. Unfortunately, their work here, especially in many industrial situations, is usually not all that precise or involved, so you, as the instructor, have to live with it.

When you have widely-different reception levels and learning modes to contend with, bear in mind that you may generally have to be a little more authoritarian than you might prefer. There may be no helping this. You can't afford to come across as wishy washy here. Otherwise, you'll end up in a struggle for leadership of your class. Once you've worked with this kind of mixed group for long enough, you might be able to loosen up considerably. But don't be too quick or anxious about doing this.

Managing your own inclinations

In developing your ability to pace your instructing styles, bear in mind your own learning preferences and inclinations, not to mention your own general receptivity. These can influence your choice and use of instructing styles at a non-conscious level. Partly for this reason you need feedback from others (preferably other instructors) on how well you're pacing your approach during teaching sessions. Feedback using audiotapes or videotapes of your instructing could help you a lot.

By pacing your learners' reception levels consistently and regularly, you'll automatically instruct more effectively. In effect, you become more attuned to your learners and this, in turn, helps you to influence them much more productively.

Learning contaminators

In an ideal instructional setting you would be able to work on your instructional pacing and produce clear reception results with your learners. In the real world, however, other factors do come into play, and these other factors can interfere with your style impact, or distort it altogether. These are 'contaminating factors', or just 'contaminators'. They take the form of intrusive people or intrusive physical conditions. Let's examine a few of them.

Have you ever attended a meeting where you had to sit in a very uncomfortable chair? Or have you found yourself going to sleep during a meeting because of the stuffiness of the room? And have you every found yourself inhibited about taking part in the meeting because of something indefinable about the general atmosphere? All of these are examples of contaminators at work.

Because instructors are often caught up in the urgencies of their preparations and their own self-doubts, they sometimes ignore the presence and impact of contaminators. This form of negligence can produce learning results of a lesser quality than might otherwise have been possible.

One way to take contaminators into account before a training session is to try putting yourself in the place of your learners. Sample the chairs they'll sit in. Or check out the sight lines in the classroom to ensure that every chair provides a reasonable view of the key places in the room. Look for leg and elbow space. If learners will have to write or draw during the lesson, ensure they will have sufficient space to do so. Think also of ventilation and temperature control. Will these enhance learning or interfere with it? Might smoking pose a problem? Can you ban smoking in the classroom? Will the lighting be sufficient? What about external noises? Will these be reasonably subdued or controlled? Give a thought to the people who might intrude on your session. What can you do about these human contaminating factors?

Whatever you can think of to check in eliminating or controlling contaminators is worth some attention. Allot a reasonable amount of time for doing this. In your lesson planning you'll find it prudent to allow a cushion of time for dealing with those contaminators that crop up suddenly or unexpectedly while you're teaching.

The possibilities go on, but you get the idea. It's not enough just to prepare your material and then present yourself to a group of people. You have to take whatever realistic steps you can to truly manage the learning situation. Some imagination and good planning will help you here. And your learners will benefit all the more.

Pollution and learning

One special form of learning contamination involves outright pollution. Our society is increasingly aware now of the reality and hazards of atmospheric pollution. But we are only just beginning to recognize the realities of indoor pollution. Some hermetically-sealed office buildings produce indoor atmospheres dangerous to human health. Particulate pollutants of all sorts, including asbestos, mould spores, arsenics, microscopic cinders, paint and varnish fumes, and so on, float around in most indoor atmospheres. In addition, a fascinating array of gases from carbon dioxide to carbon monoxide and ozone assault our lungs. Some authorities now refer to the problem of SBS or 'sick building syndrome'.

The brain uses one-third of all the oxygen the body takes in. And the brain takes top priority for available oxygen, so a lack of oxygen translates readily into sluggish body movements. Think of times in the past when you've experienced the sight of sluggish learners in a classroom setting. What was the air quality of that setting? Chances are that it was not very good. How many times is poor air the reason for learner sluggishness and not poor motivation? Physical contaminants can make people ill, and they can contaminate the entire learning process.

Because the human body is such a marvellous creation, human beings can learn in quite atrocious conditions. This is a function of the flexibility and reserve power built into the human body. Unfortunately, because human beings are capable of learning in terrible conditions, many authorities have tended to assign just those kinds of conditions for learning. This may come under the heading of 'macho training'.

The pernicious effects of corporate or institutional tradition can compound the problem of learning contaminators. Some managers or politicians have been known to say such things as, 'Well it was good enough for me when I went through, so it's good enough for everyone else'. This is a form of reasoning akin to sticking one's head in the ground to avoid dealing with reality.

Distracting noises can come at us from a variety of sources. Wherever they come from, these contaminators interfere with learning. Further, they can aggravate human stress conditions, and even cause the onset of stress problems in the first place. High enough noise levels can actually bring on varying degrees of deafness. And subsonic or ultrasonic noises may interfere with our mental processes at non-conscious levels. So even the noises we can't hear can hurt us.

Ineffective lighting can act as a major learning contaminator. Too much light or too little makes it difficult for learners to see what they're supposed to see. Low lighting levels encourage sleepiness or reduced mental activity. Some kinds of lighting flicker will induce near-epileptic responses in some people. In general, people seem to prefer incandescent lighting to fluorescent. Its yellowish tones are somehow more human. Promising developments in this area appear to be occurring with something called full-spectrum lighting.

Temperature control is an important consideration as a form of learning contamination. A room that's too hot makes people sluggish. A room that's too cold makes them irritable. Either way they're not going to learn well.

Some people react negatively to rooms without windows. They find such rooms claustrophobic, and experience a sense of psychological suffocation. For them this would be a major learning contaminator.

The list can go on and on. Open windows that lead to breezes or dust entering from a busy street, noxious smells, irritating vibrations and the like, all cause learning difficulties. Add to all this the fact that individual differences can and do enter the picture. What contaminates my learning may have no effect on yours.

Setting your instructional approach

As part of your instructional pacing or matching, you need to take into account the possible impacts of various contaminators on the individual learners you're dealing with. The presence and interfering power of learning contaminators can affect learner receptivity. They can slow down the process of growth in the learning process, or prevent it altogether, thus blunting your instructional success.

The existence of contaminators of various types should not keep you from using situational instructing successfully. They simply mean that you have to add an extra dimension to your general instructional alertness. You have to broaden the field of things you take into account, and refrain from blinding yourself to external physical events that might intrude and do damage.

Preparing yourself

Through careful examination and development of your instructional styles and an increased understanding of learner reception levels, you will become a fully effective instructor. This applies especially if you've done a good job of coping with or providing for the effects of learner contaminants. You will have better prepared yourself to design and deliver effective and worthwhile learning experiences for all the people you teach.

6 Setting Your Strategy

In examining an instructing style we've seen how important clear and well-conceived learning objectives are to an effective learning process. In effect, you can say that objectives form the core of the strategy you plan to use to provide solid learning experiences to your learners.

A strategy consists of all the means you employ to meet your objectives. In designing your strategy you make use of some or all of the resources available to you, while taking into account any risks or obstacles that may stand between you and the achievement of your objectives. Every time you instruct someone, you engage in a particular strategy. This strategy could be one you've thought about clearly, or it could be one you simply allow to happen.

Good training or teaching does not usually just happen. Most of the time it requires thought and planning. Every minute spent on effectively working out your strategy can save many minutes later on.

The learning experiences you provide, no matter how simple, go on to reflect your efforts over a long period of time. Successful learning will reflect well on you and your organization. Rough hewn or sloppy learning programmes will have long-term ill consequences for the well-being and effectiveness of your organization.

Strategy questions

In working on your instructional strategy ask yourself the following questions.

1. What are you really trying to have the learners do?
2. Do you have a clear idea of who your learners are?
3. Are you the right instructor for them?
4. What styles of instructing will you need to use?

5. Is the timing right for providing this learning?
6. Do you understand how this learning programme fits in with your organization's needs?
7. Have you worked out learning objectives for this programme that focus on the learner's performance?
8. What resources will you need to ensure that the learning objectives are achieved?
9. How will you measure the effectiveness of the learning once it's been provided?

Answer each one of these questions in turn. Writing out your responses on a sheet of paper will help you more specifically to articulate your thinking. If additional questions arise in your mind as you're doing this, try to deal with them also. These questions and your responses to them will give you a workable framework to use as a foundation for your training strategies in a variety of situations. They will also identify potential trouble spots early enough in the strategy process to enable you to do something about them.

In working through your strategy for achieving learning in others you must focus on potential or real purposes, results and objectives. To remain coherent in your own thinking as well as in your instruction, your objective or objectives for each lesson you teach must receive careful consideration.

Planting thoughts

When you instruct, you're basically trying to plant key thoughts in your learners' minds so they'll have an accurate picture (or cognitive map) of what you want them to understand. In effect, you're engaged in an act of translation that will help learners to see clearly what's in your mind. So simply pouring out your own thoughts from your own perspective will not be good enough. You have to translate your thoughts into the other person's perspective.

Your strategy needs to involve a careful thinking through and design of learning objectives assembled to provide a coherent and logical learning path. These objectives provide you with milestones of progress. They're indispensable ingredients in any training or learning strategy worthy of the name.

Thinking about learning objectives

Your task of translation works out well if you use good learning objectives. These objectives must, as far as possible, describe what your learners will do, and when. This sounds simple. But this simplicity is deceptive. Most people have a lot of difficulty in trying to word an instructional objective from the point of view of someone else. People seem automatically to word objectives in terms of their own actions, not the intended actions of others. This brings us back once again to the question of where the pressure point should be in a lesson.

When you find yourself stating a learning objective using words such as 'to show', 'to tell', 'to explain', 'to demonstrate', or 'to have', you're probably stating things from your own perspective, thus taking the learning pressure point onto your own shoulders. Use phrasings that clearly shift things onto your learners. Such phrasings could take the form of 'will perform', 'will show', 'will respond', 'will demonstrate', and so on, as long as the learner clearly is the subject.

In working through your basic instructional strategy, you'll find it helpful to go through the following steps:

1. Describe your instructional task in general terms. What, essentially, do you plan to have your learners actually learn?
2. Who are your learners? Do you have a good idea of their receptivity levels and at least some of their learning style preferences?
3. What are your learning objectives? Are they clearly worded from the point of view of actual learner performance?
4. How will you introduce the learning objectives to your learners (purpose statements)?

These steps get things off to a good, productive start. Work with them for a while, and you'll find that they start to come automatically to you. In examining this, you can see that learning objectives are essential to working out your instructional strategy. For this reason we'll now take a deeper look at the practical uses of learning objectives.

The evolution of learning objectives

Objectives in learning are not new. Ancient Roman instructors undoubtedly had some idea of what they wanted their learners to do. Medieval tradesmen or 'masters' knew the skills they wished to impart to their apprentices. And modern teachers in school settings work with objectives in their outlines and in their classes.

What's new in the past twenty years or so is an increasing focus on the specifics of the way learning objectives are worded. Loose wording is now seen as far too vague. And certain key elements have now been identified, at least by a considerable number of authorities (Robert Mager pre-eminent among them), as crucial to the writing of good objectives.

In the training and education fields much argument has taken place over the past decade about the role, value, and form of objectives for learning. As an instructor you need some idea of the nature of these arguments so that you can work out your own position regarding them.

Managing with objectives

The concept and use of objectives has not been limited to instructional activities. The application of 'management by objectives' (MBO) developed very strongly over the past twenty years urged on by such management greats as Peter Drucker and George Odiorne. This concept is not always applied well, but it does give added support to the central role of objectives in any kind of performance strategy. An objective framed within the MBO concept basically identifies:

1. The person or organization involved;
2. The performance required;
3. The time period during which the objective is to be achieved.

An objective that met these criteria might read:

> 'The sales department will increase our sales of Super Soap by 20% during the period of July 3 to October 4, 1992'.

This is fairly straightforward, and it gives management a convenient bench-mark for planning and assessing. Used properly, objectives of this type can be most helpful.

Training departments of large businesses naturally absorbed much of the MBO approach. One of their objectives might well read:

'The training department will train at least 120 students in first-line supervision within a six-month period commencing April 15, 1993'.

Notice an interesting distortion that occurs at this point. Increasing sales of Super Soap might be tangible and widely understood in the way intended. The training of first-line supervisors is not quite so clear.

How long will the training sessions be? How many people will take each session? What, exactly, is meant by 'training' these students?

In too many cases the training or education of people can simply mean exposure to training or educational activities. This is particularly true for subjects that are not perceived as mechanical or technical skills.

The behavioural focus

Since the 1930s, behavioural psychologists inspired by the late B.F. Skinner have built a very persuasive case for behavioural objectives. They based their arguments on the merits of positive reinforcement as a powerful means of shaping and building human performance. Behavioural objectives specify what an individual human being will do under given conditions. They also identify standards of performance.

Behavioural objectives found fertile ground in settings already tuned in to management by objectives. Behaviourists could even show how thoughts, attitudes and knowledge work could be interpreted through behaviours. They seemed to say that, given the right rewards, people could be conditioned into doing virtually anything desired.

A good behavioural objective might look like this:

'The subject will operate the Mark II power drill safely according to manufacturer guidelines by the end of a three-hour training session. As part of this operation, he or she will drill at least fourteen one-half-inch diameter holes through a one-eighth-inch thick steel plate. Each hole will take no more than fifteen seconds to drill'.

This objective may appear wordy, but it is certainly more precise than simply saying, 'The learner will operate the Mark II power drill'.

Behavioural theory has made massive inroads into training in business and industry. And it can claim a good deal of impressive success. But it too has its limits.

People do think. They plan and act based on their own concepts of rewards or motives. And they engage in learning for a variety of personal reasons other than behavioural reward (existing brain programming can be a powerful reason in its own right). Behavioural theory has strict limits when applied to human learning. Even so, it has contributed a great deal to sharpening up the wording of objectives for learning, thereby helping to focus training and some education much more sharply.

Good learning objectives should:

1. Focus on observable learner action;
2. Specify the standards and conditions of performance;
3. Identify clearly important time spans involved.

Practical versus theoretical

In business and industrial settings, learning objectives must relate closely to the skills actually required for competent performance on the job. You might relate this requirement to the hierarchy shown in Figure 17.

The top of this hierarchy is actual skill performance. That's where the real results lie, particularly when it comes to training. The lower levels in the hierarchy become more and more theoretical, and so removed from actual application.

The theoretical side of instructing is, by no means, inferior to actual skill performance on the job. In some cases it's actually superior. On-the-job conditions may preclude reasonable instruction in that arena. It may make better sense from your strategy's point of view to take some time to provide learners with good cognitive maps or mental rehearsals before they do get their hands on things. In using the practical/theoretical hierarchy use as your instructional entry point the level that, given all the factors you have to consider (including learning contaminators), seems most likely to work well for your instructional strategy.

ACTUAL SKILL PERFORMANCE

▲

SKILL PERFORMANCE IN A LEARNING SITUATION

▲

SIMULATED SKILL PERFORMANCE

▲

DISCUSSION ABOUT SKILL PERFORMANCE

▲

LECTURE/DISPLAY ABOUT SKILL PERFORMANCE

Figure 18: *The practical / theoretical hierarchy*

In earlier chapters we've seen how people can differ in their learning styles and approaches. In particular, we've examined the concepts of active learning and learning receptivity while relating these concepts to your own instructional style. This relating issue is, naturally, a very important part of your strategy design work. You do need to keep learner differences clearly in mind when designing your learning objectives.

Cognitive learning

You need a strong emphasis on the behavioural in stating your objectives, but you have to remain cognizant of other forms of learning, especially for learning that is not strictly at the basic technical skill level.

In recent years a field called 'cognitive science' has come into increasing prominence in the study of learning theory. This field examines the essentials of human thinking. It draws on findings in linguistics, psychology, artificial intelligence, neuroscience, biology and education, as well as other fields of human endeavour.

Cognitive science has demonstrated with EEG (electro-encephalograph) and MRI (magnetic resonance imaging) readings, biofeedback, electrical stimulation of parts of the brain, and other techniques, the power, diversity, complexity, and reality of human thought. We aren't just packages or bundles of behaviours. Action follows thought, not the other way round.

The impact of cognitive science on learning theory has, among other things, led to the use of cognitive objectives as well as behavioural objectives. These types of objectives focus on specific types of thought activities or concept working. A cognitive objective might be phrased:

> 'The learners will, during the two-day learning process, analyse the decision making used by managers within the purchasing department of the Embargo Company. They will conduct this analysis in terms of the types of language used, information preparation, decision stating, and implementation'.

Now, examine this objective from the viewpoint of an instructor trying to assess the quality of cognitive learning that takes place. He or she would probably expect the learner to identify specific examples of the kinds of statements made by the managers, the types of information used, decision phrasing, and actual implementation actions.

Learner performance tested in this type of instructional situation might well involve the instructor in asking learners to write reports detailing their analyses. At the very least it would probably involve learner responses to questions posed orally by the instructor. In other words, specific forms of behaviour would come into use to help determine the quality of the cognitive activities that took place.

We come back to the behavioural side of learning for assessing learner competence. But the behaviours that we're dealing with here are not 'pure'. They're stand-ins for cognitive activities, or they may combine with these activities. Now we can talk about objectives that might be behavioural, cognitive-behavioural, or purely cognitive.

In considering all this you might be tempted to say, 'Well it really all boils down to behavioural in the end, so why not just stay with behavioural?' You would certainly have lots of company in arriving at this conclusion. And it does make instructional life easier. You can reach a point of deciding the whole things becomes too complex. You yearn to keep it simple. Bear in mind, though, that a profound difference exists between something that's simple and something that's simplistic.

A purely behavioural approach to human learning tends to render it trivial or simplistic. It can lead to seeing people as biological robots ready for your programming. You might then have people undergo the performance of particular skills and, in this way, meet the surface requirements of a behavioural objective. But the simple performance of a task under guidance by no means demonstrates that learning has occurred. Practice and continued performance at the competent level are essential to establish full learner self-effectiveness.

Learning does involve internal mental processing. It involves brain programming, assimilation, transfer, and the association of new and existing information. It involves neurotransmitter changes and the development or enhancement of neural pathways. In the case of observable skills it requires propriocentric (total sensory awareness) coordination, and the development of a perceptual trace (a kind of internal brain template that people use to control their body movements for carrying out physical tasks in a precise manner) for the full implementation of the skill involved.

Clearly, a purely behavioural approach to the use of learning objectives is inadequate. For most human performance requirements, it just doesn't go far enough. At the same time, the behavioural aspect of learning is far too important to abandon or downplay significantly. As we mentioned earlier it sharpens the focus of learning and helps instructors to identify most effectively the areas of learning that must be addressed.

Feelings

As well as thoughts, people have feelings. These can be critical to learning. If you have negative feelings about a given task or activity, you'll probably have a hard time learning it. If you have positive feelings about it, your learning task is much easier. These feelings relate very much to your sense of motivation about your learning.

To aim at feelings or reinforce learner motivation, you might have to design objectives that fit the feelings or affective part of human learning. Such objectives would spell out how you intend learners to feel as a result of a given segment of learning. You might also term this a 'motivational objective'. Here's an example:

> 'As a result of this one-day training programme the learner will want to use the CPS problem-solving technique when

tackling general types of business problems in a typical work setting'.

A behavioural component could be added to this objective for your monitoring purposes. In this case you would end up with an affective-behavioural objective. Theoretically, you could design an objective that combined the three learning aspects: cognitive, behavioural, and affective.

Our learning domains

The three key aspects of learning are usually referred to as our learning domains. By bringing all three of these domains into use in setting learning objectives, you run the risk of having things become unwieldy, thus defeating the utility of learning objectives. In practice, you'll probably find that the behavioural or cognitive-behavioural objectives will serve most of your strategy design purposes. Just be sure to take the full cognitive issues and affective issues into account somehow in fleshing out your design.

Figure 19 helps to highlight the three learning domains. As this diagram shows, human behaviours emerge from and through our cognitive and affective domains — our thoughts and feelings. They do not take on a life of their own or operate in a remote manner, although they may work at an automode or non-conscious level.

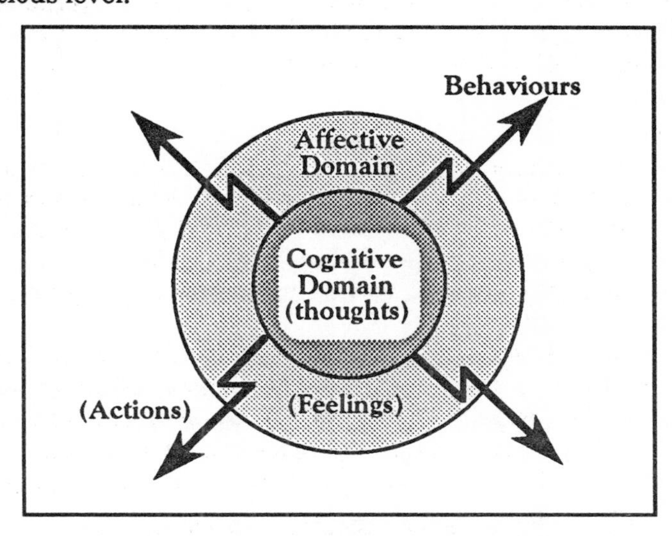

Figure 19: *Our learning domains*

When working on your instructional strategy you can take all three learning domains effectively into account by using the table shown in Figure 20.

By using this table you can set out the desired thoughts, feelings, and actions next to each other in a convenient way. Having done this, you can decide on the priority that each component really should have for your practical, on-the-job performance requirements. Out of this you will probably decide to write out key behavioural and cognitive-behavioural objectives that will give you learning performance checks for which you can effectively monitor during actual instruction.

Learning Activity:		
Cognitive Components	**Affective Components**	**Behavioural Components**

Figure 20: *Learning activity components*

These columns are arranged in a natural progression. You think about doing something, then you have feelings about it, then you act (or don't act).

The affective components column gives you a convenient place to note the kinds of things that need consideration to make sure your learners' motivational needs will receive attention. Give this attention during instructing in a general way or in specific relation to the associated action or thought/action objectives. Doing this will add an extra element of precision to your instructional strategy and execution.

In wording your objectives be sure to take into account those kinds of performance criteria that really are important. Criteria such as time, degrees of accuracy, performance results, and so on are critical to good objectives. They not only give you criteria for success that you can use during a lesson, but they ensure that on-the-job performance requirements receive due attention.

Linking to performance

Learning objectives in a business or industrial setting are meant to tune in with actual production needs. You can express these needs as 'performance objectives'. A performance objective in a given company might look like this:

> 'The personnel clerk will, when required, calculate the exact benefits due to any one of our employees, including details of holiday pay, sick benefit, medical and life insurance, and pension provisions. She or he will do this, on average, within a period of twenty-five minutes, including all related monetary details'.

This is a cognitive-behavioural objective. Because it's aimed at the actual work setting, it won't necessarily work as a learning objective. Further revision may be needed.

The objective for our personnel clerk, as written, points at the top of the practical/theoretical hierarchy (Figure 18), so it's something that needs consideration in working out an instructional strategy designed to produce someone who can carry out this task.

If it's practical, you might be able to train someone to fulfil this objective in an on-the-job situation. This might turn out to be your best strategy. Sometimes, for a variety of reasons, this course of action might not be feasible. So you take a look at the next lowest stage in the practical/theoretical hierarchy.

Skill performance in a learning situation can be attractive as the next strategy option to consider. In this case, however, it would require the use of real data for real employees, and this might not be allowable. The confidentiality of personnel records might make it difficult to use them for training purposes. And using them this way might not really be ethical.

The next level on the hierarchy deals with simulated skill performance. This might just provide the right strategy option for us to use. You no longer have to use real data for real employees. Now you can use fictional data made up for fictional employees. In other words, you can work out some simple case studies to use during the instruction. These case studies can, of course, relate to actual situations so long as confidentiality is preserved.

It's almost time to come back to our objective for the personnel clerk. But first, let's give some more consideration, from a strategy point of view, to the use of performance objectives. You can use these for describing those behavioural and cognitive-behavioural skills needed for actual work performance. These objectives are crucial for the design of learning objectives that relate well to work requirements. Figure 21 helps to show this.

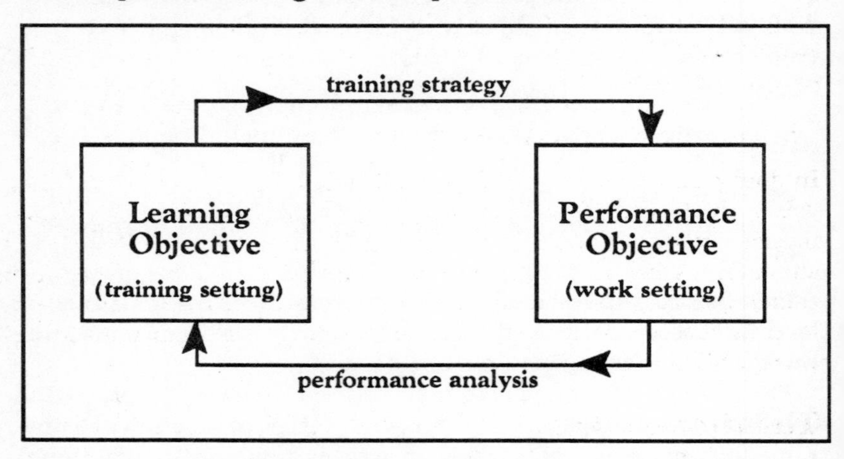

Fig. 21: *The training work loop*

Your training strategy, as this loop helps to illustrate, should always aim at the performance required at work. This performance provides the data source from which you can draw the information required to design good training. By packaging this information in the form of performance objectives, you can help to focus on those points that are most important in a given work setting. This work itself will usually lead to productivity improvements through the use of improvement strategies other than training. The clear need for new equipment or better working conditions might well become evident from the analysis of performance objectives.

For our purposes, we'll now look at the development of a learning objective based on the performance objective we've already identified for the personnel clerk. Here's what it looks like:

'The learner will, when required during a two-hour lesson,

calculate the exact benefits due to a hypothetical employee in our company. This calculation will include details of holiday pay, sick benefit, medical and life insurance, and pension provisions. This calculation, based on figures provided in a case study, will take no longer than twenty-five minutes'.

This cognitive-behavioural learning objective now forms the heart of our instructional strategy for dealing with this required chunk of training. We have incorporated standards by specifying the details needed in the calculation, as well as by specifying the maximum performance time allowable during the lesson. These standards also give us the criteria to use in affirming that the learner has reached the required level of self-effective competence.

Making adjustments

In doing this kind of strategy design work, you might decide that you want to include additional or more specific kinds of performance criteria. These you might add in after consulting with supervisors in the appropriate work locations. This is fine. Just remember that the criteria you plan to use during a lesson should lend themselves to good assessment when you do your monitoring work while instructing.

The time element

In examining our derived learning objective, you may have noticed that it specified the actual length of the lesson involved. Almost always you should include this time element in your learning objectives. It should, of course, give enough time for the actual performance required. Because learning involves more than the behavioural domain, this time element should provide sufficient time for cognitive assimilation and motivational reinforcement. It should also provide sufficient practice time for the learner to practise the skill a number of times to develop proper self-effective competence and confidence.

Concurrent needs

Human learning occurs in all three domains simultaneously. Your learners' affective and cognitive needs might well be met at the same time as their behavioural needs. Just be sure to keep all three domains in mind while instructing.

Types and levels of objectives

Different words abound when it comes to using learning objectives. Some people call them instructional objectives (Mager's original term). Others talk about learner-centred objectives. You might also come across the term 'training objectives'. In many cases, if not most cases, people are really talking about the same kinds of objectives, even though their wording differs.

The use of differently-worded objectives within the design of an instructional strategy often makes good sense. As we've already seen from the discussion of performance objectives as opposed to learning objectives, different terms have their uses. The important thing is to make sure these terms are used correctly for their intended meaning by everyone who might be involved with your strategy. Otherwise a great deal of confusion can ensue. In some cases it might even make sense to set out a glossary of terms to specify which type of objective is which.

You might reserve the term 'training objective' for stating the overall objective or objectives for a given training session. You could then group learning objectives according to their classifications under each of your training objectives. If you prefer, you might wish to call these higher-level objectives 'course objectives'.

In effect, you can work with a hierarchy or hierarchies of objectives related to training or education. The kind of hierarchy you develop for setting out the different levels of objectives is essentially up to you and your organization. But you should resist the temptation to let things become too complex here. A limit of five different levels of objectives within your general strategy design is generally fair.

One popular approach to using objectives involves the phrase 'terminal objective'. This type of objective describes the final performance a learner will be capable of at the completion or termination of a particular training or educational programme. 'Enabling objectives' are usually used with this approach as objectives subsidiary to the terminal objectives. Enabling objectives literally enable the terminal objective to be met.

Because the word 'terminal' often has unfortunate connotations, the term 'completion objective' might prove a happier choice of phrasing.

Objectives in your strategy

Objectives lend themselves to flexible use. This flexibility allows you to use them in the contexts of many different training and education systems. Just be sure, when you do use them, that you tune them in well with the real needs of your own organization.

By using learning objectives and using them well you will provide clarity, precision and strength to your instructional strategy. You'll also find that objectives in learning situations have beneficial effects simply from their predictive value. By stating that something ***will*** happen, you increase the chances of that actually turning out to be the case. You've set in motion a potential self-fulfilling prophecy (the 'Pygmalion effect').

The way you finally set out your instructional strategy is your choice. You have to decide what's most likely to prove effective in helping people learn well. And you have to decide what must be learned (or find out what must be learned from the key decision makers you have to deal with). These components are vital to your strategy.

Whatever you have to deal with or consider in examining the learning needs your instruction must meet, you do require some form of strategy. Learning objectives will form an essential part of this strategy. They should lie at its core. Given enough thought and enough specific laying out, a good strategy will help you and your learners truly succeed.

7 Designing Lessons

Once you have your strategy for instructing worked out, you need a plan that will help you to implement that strategy. Planned and prepared lessons are fundamental to good teaching. This statement is so obvious that it's almost a truism. Yet this type of planning often receives too little attention.

Many organizational managers and administrators tend to see the time allotted to the planning and preparation of lessons as being akin to slack time. The actual delivery of instruction is what counts in their eyes. It's almost as though they think this is something that just 'happens' when you bring an instructor into contact with his or her learners.

If costs are being questioned or cut for training or education, planning and preparation generally suffer. This is truly a false form of economizing. Poorly planned and prepared lessons are poor teaching instruments. They harm the learning process. Damaged or ineffective learning hurts any organization in which that learning is applied. It detracts from excellence, and, ironically, in the longer run it costs more too.

How detailed?

Lesson plans can be simple or complex. A lot depends on the experience of the instructor with the subject and learners concerned. And a lot depends on the technical intricacies that may be involved in the subject matter itself. A simple one might be a mental one that exists only in the mind of the instructor. A complex plan must be written out in a way that will permit ready information access by the instructor during the conduct of the lesson.

The objectives core

Learning objectives form the core of your instructing strategy. Similarly, they provide focus to lesson plans. You must have a clear idea of what you want your learners to think, feel and do as a result of your lessons.

The body of your lesson plan basically contains the key steps involved in helping your learners to acquire the objective or objectives desired. You may further subdivide these key steps into subsidiary tasks or notes. Organize these steps, tasks and notes generally in the order in which you expect to deal with them during the lesson.

Remain flexible

An important point should be made here. Never feel that a particular sequence is cast in stone. Methods, technology and circumstances can change the logic of sequences. A good instructor remains prepared always to deal with such changes as they occur. Flexibility of use is crucial to using lesson plans. In some cases, this may even mean throwing away your lesson plan and just going with your learning group (although one hopes this will not prove necessary too often!).

Pre-instructing planning

You can make a good start on any lesson plan by using the pre-instructing planner shown in Figure 26. This allows you to sort out your basic ideas in convenient form.

Most of the questions given in the planner are straightforward. But a couple of them may need a little more elaboration.

Question 1 basically points towards the *learning objective* or *objectives* you want your learners to reach. You can work your response here in general terms, but it must outline planned performance for the learners as a direct result of the lesson.

Question 2 points towards the cognitive skills your learners will develop. Your response here too can be generally written. The key thing here is to have some focus on mental activities.

The associated feelings asked for in question 3 may be a little difficult to think of at first. But they are important from the standpoint of learning effectiveness and learner motivation.

Associated feelings you might wish to consider could include the feelings of comfort, concern, enthusiasm, care, joy, excitement, vigour, delight, aloofness, involvement, passivity, relish, fervour, sincerity, empathy, desire, acceptance, repulsion, and so on.

1. What will this lesson enable my learners to do — for what purpose?

2. What thinking skills do I want my learners to develop during the lesson?

3. What associated feelings do I wish my learners to acquire during this lesson?

4. What specific things will the learners themselves actually do during this lesson?

5. In teaching this lesson I will basically:
   - (a) Tell the learners what they should think or do concerning the lesson's subject matter ❐
   - (b) Sell the learners on the subject matter ❐
   - (c) Support the learners in continuing to do what they are already doing with this subject matter ❐
   - (d) Join the learners as an equal among equals to work on the subject matter along with them ❐

6. In light of the style chosen in (5), what special considerations will I need to take into account in this lesson?

7. What key points of information must be included in the content of this lesson?

8. What other types of communication or instruction will I need to supplement this lesson before, during, or after its conduct?

Figure 22: *The pre-instructing planner*

Feelings, or the affective domain, give depth and shape to the things we learn. They influence us deeply in doing certain things or in avoiding certain things. For our thinking and our behaviour to be fully effective, the associated feelings must be in tune with them. Otherwise, the fundamentally important mental traces we develop for performing learned functions will be seriously flawed.

Question 4 highlights an important aspect of most good lessons. Instructors can become so caught up in their own performance before and during their lessons that they forget or downplay performance by their learners. In effect, they put the *performance pressure* on themselves, not their learners. Yet learning must almost always place performance pressure on learners. The wise instructor asks him or herself often where the pressure point is in a teaching session, and makes quick corrections as needed.

Question 5 brings out the basic instructional style you plan to use. The 'a' choice is the *director* position; the 'b' choice points to the *persuader;* the 'c' choice gives you the *developer* style; and the 'd' choice is the *associate.*

In thinking about the style you will use, you can also think about its consistency with the other areas of your planned lesson. Clear thinking can enable you to spot inconsistencies or inadequacies of style before you actually teach the lesson. Similarly, while teaching the lesson, you can check with yourself from time to time to ensure that your style actually is consistent with what you want to have happen, including the development of your learners' receptivities.

In a given lesson you might not wish to be confined to just one style. You may plan on switching from one style to another as the lesson goes along. Or you may wish to try using combined styles. You can indicate more than one style by ticking more than one box in responding to the choices in question 5. The choices are yours to make, and they can certainly make for more effective lessons.

Question 6 acts as a reminder of things to look for that will help you use your selected style or styles most effectively during the course of the lesson. You may need to have certain supplies or equipment available for your learners. You may need some adaptations in your learning location. You may need arrangements with administration for equipment or facilities. The possibilities are many. But it is important to open yourself up to thinking about them.

Question 7 provides your initial layout of content for the lesson. In some cases this may be sufficient for the body of your lesson. Most of the time, however, you will need to do some more work with this information. You will have to consider its sequencing and its expansion. You may also have to consider including such things as definitions, diagrams and so forth.

Question 8 too is an important one. Other types of communication might include learner preparation messages, applied technology information, administrative support statements, post-instruction follow-up of various types, on-the-job co-ordination effort, or general publicity information.

The pre-instructing planner allows you to sort out much of your lesson design ahead of time, and this is very important. Far better to anticipate problems than to endure them. The planner allows you to anticipate, and thus be prepared.

The 'thinking tree'

Question 7 of the planner, as pointed out already, may well require additional work after you've filled out the planner for a particular lesson or learning design. The content you select, and the way you organize it can be crucial to the effectiveness of your lesson. The device called the 'thinking tree' can help you with this.

To produce a thinking tree you first need a blank writing surface of some kind. A sheet of plain, unlined paper, a chalk board, a white board, or a sheet of flip chart paper can serve well here. At the top of your blank writing surface write in the topic about which you'll be bringing out your thinking. Then start writing down the key points that occur to you about this topic the moment they arise in your mind. While writing these key points it's a good idea to enter them all over the surface you're working on at a variety of different angles. This helps you to open up your thinking to include the right cerebral hemisphere of your brain, thereby enhancing your creative output.

As you bring out the key points on your thinking tree, you'll find that some points seem to spin off naturally from at least some of your key points. When this happens, draw in a line from the key point concerned and write in the spin-off or 'branching-out' point along this line. Similarly, some subsidiary points may branch out from your initial branches. Draw in growth lines for these points too, and write them in along these new branches. This branching-out effect gave rise to the term 'thinking tree' in the first place.

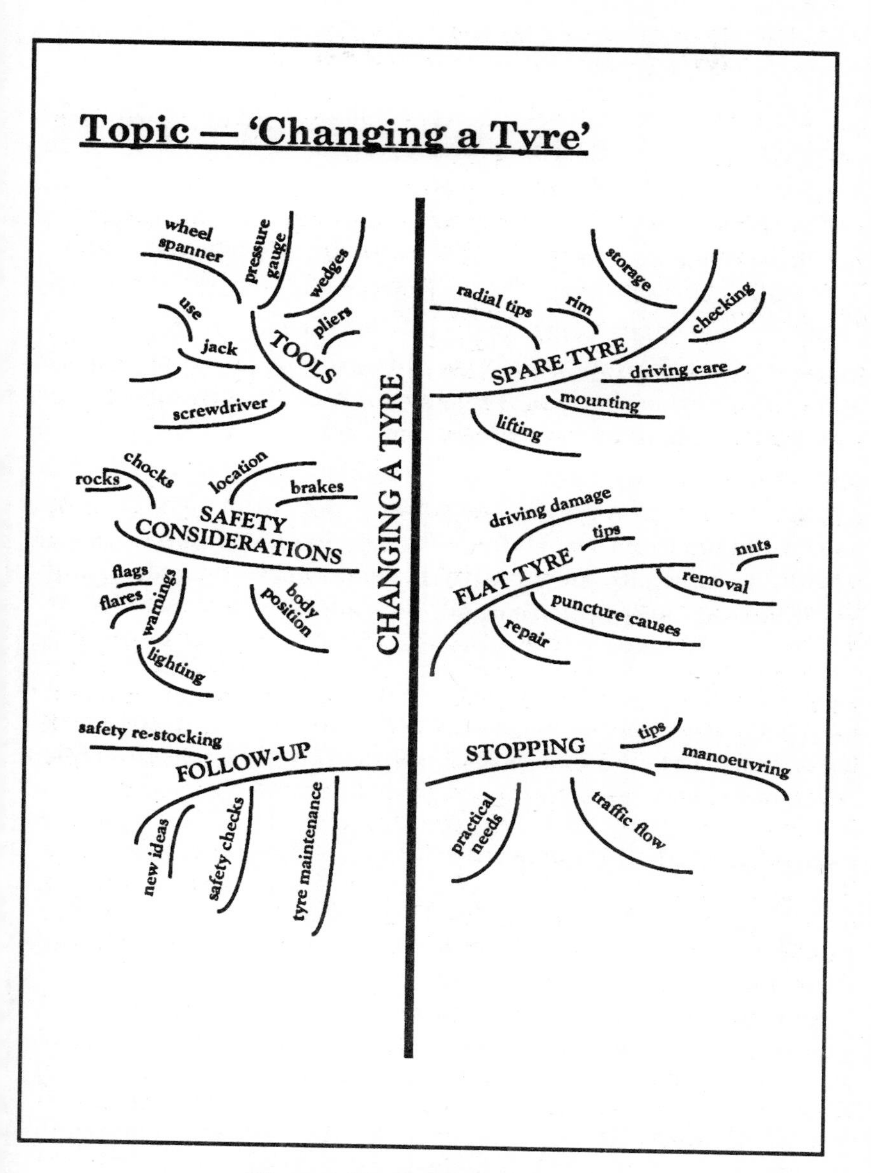

Figure 23: *A thinking tree*

Take a look at Figure 23. It will give you an idea of what a thinking tree developed for a lesson on the topic of 'changing a tyre' could look like.

Once you've identified all the key points and their spin-offs, write in numbers next to each key point corresponding to the order in which you think you should deal with them in teaching. After you've done this you can reproduce the information on another sheet of paper in the order shown by your priority numbers. This will lay out your content in key point order along with the subsidiary points that apply for each key point.

Some people like to refer to this process as brainstorming. They're incorrect in doing so. Brainstorming involves generating all sorts of ideas fast — the wackier the better. Working too fast and bringing out wacky ideas would interfere with using the thinking tree process most effectively. You want points to rise naturally and comfortably here from your own brain knowledge. This can be quite slow and deliberate work. In effect, you're 'mining' your own brain contents.

Once you catch on to the ins and outs of using this process, you'll apply it to all sorts of planning activities, from deciding what to do on your holidays to thinking about your need for a new wardrobe. The possibilities are endless. And the results will speak eloquently for themselves.

Associated activities

While you're planning a given lesson, you may find that you can start the ball rolling on various items that need attention prior to the conduct of the lesson. These could include room arrangements, audiovisual arrangements, equipment requests, instructions to learners, contact with subject experts and such. Good lesson planning should point the way automatically to these associated preparation needs.

Date/time of lesson: | Location:

LESSON TOPIC:

Equipment needed:

Learning objective(s)
(what you want your learners to do, when):

Content

Time	Key points/questions	Audiovisual/ hands on

Fig. 24: *Lesson plan format (first page)*

Content		
Time	Key points/questions	Audiovisual/ hands on

Figure 25: *Lesson planning (middle page)*

Content		
Time	Key points/questions	Audiovisual/ hands on
Special considerations for this lesson		

Figure 26: *Lesson planning (last page)*

Lesson plan format

No lesson plan format can be described as *the* correct format. Various types have various merits. You will probably want to work out and use your own format. Bearing these limitations in mind, the preceding lesson plan formats may prove useful to you.

Entering the *date/time of lesson* on your lesson plan helps you to set things within an overall plan or strategy. It also gives you a convenient reference point for future review, should you need to conduct this particular lesson again. Then, if some factual information has changed, you'll be able to update things quickly.

Notes about the *location* of your lesson are important, as they can alert you to particular points you need to take into account in your preparation and delivery. The location may also preclude or enhance some activities in your lesson. The more you can know about your precise location ahead of time the better.

The *lesson topic* and *learning objective* boxes should be self-explanatory. Noting them accurately is an important aspect of good lesson planning.

The *equipment needed* box contains vital information, especially for a technical lesson of some sort. Here is a place to remind yourself that having sufficient equipment for everyone to perform any skills required often marks a highly productive teaching process. In fact, if insufficient equipment is available, this will often seriously mar even the best of teaching.

Your *key points* are those you've worked out in your process of deciding on the emphasis and priorities for the contents of your lesson. Right alongside each point (key and subsidiary) noted in the key points column is space for entering your time estimate for the point in the lesson when you think you're likely to hit the point concerned.

On the right-hand side is a column for notes about your use of audiovisual equipment or hands-on work. These notes are vital to a well-run lesson. They enable you to sort out and anticipate all your audiovisual needs in conjunction with your instructional progress towards the learning objective or objectives concerned. Additionally, being able to set out hands-on work helps to make sure you include the kinaesthetic and behavioural side of learning to full advantage.

Most lessons would require at least two pages of lesson plan. The second diagram shown in Figure 25 gives you a format to use for any middle pages. The third diagram gives you a good last page. So if your lesson plan will be two pages long, use the first and last pages shown here. If it's longer, use the first and last pages along with as many middle pages as you need. This way, even for the longest lessons, you'll end up with a logical, comprehensive plan.

The *special considerations* block at the end of the last page of this plan makes it easy to note particular points about content or the conduct of your lesson that are important, and that aren't necessarily taken care of in other parts of your plan. It also provides you with a handy place to make 'process' notes while you're actually conducting the lesson. These notes cover such points as whether or not your time estimates were correct, how learners reacted to certain events, and ideas that occur to you for future conduct of the lesson. Used well, this block gives you an excellent mechanism for automatically updating your lesson plan as you go.

Lesson plans are the basic building blocks for training courses of all types. For this reason many organizations make extensive use of them for training design purposes. This can be a good thing to do provided effective co-ordination of the design work is arranged, and provided the lesson plans really do address organizational performance requirements.

You can't take everything into account in your lesson plan, but you can certainly make things a lot easier on yourself by taking a good look at the different parts of your lesson beforehand, and deciding how these might best be dealt with for the learners concerned.

Lesson plan layout

When writing your lesson plan in its final form, remember to be fair to yourself with the size of print and illustrations you use. It's one thing to consider different points in your lesson plan while working at your desk, but quite another to look at your lesson plan from time to time while actually teaching a group of people. Underlining, colour highlighting, point form and diagrams make things much easier for you once you're using your lesson plan 'live'.

Because it's almost impossible to predict everything that might occur in a particular class, you must always bear in mind that almost no lessons will actually go according to plan. So you have to remain flexible at all times. Don't let yourself become upset if you deal with things while instructing in a different order from the one you had anticipated in your plan. Go with the changes as naturally as you can during a lesson. Simply ensure that all your key points are dealt with effectively by the time the lesson ends.

In working with lesson plans it is very important to remember never to allow yourself to become trapped or limited by them. Treat them as guides, not commandments. Similarly, remember that lesson plans are very individual devices. Ideally, you should always use lesson plans you've produced yourself. If you must use lesson plans prepared by someone else, translate them for your own use. In essence, 'personalize' them.

Technical manuals

Detailed lesson plans, particularly for technical subjects, often become sections in training manuals; these manuals, in turn, can become informal technical manuals. This tendency is one that bears cautious monitoring.

As a general rule training manuals should not serve as technical manuals. If they do, the tail is wagging the dog. Technical manuals should be of and by people concerned with day-to-day work activities, not people concerned primarily with training. While technical instructors can usually offer a good many points for technical application, and they have unique access to technical information, it is unfair to expect them to take charge of technical documentation, unless specific provision is made for this function in their job descriptions and their spheres of authority.

Ideally, up-to-date technical manuals should be provided to instructors for use as references. Lesson plans can then be linked into these technical manuals with appropriate referencing. Often this referencing will occur as part of setting out the standards for learning objectives. Then too the special considerations section of the last page of the lesson plan provides a good place for more general references.

Clear linking of lesson plans to technical manuals within an organization can help to bring about effective cooperation between line people and training people. A clear connection then exists between the information imparted in training sessions and the information used in on-the-job applications. And this helps to ensure that training is well grounded in practical realities.

Time to plan

The time spent on the planning and preparation of any instructional session is nearly always well spent. This almost goes without saying. But how much time should it take you? The answer to this question depends on a number of factors. How familiar are you with the subject matter? How many times previously have you taught the lesson concerned? How receptive are the learners involved? What are their general learning modes and patterns? How supportive is your organization in providing help? These and other such factors all make a considerable difference.

One widely recognized ratio for planning time compared to delivery time is 10:1. For every hour of delivery time you should have ten hours of planning time. Now, like many formulas, this is not a hard and fast figure. For very new or innovative lessons the ratio should shift to figures higher than 50:1. By the same token, routine and well-rehearsed lessons might need ratios of as little as 1:4, or one hour of planning time for every four hours of delivery time.

A key point here is that all lessons require some planning time no matter how often they have been conducted in the past, and no matter how well laid out their lesson plans.

Full-time lesson planners

Some organizations make use of full-time lesson planners. These people spend most of their time planning and reviewing lessons that will be delivered by other people, usually part-time instructors. This can be a useful system. But careful integration of the instructor's ideas and skills with the content and frame-work of the lesson plans so produced is still necessary. Without this careful integration, instructors can come across to their classes in a wooden and ineffective fashion.

Preparation time

Lesson planning time prior to lesson delivery is one consideration you need to bear in mind. Another is preparation time. Preparation, as opposed to planning, involves making all the arrangements of yourself and the organization that are needed to support your lesson. It can include your manner of dress, the materials and equipment you must carry with you, classroom arrangements, audiovisual arrangements, travel and accommodation arrangements, the delegation of various tasks or activities, refreshment and meal arrangements and so on. These little things can take up a lot of time. But if they aren't seen to ahead of time, they can bring havoc to what should have been a good lesson or workshop.

The rule of three

In working on the time-planning part of lesson design, the rule of three will help you a great deal. Basically, it tells you to take whatever time is allotted for your lesson and divide it into three components: *start-up, conduct* and *completion.*

The start-up component involves all those things you need to do to get a lesson underway. This could include getting people settled down, making out name cards, taking attendance, last-minute administrative work, and providing the learners with the introductory information they need to prepare them for the lesson.

The conduct part includes all the details involved in the actual learning up to and including achievement of the learning objective or objectives. It is the heart of your lesson.

The completion part involves all those things required to, in effect, bring the lesson 'in for a landing'. This should include a summation or recap of the lesson, time for some fine tuning, and time for people to get ready for their next lesson or going back to the workplace.

When first thinking of the time needed for each of these components, divide the time you've been allotted into three equal parts (rounding off to the minute and in favour of the conduct part). So if you have a total of forty minutes, your time allotments would be 13, 14 and 13 minutes. In this case, you might say that a forty minute lesson really becomes a fourteen-minute lesson.

You have to exercise some judgment and experience here. If it's the first lesson in a given programme or a session you're conducting as part of a conference, or you have to help people adjust their minds to being in a learning situation as opposed to some other situation, then you might need to use the time allotments we arrived at through even dividing. In other situations, you should build up the conduct part.

If your lesson is one in a continuing series dealing with the same subject, you might be able to build up the conduct part to thirty minutes out of the forty. But, no matter what the lesson, you must always leave time for start-up and completion. A good rule of thumb here is to consider five minutes as your minimum time allotment for each of these components.

When you're in doubt about the exact arrangements for the location and timing of your lesson because of factors beyond your control, be conservative in using the rule of three. Better to risk finishing a lesson early than risk having it cut off in mid-flight.

You can build these time components into your lesson plan, or focus your lesson plan only on the conduct component. Whichever route you choose, make sure you plan for all three, and that you don't give short shrift to the start-up and completion.

The time imperatives of learning objectives

In brief, people achieve real learning objectives in whatever time it takes them to achieve such objectives, not the amount of time that some remote administrative authority decides arbitrarily to allot them.

When your learning objectives contain a strong behavioural focus, as most learning objectives should, performance time becomes critical. If you want people to perform a task or demonstrate a skill, the time allotted must be realistic for the task or skill concerned. Otherwise the learning process is debased.

Careful observation and measurement will determine the time spans needed for the average learner to carry out specific acts of skill performance. These should be the times used for lesson planning purposes, not the timings that might be convenient to administration.

If learners have not actually performed the behavioural portion of the lesson objectives concerned, then they cannot be said to have achieved those objectives. This is a fundamental principle of good lesson design work, and cannot be overstated.

When instructors talk of 'covering material', beware. They're almost announcing that they propose to teach in a broadcasting, open-loop way, without proper regard for the actual learning that takes place. Yet the covering material approach takes place constantly.

The driver can't open the doors of the bus to let passengers out when the bus stalls at a level crossing. Several people die and more are injured when an onrushing train cannot stop in time.

In the subsequent coroner's inquiry the trainer involved in the driver's training testifies, 'Well, we did cover how to open the doors in an emergency. The driver should have known.'

Where does the blame lie here? All too often people in positions of authority will try to blame learners, 'who should have learned'. The question that is too seldom raised is, 'Who confirmed that the learner could actually apply this skill?'

Educational excellence, training excellence, learning excellence — all sorts of excellences related to having people acquire new knowledge or skills are talked about these days. But excellence is just not possible if the time needed for actual skill performance during training is cut down arbitrarily, or is not allotted at all.

Quality training or teaching takes time. It cannot be rushed arbitrarily. It is a professional and ethical duty of anyone involved with training or education to ensure that the arbitrary approach is resisted and denounced wherever and whenever it occurs.

Checklists

ADMINISTRATIVE CHECKLIST FOR WRITING WORKSHOP

1. Travel/accommodation arrangements ❒
2. Lesson plan notes ❒
3. Reference books ❒
4. Hand-outs for all participants ❒
5. Pens for OHP and flip chart ❒
6. Spare pencils ❒
7. Supply of blank paper ❒
8. Transparencies for overhead projector ❒
9. Self-contained and noise-free classroom ❒
10. Sufficient chairs and table space for all participants plus at least four extra chairs ❒
11. Overhead projector with low stand ❒
12. Flip chart (with full pad of blank paper) ❒
13. Electric outlet convenient to OHP ❒
14. Twelve-foot extension cord ❒
15. Tea, coffee, or juice available three times a day (start of day, morning break, and afternoon break) ❒
16. Name place cards for all participants ❒
17. Convenient access to photocopier ❒
18. Name and phone number of administrative contact person ❒

Checklists are highly useful for good preparation. Like a good pilot preparing an aircraft for take-off, a good instructor must prepare her or his lesson for successful delivery. The checklist just shown gives you an example of a form you might use prior to conducting a workshop dealing with written communications.

This checklist could be useful in a number of ways. You could use it for your own personal memory jogger or as a reference for arranging things with a client. Interestingly, you could also use it as a means of reassuring yourself that everything is set before starting a training session. And this kind of self-reassurance will go far towards helping you feel less nervous and more confident at the outset.

The points to list in checklists of this kind generally would suggest themselves to you for particular subject areas over a period of time. You need only forget something important once to realize how useful a good administrative checklist can be!

Designed lessons

The designing of lessons is an important activity. It should not receive short shrift, no matter how convenient this might be for administrative purposes. All lessons need designing and, over a period of time, they need re-designing.

Continuing attention to lesson design work reflects itself in the quality of the lessons concerned. This, in turn, comes through in the general quality of training provided by those lessons. While designing your lessons must receive careful attention, flexibility must remain a keynote. Well-designed lessons can be invaluable. But they must never become instructional traps. Rather, they should be well-conceived guides or pathways for learning.

Working on your lesson designs certainly takes a little effort. And you may often find yourself tempted not to make the effort, particularly if you seem to do all right in your instructing without giving much care and attention to lesson planning and preparation. Nevertheless, to provide excellence in your teaching activities, make sure you give continuing and good attention to your design work. It may not make all that much difference in the short run, but over the longer course of events it will make an enormous difference. And it will provide you with an instructional track record of which you will be proud.

8 The Power of Positive Guidance

Events occur around us all the time, whether we notice them consciously or not. Sometimes these events are random, sometimes they are deliberate, and sometimes they are important. The main thing, of course, is that you notice and do something effective about the important events that occur in your surroundings. The ability to monitor well in your surroundings is very important, and this applies especially when you're actively instructing people.

When you last went shopping, what information did you take in? Do you recall the hair colour, facial features, or clothes worn by the cashier at the check-out counter? Can you describe the smells you experienced or the feelings that were aroused in you? The questions about the details you observed while shopping, or during any other daily activity could go on almost forever. And you could probably answer only a small number of these questions accurately. Once again we're looking at receptivity — your receptivity.

In any learning situation the accuracy of observations made by the instructor is crucial. This importance lies not so much in the need for making personal evaluations or assessments of learners, although these activities are important, as it does with the design, conduct, and long-term development of truly excellent learning in any setting.

Cybernetics

In the 1950s Norbert Weiner developed the term 'cybernetics' to describe the study of feedback in the operation of dynamic systems. Cybernetics has proved essential in the development and maintenance of a wide variety of physical systems. And, of course, it is applied everywhere in the field of computer science today.

But cybernetics really applies to people as well. Individual human beings are themselves 'dynamic systems'.

Think of it. Whenever you do something, no matter what it is, you make use of feedback. Sometimes the feedback comes from the physical movements or reactions of an object or process, and sometimes it comes from the comments or actions of other people. Whatever the source, we do react to feedback in tangible ways. This happens even if the feedback occurs at a non-conscious level of receptivity. We can and do respond to things happening around us, including other people's comments, without realizing we're doing so.

In cybernetics positive feedback tends to increase the occurrence of a particular dynamic, while negative feedback tends to decrease that dynamic. Neutral feedback tends to keep things in a steady state. In effect, you have the idea of an accelerator and a brake. Thermostats provide this form of feedback for maintaining a steady temperature in buildings. When you turn the thermostat up, you provide positive feedback, leading to an increased temperature. When you turn it down, you provide negative feedback, leading to a decreased temperature.

In human beings you have similar occurrences. If you are running a race, and the crowd starts to yell, 'Faster, faster!', you tend to increase speed. Similarly, if you're driving along a motorway and spot a police car, you tend to slow down (at least until you've checked what speed you're doing!). Our bodies are maintained in a steady-state condition at all times unless we're ill. This bodily state is called 'homoeostasis', and its main feedback system is our blood.

The human brain continually processes feedback in many forms. In line with the findings of modern research this processing begins even before birth. Our environments have a profound impact on our brain development which, in turn, shapes our personalities to a remarkable extent. Early feedback seems to have a bearing on the physical structuring of our neural pathways. So, in many respects, we become 'hard-wired' in our thought processes. This phenomenon alone has deep implications for the field of early childhood education.

One of the most important means of providing human feedback involves the use of language. The words we hear and the way we hear them are deeply significant to us. Again, words can have positive, negative, or neutral impacts on us. The right words help people to work marvels. The wrong ones ruin performance. The old children's rhyme about 'sticks and stones' is incorrect. Words can hurt us — deeply. Clearly, instructors can use words with their learners for good or ill.

Positive reinforcement

The power of feedback has intrigued psychologists for many years. The nature of its power has sparked a good deal of debate and controversy, most of which has not been settled to this day. But, given the significance of some psychological theories for business, industry and education, you should have at least some idea of where the dispute areas lie.

The core of the controversy is the impact of behaviourism, especially strict behaviourism as represented by the teachings of B.F. Skinner. Probably the most important tool developed by his teachings is that of 'positive reinforcement', a tool that emerged from his experiments in the *operant conditioning* of animals.

In operant conditioning an observer closely monitors the subject (Skinner used the term 'organism', even for human subjects) and provides reinforcement as the subject moves towards and achieves a desired behaviour. Less frequent and less intense reinforcement is provided to sustain the subject in the desired behaviour.

The classic experiments in operant conditioning used seeds or food pellets with pigeons or rats in 'Skinner boxes'. These creatures could be taught to trigger food dispensers when desired, or to navigate confusing mazes successfully. This careful work has now been extrapolated to human beings using the apparent human equivalents of seeds and food pellets as rewards.

What human beings find rewarding can, of course, be quite diverse and complicated as we saw in Chapter 3 'Motivation for Learning'. But the theory of positive reinforcement as applied to people basically says that people will respond to such tokens as prizes, presents, positive remarks, time off, promotions, money and so forth in much the same way as pigeons and rats respond to their food.

Positive reinforcement has had a great impact on human institutions of all types, particularly business institutions. As a tool it seemed to offer the ultimate means of managing people and turning them into good, productive employees. The results over the years have been decidedly mixed.

Just as Skinner's 'teaching machines' with their programmed instruction technology did not revolutionize education, positive reinforcement did not revolutionize management or training. This is not to say that it lacks merit. The main problem seems to be that it is incomplete.

The human mind

Positive reinforcement has definite limits with human beings. The mind has reasons and inclinations of its own. Each one of us is unique, as we've now seen in examining our different learning styles and reception levels. Different things reward us, and we work and learn basically for our own motives. The cognitive and affective domains of our psychological structures can override the behavioural.

More complex forms of learning, such as the conceptual reasoning required to understand the workings of a nuclear reactor, cannot be reduced to discrete behaviours, no matter how hard behaviourists may try to do so. In the fullest sense, people must apply their minds as well as their hands to complex operations. And their feelings enter directly into the degree of motivation that influences what they'll do.

Using the right context

For it to be most useful as an instructing tool, the good qualities of positive reinforcement must be placed within a context that allows for the cognitive and affective domains of human learning. When this is done properly, excellent teaching can ensue.

In the previous chapter we developed the concept of learning objectives within a fuller learning context. Now we can do the same thing with the concept of positive reinforcement. We will develop this fuller context within the framework of a general instructional technique called 'positive guidance'.

Positive guidance

Positive guidance involves using feedback from the instructor to the learner based on work by the learner towards given learning objectives. At this point we basically have the positive reinforcement approach. Add in learner motivation, as discussed in Chapter 3, and you have positive guidance.

This process is framed from the start within the learner's perspective. It stresses learner needs and goals. These needs and goals are then related to learning objectives. In some cases they may well become learning objectives themselves. So learner commitment to learning objectives is developed at the start of a given learning session. This motivation-building aspect of positive guidance is sometimes called 'building the learning contract'.

Self-directed guidance

One of the important elements of positive guidance is that of helping learners help themselves towards specific learning outcomes. This element applies to individual as well as group learning activities. It also means that learners can, to some extent, provide their own guidance through effort and feedback. Self-directed guidance becomes positive when the learner receives positive feedback. This kind of feedback need not come from another human being. Simply finding out that something works provides the human brain with immediate positive feedback. I push a button and lights come on — I've received positive feedback.

We provide ourselves with positive guidance every day of our lives. When we find a great new restaurant, we've positively guided ourselves. Similarly, when we find a shop that stocks a lot of the kinds of things we want to buy at a good price, we've positively guided ourselves. Even grabbing a vacant parking space before someone else does involves self-directed positive guidance.

The element of self-direction in human learning (as Malcolm Knowles and Allen Tough have brought out in their work) is a very important one. People enjoy achieving things on their own. When people are learning a new computer program, for instance, they often put the manual aside and just fiddle with the computer. When they do this they're relying on feedback from the computer to guide them in their learning. It seems to be instinctive.

The wise instructor continually looks for ways in which learners can have this self-directed enjoyment while working toward important learning objectives. This provides an important element of sustained learner motivation.

Discovery adventure

If possible, learners should be guided through tasks, especially skills, as a sort of discovery adventure, rather than having the instructor demonstrate what needs to be done. In a sense, you might say that the instructor needs to resist the temptation to steal the learning fun for him or herself. This form of self-discipline on the instructor's part goes hand in hand with the need to put the pressure point in learning on the learners and not the instructor.

In Chapter 5, 'Styling Your Instructing', we brought out the concept of the instructor shifting from active mode to passive mode as the learners raised their reception levels. The positive guidance concept essentially urges that this shifting process move fairly rapidly. You want to plunge your learners into active learning as quickly as possible.

The learning guide

In using positive guidance you act as a learning guide. You give your learners directions, tips and clues as you see these are needed to help them through the learning experiences you've arranged. You provide learners with information they can use in their learning. And one essential form of information they need is honest feedback on what they're doing and how they're doing.

You should not deliver learning information in a harsh or unduly impersonal way. Keep your comments generally warm and supportive. And keep your supply of information as subtle and simple as possible. Don't overload learners with an overwhelming amount of information. Remember the KISS principle ('Keep it short and sweet', or, if you prefer, 'Keep it simple stupid!'). Gestures, facial expressions and other such non-verbal language will provide adequate information to most learners.

The basic positive guidance approach is laid out in Figure 27. This diagram sums up most of what we've already seen of the positive guidance technique. The learner aims at a learning objective and engages in activities directed towards that objective which produces her or his performance in the learning situation. The instructor (who can be the learner in self-directed learning) monitors the results of the learner activities as well as the activities themselves. Based on this monitoring, the instructor may provide information to the learner to alert her or him to areas of performance needing adjustment. Finally, when learner performance is truly in line with the requirements of the learning objective, the instructor gives information to the learner in the form of positive feedback. This feedback, in turn, reinforces the learner's motivation by reassuring her or him that the objective has fully been achieved.

Careful monitoring of learning behaviours is crucial. Through this monitoring you can see how things are going and provide feedback in a timely and positive way. Accuracy, timing and a positive bias are essential ingredients here. The quality of your monitoring work depends to a high degree on your own general receptivity. What do you look for and how well do you look?

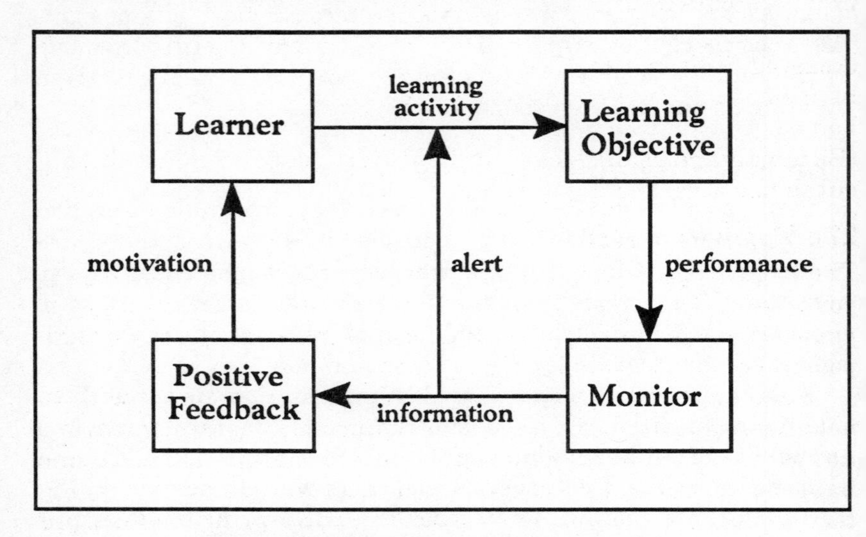

Figure 27: *Positive guidance learning*

Ill-considered or inaccurate feedback given to another human being can be most injurious, and its effects can be long-lasting. This injurious effect sometimes occurs despite the best of intentions on the part of the person giving the feedback. Inadequate receptivity in the monitoring process will lead to this. No matter what the reasons might be, incompetent or sloppy feedback is dangerous. It can easily hurt or destroy learner motivation in a fundamental way.

Monitoring distortions

Because the process of monitoring is so important to effective positive guidance, you must develop a good awareness of the ways in which our monitoring can be distorted. Things aren't always as they seem. First impressions can certainly be misleading. Very often in teaching *suspended judgment* becomes the best kind of judgment. When you see or hear something and find yourself making some kind of judgment about it, always be prepared to say to yourself: 'Now am I sure of this?'

Our expectations

We fit the events we notice to our own expectations. And these expectations are built into our brain programming. This building process occurs for the most part at a non-conscious level. So it can distort our view of things without our realizing the distortion has occurred. This can cause us to 'see' or 'hear' things that did not happen at all. Your observations about someone else can be quite honest to your conscious mind, but quite wrong in actual fact. (Elizabeth Loftus has done excellent work on bringing this point out in her work dealing with human memory.)

The 'Pygmalion effect'

The Pygmalion effect can also distort our monitoring accuracy. If you expect someone to perform well, you will tend to see that person perform well. Conversely, if you expect someone to perform poorly, you will tend to see that person perform poorly.

When we already think poorly of someone, we will tend to notice every time she or he does something wrong. And we might not notice when she or he does something right. The reverse happens, of course, with someone that we think well of. We tend to fit the actions of others into our own expectations. And we do a lot of this automatically at a non-conscious level.

Your own way

Another form of monitoring distortion can occur when you mentally compare the way someone else is doing something with the way you personally would tackle that same task. In effect, you link everything that person does to your own brain programme for that task. This can cause you to make assumptions about the quality of a given learner's work. And these assumptions can lead you to make erroneous judgments about the learner's performance.

Because each of us possesses an individually programmed brain, we each have different ways of doing things, from the way we hold our hands to the way we describe our experiences. This makes it quite possible for the same task to be approached and performed in a number of different ways, and each of these different ways might be correct in terms of results.

Check your monitoring

Before you decide a learner is doing something wrong, check your monitoring. Be sure you're seeing, hearing, or sensing what you think you're seeing, hearing, or sensing. And remain alert to the possibility that the learner is simply doing something differently from your own personal approach while obtaining the correct result.

Accurate feedback is critical to the success of positive guidance. You cannot base it on hasty judgments or half-formed thinking. You must base it on sound monitoring.

Providing feedback

You can see a useful analogy for using feedback within a positive guidance process in the task of helping someone throw a ball into a bucket on the other side of a high wooden fence. The thrower (learner) cannot see the bucket, but the observer (instructor) can. So the observer can give performance information to the thrower.

The thrower knows the objective is to get the ball into the bucket, so he or she listens carefully to the observer's description of where the bucket is (guidance). He or she then throws the ball (learner activity).

The thrower probably wouldn't land the ball in the bucket on the first toss, although 'holes in one' are always possible! The observer would provide feedback information to improve accuracy. While reporting on where the trial tosses fall, the observer can make positive and encouraging comments: 'A little more to the left, and you'll get in!', or, 'Try dropping it just a little shorter!', and, now and then, 'Keep going, you're doing fine!'

If the fence were not in the way, naturally, the person throwing the ball could actually see the bucket. But he or she would still be using feedback, only it would be feedback going instantly into the brain (high receptivity). In this case you would have self-directed feedback.

Timing your feedback

As an instructor you must take care when using positive guidance not to provide feedback at inappropriate times. To do so can interfere with effective learning. You would become a contaminator for the learner, not a guide.

Consider what happens when you learn to operate something like an electronic calculator. You require some cognitive mapping to understand the function of a calculator in the first place, including a good idea of your objective in using it. Then you need to find out how to switch it on and how to use its buttons and the display window. You experiment to find out what happens as you input numbers or perform certain functions (discovery adventure).

All the while your brain is actively taking in information to incorporate in your brain programme for using electronic calculators in the future. Your fingers send back pressure, feel and spatial data. Your ears pick up clicking and beeping noises. Your eyes note details of form, colour and brightness. Your nose might even pick up the smell of ink or paper. And all of this information rushes into your brain at top speed, most of it non-consciously. You might say in this case that your brain programmes itself.

An instructor who interrupted this automatic brain programming would interfere with learning. She or he might even introduce a permanent fault (bug) into the learner's programme for carrying out the learned operation in the future. Premature or clumsy activation of conscious thought in the learner while automatic and effective feedback is occurring is a real hazard in learning situations. And this is a hazard that is virtually inexcusable in a competent instructor.

Safety or cost interference

Some instructors interfere with learning for safety or cost reasons. And such considerations are important in their own right. But these considerations must be weighed against future safety and cost considerations. If someone learns a distorted approach to climbing a wooden pole in a learning situation, for instance, this distorted approach could have long-term poor consequences for performance in the work setting. And, ironically, these long-term poor consequences could include less safe and cost-effective work.

Learning through positive guidance

In using positive guidance here are some important points to apply:

1. Identify the learning objective(s) with the learner (gaining commitment or setting the learning contract).
2. Provide the learner with a general outline of the approach to take to achieve the learning objective(s) (guidance information).
3. Involve the learner as quickly as you can in the mental and physical activities required.

4. Provide careful guidance tips and feedback (learning cues) to the learner as she or he moves towards the desired objective(s).
5. Provide for learning experiences that will give the learner a real sense of discovery adventure.
6. Monitor learner actions with care, being sure to form opinions or make judgment calls that really are justified.
7. Ensure that you continue to provide the learner with encouragement as he or she successfully moves towards achieving the learning objective(s).
8. When the learner achieves a learning objective, be absolutely sure that she or he knows it.
9. At a later point in time follow up on the learning to ensure that the learner really did assimilate the learning and is still applying it.

These points will serve your instructional needs well, and you can apply them in a wide variety of circumstances. With a little modification, for instance, you can use them as guidelines for supervising people at work. Over a period of time you can make sure that the elements of positive guidance infuse all your instructional activities, and this is certainly worth striving for.

Improving your receptivity

Productive receptivity is essential, as we've seen, to skilful application of positive guidance. Effective monitoring and feedback are clearly impossible without it. But how can you make your own receptivity more productive?

Through deliberate practice and repeated self-reminders, you can, bit by bit, learn to take in more of the events (signals) that occur around you. You can see more actions by people and spot more things in your environment. You have the ability to sharpen your total *sensory acuity* or *information alertness*.

When you travel observe the little things that people do. Watch the way they hold their hands, place their feet, or move their eyes. You can play little mental games such as seeing how many people fold their arms while waiting in a queue, or how many people rise up on the balls of their feet while talking. The possibilities are endless. The point is continually to train yourself to be more and more aware of what's going on around you in this world.

When you instruct people, observe their behaviours carefully. Always try to avoid the TNTWIWDOI phenomenon (That's Not The Way I Would Do It!). Keep yourself from making hasty judgments about what your learners do. By being more open to the different things that occur in your classroom you will learn much more yourself.

You might not be able to become a completely objective observer of events, but you definitely can become more objective with practice and effort. And this increased acuity will serve well when you seek to provide feedback to people about what they've done or haven't done. This, in turn, will lead others to place more faith in what you have to say about their work, thus building a better sense of trust and accomplishment.

Learner control

When learners have a good idea of what they're trying to learn, and receive good feedback about their progress in learning, they can start to exercise better and better control over their own behaviours. And this increased self-control helps them to become more self-effective. They will increasingly be more efficient and effective in using feedback from sources other than yourself, thus helping them better to direct their own learning activities.

Mental rehearsal

Our brains work well at imaging things. With good imaging guidance through the details of a task, similar areas of the brain are activated to those brought into play actually to carry out the task concerned. This is the basis of the *mental rehearsal techniques* used so successfully in sports training. As an instructor you can use the same technique when explaining learning activities.

Try to 'walk' the learner mentally through the activity concerned by engaging his or her imagination. This will help the learner develop a good mental trace or cognitive map for the desired learning. And it increases the chances of the learning occurring correctly on the first attempt. Mental rehearsal can speed up learning markedly, and it is certainly helpful to learner motivation.

To use the mental rehearsal technique you need to do some careful planning. In particular, you have to possess a good grasp yourself of the task involved. If you do not already have this grasp, you may be able to obtain the details you need from technical references of various types or from other people. Sometimes, of course, you can work out the required planning in your mind without the need for outside references at all.

The thinking tree technique (p. 113) lends itself well to helping you access points of information and procedure from your own non-conscious. It aids you in tapping into resources in your mind that you would not consciously be aware you had.

When working out the cognitive mapping you plan to use, remain aware of the need for some discovery adventure for the learner. Build in points on the map where you'll ask the learner a question or drop a clue that the learner can follow up on. This helps to keep the learning process interactive, which makes it much easier for you to monitor the learner's developing understanding of the subject concerned.

Task guidance

In the case of hands-on types of skills you can develop the cognitive map in association with the learner actually walking through the task. Provide enough information for the learner to make progress without a lot of floundering. But don't overload him or her with information. And be sure to allow the learner to discover a few things on his or her own.

While the learner is assimilating the skill, be careful not to interrupt unless you absolutely have to. Otherwise, you run the risk of disrupting learning while it's still at a critical stage. If the learner asks for assistance, provide it in as indirect a manner as you can, so that she or he will still work out most of the activity in her or his own mind. While doing all of this, remain patient, positive and supportive.

After completing the learning of a skill, have the learner review how things went from his or her perspective. And allow this to happen as naturally as possible. Avoid turning this 'debriefing' into an out-and-out interrogation. But do look for points to reinforce or clarify.

Verbal guidance

In the case of learning that does not involve hands-on types of skills, you can work things in a similar manner using verbal interactions. You can build this into a variety of different methods. The main thing is to ensure that the method you use will give learners clear mental pictures of the material they need to learn, while allowing you some means of monitoring how well they're assimilating it.

Importance of relaxation

When people receive accurate feedback about their behaviours, they can adjust the way they do things quite readily most of the time. If they are inwardly relaxed while doing this adjusting, their brains and bodies will automatically tend to carry out learning tasks effectively. But they must be as psychologically relaxed as possible.

Positive emphasis

Within the context of positive guidance feedback should, as far as possible, concentrate on the positive or good aspects of the learner's activities. This helps to enhance those things the learner does well, while avoiding putting too much weight on those things he or she does not do well. Over time the positive behaviours will tend to drown out the negative ones.

Dangers of negative feedback

Negative feedback can damage in a number of ways. It can be quite de-motivating. When confronted with a few negative comments, a learner can feel that he or she is being subjected to a barrage of abuse. This can bring about a personal concentration on negative feelings, rather than on the points of information delivered in the criticism. Such negative feelings interfere with effective brain programming, so they constitute another form of learning contamination.

Negative feedback delivered too vigorously can cause learners to do things under pressure. But this kind of 'forced' learner performance will not usually lead to good long-term learning. The learner will simply learn to perform only when someone is present to provide continuing feedback, because she or he will not have integrated the learning comfortably into her or his own frame of reference, or really taken possession of learning in a meaningful way.

Malicious obedience

Negative feedback can cause resentment, and this resentment can lead to poor results over time. When faced with apparent hostility and a sense of personal powerlessness, people tend to engage in malicious obedience. They will obey instructions to the letter, even if they know those instructions will cause something to go wrong. Or they may do certain things because 'the book' says they should be done, even though common sense may say they shouldn't be applied in some cases.

Operant escape

Negative feedback can lead to operant escape. This is the process whereby a person (or animal for that matter) will carry out a particular task to escape from an unpleasant situation or occurrence. This avoidance learning may lead the person involved to look for ways of avoiding carrying out the task at all in the future. And this avoidance behaviour could occur at a non-conscious level, so people learn to avoid doing certain things without necessarily being consciously aware of their own avoidance.

Most learners can recognize when they're not performing up to standard. If they're approached in a positive way, they can usually come up with good personal solutions. Given this opportunity, they can even feel good about themselves despite some inadequacies of performance. They will avoid learning to think of themselves as failures or losers.

Success orientation

Success breeds success, while failure breeds failure. Self-reinforcing cycles are at work here as well as the Pygmalion effect. Productive feedback should always focus on information that will lead the learner to success. This type of feedback does not just happen. It requires excellent monitoring and detailed concentration on your part.

The following points can help you to use feedback well in your positive guidance teaching activities:

1. Bear in mind always the need to establish a climate of trust for your learners.
2. Make sure you are clear in your own mind about the learning objectives concerned.
3. Make the feedback you use objectively descriptive rather than judgmental.
4. Be specific and relevant in your comments to the learner, but not overwhelming.

5. Direct your feedback towards those types of things the learner can actually do something about.
6. Keep the needs of the learner clearly in mind, particularly from a motivational point of view.
7. Frame what you have to say positively.
8. Concentrate on performance, not the person.
9. Give feedback as soon after performance as possible.
10. If you can, arrange things so that the feedback is solicited by the learner, rather than being imposed by you.
11. Remain flexible in your approach at all times.
12. Keep your feedback within the context of the learning as a whole.
13. From time to time verify with the learner what he or she actually hears you saying, and modify your comments as necessary.
14. Keep your tone as supportive as possible throughout.
15. If it seems likely to be productive, give a practical demonstration to illustrate a key point of feedback.

Providing good feedback to your learners does not come easily or automatically. But it is essential to using positive guidance properly.

Before you give feedback to someone else, go over all the details of what you plan to say and how you plan to say it. When you do this, picture it happening in your mind, complete with the learner's likely reactions. 'See' the kinds of approaches and comments that are likely to bring out positive and productive reactions from the learner. By doing this, you harness the power of mental rehearsal for your own performance as a feedback giver.

The indispensable tool

The positive guidance technique gives you an approach to instructing that's invaluable. It doesn't allow you to programme people against their wills, but it does allow you to help them learn in a highly effective fashion. It's a technique that works in a wide variety of settings, and it can be infused into a variety of instructional methods and styles.

Positive guidance based on sharp monitoring and feedback requires attention to detail and patience on your part. But you should consider it an indispensable tool to use in all your instructing. It enables you to guide someone else's learning with care, respect and dignity. You act as a learning guide, not a learning dictator. And, very importantly, you enable your learners to become fully self-effective in their work.

9 The Ma

ur Words

The language you use
of great importance. I
helps you to achieve tl
far towards defining yo
A language is much
memorize all the wo
command of language
attempts to have con
foundered. When you re
with language is a truly
other creature on this pl
Through the consider
out tasks clearly for oth
mance feedback, and ger
Your use of language
Clear language tends to
recent years shows that
connected with the deve
use of a particular langu
the physical development
People deprived of huma
life are permanently imp
tion in our society is conce

Language programm

Language has subtle impa
and 'turn off' phrasings,
murmur a word of approva
word, that person will gra
more, without necessarily

it as an instructor are
relate to others. It
chieve. And it goes
ur learners.
words. You could
till not have a
n which many
nguage have
ur capability
rt from any
ou can set
performance
rning.
think.
ch in
dly
he
n

acc
, dis
omen
nd yourse
came from
have you no
and over again
hrases up in a pa
use a personal co
phrases can be qu
In their best-s
and Peters found
had a lot of p
repeated them
continually.

How far have you b... or 'programmed' at a non-conscious level in the ... respond to language? It's a difficult question to ... would be foolish to think that any of us are free o... ng.

The way you u... guage has a profound effect on the degree to wh... ce others and on the degree to which they care...

Language ... ism of interpersonal and organizational c... daily lives it is the most important tool ... es doubly to those of us who are instruct...

Like ... be looked after properly if it is to do th... like most other tools, language ma... as deep psychological implications. A... age implies a re-structuring of your ... n re-structure you as a person.

... n with the ability to make all the ...) of all the languages in the world. ... learn to make only those sounds that ... hich they are raised. With few excep- ... to make those sounds that aren't used ... The language centres in their brains ... as a result of receiving no supporting ... world.

... bject to the subtle language influences of ... ou ever travelled to a region that uses a ... ent from your own and, after some expo- ... covered that it's starting to influence your ... n can be disconcerting, if not downright ...

... lf using sayings, and then realize that these ... your parents or a favourite uncle? In your ... ticed that you tend to use certain pet phrases ..., and then realized that you picked those pet ... ticular work environment? (By the way, if you ... nputer, using the 'search' function to find such ... te revealing — and fast.)

... elling book, *In Search of Excellence,* Waterman ... that slogans and the sayings of key individuals ... wer. Employees picked these phrases up and ... to each other, thereby keeping them in mind

Language provides us with ideas and shapes our concepts. Repeat the same words over and over again, and their content will have an ever-deepening impact on you and your beliefs. This, of course, smacks of brain-washing, and so it is to a degree. But, if your brain has been well programmed to begin with, it's difficult to sway you into paths you don't wish to tread simply by the use of language.

Mental language

When you learn how to do something, a major portion of your learning involves the acquisition and use of language. Mentally, you talk yourself through the steps needed to carry out the task you're learning, whether the task is physical or mental. The instruction may help you with this talking, at least to some degree. During the earlier stages of your learning, little rhymes might be used for this purpose when it comes to applied skills. In learning to use a magnetic compass, for instance, you may learn, 'Variation west, compass best; variation east, compass least'. Sailors have often learned, 'Red sky at night, shepherd's delight; red sky in morning, shepherd take warning'.

Words stay in our minds with our learning in particular orders and particular structures. In checking out someone's understanding of a particular task, job, or concept, you'll find that it's a good idea to have that person describe how he or she goes about doing the task or job, or conceives of the concept. When this is done in a detailed and careful way in the field of brain research, it is referred to as the process of 'protocol analysis'. We all have particular protocols or steps we can verbalize to describe the skills we possess and use regularly.

By ensuring that a person has a good verbal description or protocol of a skill or area of applied knowledge, you can help to ensure that person's success in carrying out the actions required. Bear in mind, however, that people with a great deal of experience in a given area may have incorporated this verbal information into their minds at a non-conscious level. So they may need extra assistance to bring this information to the conscious level. For this reason you must be cautious about deciding that someone is incompetent or 'past it', simply because of an inability to verbalize a given skill quickly — this applies especially to routine kinds of skills.

Cues or little 'signals' for the mind can prove quite helpful in assisting people to describe skill protocols. Such cues can take the form of key 'trigger' words, pictures, drawings, models, or other devices that help the learner's brain retrieve and set out the right information. Cues can also be very helpful during learning, as they provide people with memory links their brains will put to good use.

Meanings

In considering the use of language, words, naturally, play a major role. But have you thought of all the general meanings or implications that a single word can have? Here is a listing of key aspects of word meaning:

DENOTATIVE	The meaning or meanings given in general references such as dictionaries or thesauruses.
CONCEPTUAL	The apparent concept structure referred to.
REFERENTIAL	The person, object, or event referred to.
SOCIAL	The implications that emerge from the social setting involved.
EMOTIONAL	The speaker/writer's apparent feelings.
CONTEXT	The significance and relationship of surrounding meanings.
ASSOCIATIVE	Other senses of the same terminology that may come to mind.
JARGON	Specific meanings that may relate to a particular field of activity.
BEHAVIOURAL	The relationship to the speaker/writer's known behaviour pattern.
THEMATIC	What is communicated by the way the message is organized in terms of order and emphasis.
FORM	The physical or graphic characteristics of the statement.

Other such categories exist, but you get the idea. Additionally, any given word you look up in the dictionary will have several stated meanings. For example, the word 'quotation' could mean a repetition of a statement made by someone. Or it could refer to the price of a stock. Now the word 'stock' could refer to a holding in the ownership of a company or it could refer to the wooden support structure of a rifle. And on we go.

What we're dealing with here in a superficial way is the field of 'semantics'. This word refers to the study of meaning. But some people find this study so confusing that they've come to regard the word 'semantics' itself as another term for confusing issues. But it's not semantics that causes confusion, it's language.

Language precision

When you're precise in your language use, and this includes tuning in well with the people who will hear you, language will work for you. When you're sloppy, you can be sure that it will work against you, perhaps not right away, but sooner or later.

Even in the most mechanical of training situations you can influence learners to a marked degree with your language use. They learn new terms and have new thought vistas opened up for them. They make new connections and absorb new capabilities. And even in the most ordinary of lessons, they grow as people in the wake of your words.

When adults review and re-structure their language capabilities through significant learning experiences, they undergo some soul searching. The deeper or more significant the learning experience, the more probing the soul searching. And most of this is done through using language internally (thinking) or externally (speaking, writing).

As an instructor you cannot afford sloppiness in language use if you are truly concerned about learning excellence. Key terms that you may use, especially if you use them repeatedly, will embed themselves in learners' minds, often non-consciously. So you need to exercise sensitivity, care and precision in your words. Are you really using the right words, and are they having the right effect on your learners? Look for feedback from them to find out (monitor).

Your language must be consistent. You can't afford to chop and change the technical terms you use. You have to sound convincing and definite. Your language must seem organized and logical. If you wander all over the place in your talking or writing, your learners will too.

High-flown technical or academic terms can become blocks to good communication. Far from impressing, they can depress, confuse, or bemuse learners. Simplicity is a virtue in language, especially when the language is used to instruct. By the same token, if a particular term is important in its own right, then use it, but make sure your learners understand the meaning as fully as possible.

Some sense of direction should come through in your language. This is another area in which learning objectives help. They enable you to state clear purposes to your learners, and keep you on track in your comments.

When used to help learning occur, language should be as practical as possible. It should be truly relevant to your learners and what they must achieve. Images, anecdotes, practical examples and illustrative stories can all apply to ensuring practicality and relevance.

Embedded suggestions

In hypnosis and neurolinguistic programming, embedded suggestions are very important forms of language use for effecting changes in the cognitive, affective and behavioural domains of people. Similarly embedded suggestions in instructional language have real power. Key points should be brought out and repeated in a number of different ways. When it comes to helping people learn, some redundancy can be a good thing.

Language by decision

When you work on your lesson designs, you use language in several ways. One way involves thinking. In a sense, this is talking to yourself. Some people even find it helps to talk out loud to themselves when they're thinking. Similarly, when you use the thinking tree process, you encourage words to emerge from your own brain — language again. The words you actually put down on your lesson plans again involve language — in its written form. And we've already considered these types of language use in the earlier chapters dealing with learning strategies and lesson designs (Chapter 6 and Chapter 7). We have not yet, however, taken a fuller look at language in its spoken form.

Your voice

Your voice can be a major asset for instructing. It allows you to give directions to others, to outline theories and possibilities, and generally to communicate in a wide variety of different situations. In fact, the voice is so useful for instructors that many teachers are tempted to use it far too much!

Your voice, its cadence, its accent, its volume, its clarity, its depth and its vigour, is a product of your education and experience. It's not just a given. It is susceptible, however, to change or improvement. It can change naturally through experience. Or it can change deliberately through practice and effort on your part.

How are you heard?

How does your voice come across to other people? Do they find it rich and pleasant to listen to? Or do they find it irritating and harsh? The reactions of others have a major bearing on the effectiveness of your voice as a teaching instrument. If you have an interesting voice, people will tend to listen to what you have to say. But if you have a dull, flat voice, people will tend to close you out, perhaps doing so at a non-conscious level.

Improving your voice

You can improve your voice in a number of practical ways. You just need to start with a good understanding of your voice as it is now. Tape recordings can give you good feedback. You can record your voice in many different settings. Sometimes you might wish to have friends or colleagues help you. One good way to record your voice is to take along a small cassette recorder when you have to deliver any kind of presentation. Place the recorder in a discreet location, switch it on, and later you'll have a recording of your voice taken in as realistic a situation as you could wish to have.

You may be one of the many people (probably in excess of 90 per cent of all adults) who loathes the sound of your own voice. In fact, at times your might deny that it really is your voice when the cassette recorder plays back, even if people assure you that it is.

The personal impact of hearing your own voice for the first time can be deep and sharp. You suddenly realize you're not entirely the person you thought you were. But bear with it. Your voice almost never sounds as bad to other people as you think it does. Usually the real problem is that you're not sufficiently well acquainted with the true sound of your own voice.

Our skulls act more or less like 'sound boxes' to change the sound of our voices when we hear ourselves speak. Other people hear your voice outside the confines of your unique sound box. So you're the only person in the world to hear your voice the way you do. This is a major part of the reason why the sound of your own voice coming back to you through some form of recording can be such a shock the first time you experience it. In effect, you're listening to a stranger's voice, but everyone around you insists it's yours!

Using the 'CALM VOICES' approach

Once you overcome the shock factor of hearing your own voice, you can start to do something with it. The main thing is to decide exactly what you really want to change in your voice. For this purpose a form of checklist comes in handy. Think of the phrase CALM VOICES. The words in this phrase break down as shown in the following box.

Clarity
Aim
Language
Modulation
Volume
Openness
Images
Confidence
Enthusiasm
Speed

These words summarize most of the key points you need to consider and apply to develop a good voice, if not an excellent one. Let's look at each of these words in a little more detail.

Clarity

The clarity of your voice comes from the precision of the words you use, including their specificity, as well as the way you pronounce them. Precisely chosen words used in specific ways carry excellent impact with your listeners. They help to create an aura of definiteness and conviction, leaving the listener in little doubt about your position and meaning.

Of course your well-chosen words must have the correct pronunciation if they are to work effectively. Many people have a habit of 'mouthing' or swallowing their words. They don't enunciate all the syllables in the words they use. So *want to* becomes *wanna,* or *underground* becomes *unagran.* Similarly, *roundabout* becomes *ranabat* and *comfortable* becomes *comfable.* Intoxicated people mouth their words horribly. This is one of the reasons we know they're intoxicated.

Once you're alert to this form of verbal sloppiness, you can start to detect it quite readily in the speech of others. This will make it easier for you to work on eliminating it from your own speech.

Aim

You aim your voice in a couple of important ways. You can aim it directly at your audience and you can aim it directly at some specific purpose. Both are important.

To aim directly at your audience place yourself so your voice will project to their ears by the most direct route possible. This means facing your audience directly, trying to keep clear of any physical obstructions that might lie between you and them.

In aiming at your audience, keep in mind the phrase *eye contact.* Look people directly in the eyes, but not to the point of staring or causing embarrassment. This process forces you to aim your voice well at other people.

The other part of your aim concerns your reason for speaking in the first place. An audience needs some direction and some idea of the destination your words will lead them to. To put it bluntly, what's in it for them? You can answer this question by stating your lesson purpose at or near the beginning of your lesson. And this purpose must derive from the learning objective or objectives you intend to help everyone achieve.

Language

Language concerns word choice and the actual use of words. Decide if your words will convey the right tone. Are they simple, yet effective for your purpose? The right words will do credit to your voice, but the wrong words will damage even the most melodious of voices.

Spoken language still needs to observe at least the basics of good grammar. Like written language, it contains sentences and paragraphs. And these sentences and paragraphs should conform to exactly the same grammatical rules as written language, although a lesser degree of formality is often acceptable. Some speakers, of course, deliberately flout the rules of grammar for effect. This is fair enough if you really know what you're doing and the effect is worthwhile. But if your grammar is poor for reasons other than special effect, it will reflect poorly on you. This applies also to the repeated use of hackneyed terms such as 'bottom line' or 'last but not least'.

An excellent way to check your spoken grammar is to record a good sample of your own speech, and then have this transcribed into writing. This will enable you to examine your spoken language very carefully. If you have doubts about your ability to pick up on grammar problems, get someone you trust to help. This effort can yield positive results for you in making all sorts of presentations.

Language not only provides us with a means of communication, but acts as an organ of perception for us as well. Once we use words to describe something, these words can themselves virtually allow us to sense fully the thing described. In effect, words can substitute for the objects or actions they describe, at least to a degree. This is part of the reason why people can often delude themselves into believing they've reached an objective simply by talking about it.

If you lead learners through the performance of some task with words alone (a cognitive instructional approach), you activate similar areas in their brains to those activated if they were actually doing the task described. This is the essence of the use of mental rehearsals in instructing. But this kind of positive guidance through words requires a very detailed and imaginative use of language. In particular, it requires the use of carefully chosen and accurate images that people can work with in their minds. This is an area in which well-chosen audiovisual illustrations of various types can reinforce your guidance.

In thinking of the perceptual power of language for humans, remember the dangers of inaccurate, premature, or negative *labelling*. When you pin arbitrary labels on objects, actions, or people you can cause long-lasting damage. By embedding such labels in your learners' minds, you contaminate the quality of their learning, and this can lead to very unpleasant consequences in the work-place.

Words have their greatest power when people find them personally meaningful (they're receptive to them) and when they evoke good mental images. The right words used well at the right times will stay with people long after a training or education programme has ended. They play an invaluable role in achieving productive learning at both a conscious and non-conscious level. All the more reason to take special care in your language use for instructing.

Modulation

Modulation involves the injection of a sense of rhythm into your voice. You can help yourself to do this by thinking of singing. When you sing you change notes and move your voice up and down the scale. In normal speech this kind of rhythm is modulation. You seek to provide an interesting *melody* in your speech to help your learners listen comfortably and attentively to what you're saying.

If you listen closely to the voice of a professional radio or television announcer, you will hear a voice that uses modulation to very good effect. You can practise your own use of modulation by recording a professional announcer's voice on tape. Play back this recording, listening carefully, and then record your own voice on the tape immediately after the professional announcer's, making a deliberate attempt to modulate your voice in the same way. Use this procedure frequently for a few weeks and you'll find your modulation improves markedly.

Make a habit of listening for the way different people modulate their voices in your everyday activities. You'll quickly notice that some people are very good in their voice control, while others speak regularly with flat and monotonous voices. Take your lead from the well-modulated voices you hear. Your voice will become more and more pleasant for people to listen to.

Volume

The use of voice volume in instructing differs to some degree from its use in everyday conversation. You can, for instance, speak with a conversational volume in a classroom setting and actually have people hear you. And yet your volume might really not be high enough.

Instructing requires a volume a little bit louder than the volume needed simply to be heard. You should be trying to use your voice as a *command* or *attention* device, and it's difficult to command attention if your voice lacks good volume.

You can learn to produce more voice volume through the control of your breathing. Your voice, after all, is produced through the expulsion of air from your lungs through the vocal cords of your larynx. These vocal cords are pairs of folds that produce humming sounds. You produce speech with these sounds by changing the air pressure and varying the tension in your vocal cords controlled by muscles in your larynx. Of course you're not usually consciously aware of this, since the speech centres in your brain handle things automatically.

Good breath control is essential to good speech, particularly when it comes to having sufficient volume. Many, if not most, people do not breathe deeply enough. Full breathing, as the yogis point out, involves the use of your stomach along with your chest. Part of the reason many of us don't breathe deeply enough has to do with the idea of tummy expansion. Too many of us may feel our tummies are expanded enough already!

Anyway, try taking in a deep breath and making sure your tummy does expand. You'll notice this gives you lots of air for your system to work with. All you have to do now is to make use of this extra air for giving more volume to your voice.

Place the tips of your fingers gently at the bottom of your rib cage. This is roughly the location of your diaphragm. Now make a loud noise with your voice. A hum or the sound *ah!* will do. If you make this sound loudly enough you'll feel your diaphragm vibrate under your fingers at the same time as you make the sound. Quite literally this gives you the *feel* of your voice at work. You can enjoy doing this while taking a shower. A rendition of your favourite aria could easily give you lots of sound to work with!

If you have a friend or relative who will cooperate, practise your voice volume with him or her in a large hall or outdoors. Try shouting instructions, being sure to project and support your voice volume from your stomach and not your throat. If your friend or relative can hear you and carry out your instructions (e.g. 'Touch your toes'.) at a good distance, you'll know you have volume working well for you.

By supporting your voice volume with stomach breathing you take a lot of strain away from your throat. This, in turn, reduces the chances of your becoming hoarse or losing your voice as a result of too much public speaking. If you do find yourself going a bit hoarse, you're probably not using your stomach effectively. Either that or you've got a cold coming on. Remind yourself now and then of the importance of deep breathing for voice control and volume.

If you're nervous at all, your voice tends to rise up into your throat. This automatically interferes with effective volume. Deep breathing will help calm your nervousness as well as providing you with better voice volume.

Openness

You can convey openness in your voice through the words you choose and the way you emphasize them. There's a certain quality or timbre of voice that gives others a sense of your honesty and sincerity. You enhance this effect through the directness of your eye contact and the relaxed flow of words you produce when talking.

Your *body language* too influences your apparent openness to quite an extent. Make sure your hand doesn't cover or partly cover your mouth. Try not to speak out of the corner of your mouth. And don't speak through tightly controlled lips.

Your posture and gestures reinforce or detract from what you're saying. Crossing your arms, for instance, may convey defensiveness to your audience. Tightly clasped hands may signal nervousness to others or, worse, disbelief in what you're saying. If you're trying to affirm something in your speech, but shake your head from side to side while doing so, you're sending out mixed signals. The same thing occurs, of course, if you're trying to negate something, but you're nodding your head at the same time.

If you genuinely *think* honesty and sincerity, this will tend to come through in your voice. You've noticed this before in listening to other people. When you really think about it, the openness with which people speak influences what you think of them very much.

Guarded or fuzzy words destroy openness. So take care in putting too many qualifiers in your words, particularly with audiences or classes that might not really appreciate the need for fine or careful distinctions. Take their reception levels into account. Academics, in particular, have to take care here.

In setting a good climate of openness, you must not only try to be open with your audience, you must try to be open about yourself as well. Share little titbits of personal information with your audience. You don't have to drag out all sorts of embarrassing details about the 'closet' areas of your personality, but it helps if you can put a little flavour of yourself into what you say. This makes it easier for others to relate to you and the information you seek to impart.

When it comes to conveying a sense of openness to others, little things mean a lot. For this reason it's worthwhile taking a look at yourself on a videocassette recording. Objective viewing will provide you with a lot of little details about your speaking manner. And these details will help you to identify the aspects of your approach you wish to enhance, eliminate, or include in your future instructing work.

Images

Using images is very important, as I've pointed out a number of times already. Most people think with images. We see things happen in our minds. We can even programme ourselves to see things that might not actually have happened or that happened in the remote past. The right image helps us grasp even complicated concepts quickly.

Consider some samples of image language. Something that's been held back might be described as *dammed up*. A remote or lofty idea might be described as *in the clouds*. Solid or practical suggestions might be called *down to earth*. Feelings can be *bottled up*. Roads can *snake* through hilly terrain. Determination can be *solid as a rock*. Thinking can be *woolly*, and on it goes. Images carry your messages quickly, effectively and dynamically.

Sometimes, when you're preparing a lesson, you might find it difficult to conjure up useful images. If this happens, try to get you mind to focus on something else for a while. Relax. Take a walk. Anything to take your mind off the lesson for a while. When you come back to work on your lesson plan after an hour or so, the chances are good that you'll have come up with some new and useful images.

If different activities don't seem to help you come up with good images, try being a little more deliberate in your brain work. Leaf through a dictionary looking at words selected at random. Examine a particular object in your immediate surroundings, such as a lamp or a vase, to see what thoughts arise in your mind that might produce useful images.

Deliberate effort and a little imagination will lead you to develop numbers of useful images to help people grasp the points of information and ideas you want them to take in. And you'll enjoy the process of coming up with these images too.

Confidence

This concerns the degree to which you seem to believe in what you're saying yourself. It is built and reinforced to a large extent by your effectiveness in handling the other aspects of speaking. But it has some attributes of its own that are well worth considering as well.

Before you speak in front of any group, be sure in your own mind that what you will say makes sense and is accurate. In short, believe yourself. This will help you speak without hesitation. And when you speak, be definite, ending your sentences with vigour. Don't just let them trail off leaving a sense of limp vagueness.

The KISS principle will help you project confidence. Keep your words short and sweet most of the time. But be careful not to be too short or too sweet at times. You can remind yourself of this by thinking of the acronym KISSBAC instead of just KISS. The KISSBAC principle refers to the words, *keep it short and sweet, but accurate and complete*. It reminds you that sometimes accuracy and completeness must prevail over sheer brevity and sweetness.

Confidence is helped too by the sense of determination you project. Emphasize certain words and terms. Give some of your more important words a sense of 'bite'. This makes them stand out better in the minds of your learners and penetrate deeper.

Once you've said something, leave it alone. Don't torture it with a lot of qualifiers or afterthoughts. This gives people a far better chance to hear and understand what you're saying. And they can focus more easily on the thrust of what you're trying to convey.

Body language, once again, is important. You have to look convinced yourself to help your audience become convinced. If you want something to come across strongly, look strong. Don't let a weak little smile belittle the worth of your words. If you want your audience to laugh, try to look happy yourself. Seeing yourself on a video play-back can help you see if your body language is consistent with the confidence you want to project.

Enthusiasm

A sense of enthusiasm on your part can help your learners become enthusiastic about what you tell them. And if they become enthusiastic they will tend to develop a better level of motivation about you and the subject at hand.

You can convey enthusiasm in a number of ways. Try injecting a special sense of energy and vigour into your voice while reinforcing this with your body language. Rise up a little on the balls of your feet now and then. Lean towards your audience when you want to emphasize particular points. Use some calculated gestures to hammer ideas home. Try to put a little sparkle in your eyes. These types of actions will help to build an atmosphere of enthusiasm for everyone.

As with confidence, you have to develop some enthusiasm yourself before you can put it across to other people. If you're not really enthusiastic about what you're doing or saying, you can hardly expect anyone else to be enthusiastic either.

You might have talked on the subject concerned many times before. And this can cause some lack of enthusiasm (incipient 'burn-out') to creep in. It might even cause you to feel bored about your own topic. If you don't do something about it beforehand, your own lack of enthusiasm or your sense of boredom will come across very quickly to your learners. And this is not only unfair to them, it's unfair to you as well. You really don't want to gain a reputation as a boring teacher!

Concentrate on the good things you will give people through your speaking. And remember, it may be old stuff to you, but it's new to them (or it should be). Leave aside doubts and mental hesitations. Work on convincing yourself that what you say really matters. And pretend you've never said it before.

Look for signs of interest in the faces of the members of your audience. Reinforce your own sense of interest through the interest shown by others. And don't worry too much, at least at the start, about those people who may appear uninterested. You can't always expect to keep everyone interested, no matter how good a speaker you might be.

Great actors work hard to develop their sense of projected enthusiasm. They might play their roles a hundred times or more, but they know that each time they replay a role, it must seem as if it's being played for the very first time. Keep this in mind for your speaking. You can convince yourself to be enthusiastic with just a little patience and effort.

Speed

The speed with which different people speak can vary a lot. Fast talkers can speak in excess of 200 words per minute. Slow talkers talk at a rate something less than 100 words per minute. Your own speed is probably somewhere between these two extremes.

Many people have been taught to speak slowly when making a speech or presentation. The idea has been that slower speech makes for better comprehension on the part of listeners. But this is not necessarily so. It might even have the opposite result. Speech that is too slow might simply put people to sleep.

Our brains can think verbally at a rate in excess of 1000 words per minute with good comprehension. Words coming into our brains at a speed of only 100 words per minute leave a very big thinking gap. In our daily activities we tend to fill in this gap with many thoughts beyond those someone might be saying to us. This is one of the causes of ineffective listening.

No one on earth can speak at 1000 words per minute. With compressed audio recordings a human voice might come across to you at a speed of about 400 words per minute. Without artificial assistance, some people can speak at about 240 words per minute. Some of them are employed in fairs or similar public places. Hence our mental associations with the term *fast talker*.

You probably don't want or need to speak at a fast talker clip. But you might, from time to time, want to talk at a speed of up to 180 words per minute. This is a pace somewhat faster than most public speakers use, and for this reason alone it can help to focus learner attention without seeming too fast to most people.

By injecting important concepts or interesting titbits of information into your language you help your audience to increase their subject reception level. They can chew over these morsels of *food for thought* in the gap space between your talking speed and their thinking speeds. This will help them deepen their understanding of what you have to say.

You can calculate your speaking speed fairly simply. Record five minutes of your speaking before a given group of people. Then have this recording transcribed. After this you simply have to count up the number of words you spoke, divide by five, and there's your speed. Alternatively, you can read aloud a page containing a known number of words using a stop watch to check the amount of time it takes. Just try to be sure that your reading-out-loud speed is close to your usual speaking speed. Someone else might be able to help you here. Or an audio-cassette recording could let you make this check.

Speeding up your talking at times and slowing it down for special effect at other times will work well for you. Be sure you don't get into the habit of always speaking at one speed, fast or slow. You can use speed to reinforce your use of the other key points we've brought out here. And it will reinforce them for you very effectively.

Regular use

By making regular use of the CALM VOICES approach to using your voice for teaching you'll find that all of its aspects soon come quite naturally to you. By checking your audio or video recordings now and then you'll notice the progress you're making with your voice. And, most importantly, you'll be getting better results with your learners as well. The points are all here. You can use them.

Stage fright

One aspect of speaking in any kind of public setting, of course, concerns dealing with so-called 'stage fright'. For most people this is a problem. But it's one you can deal with.

First, consider the word 'fright'. What does it really mean? Essentially, it's an indication of an immediate, somewhat terrifying reaction to a sudden occurrence of some kind. So if a truck almost runs you over in the street, you experience fright. The same thing happens if a sudden loud noise occurs very near to you.

We can all become frightened. The fright reaction is really a built-in biological factor. And it's probably a good thing. It readies us for fight or flight when danger threatens. Fright is an immediate and automatic reaction to something that seems dangerous in our environment.

Stage fear

Now let's consider the word 'fear'. This word describes our mental reactions to anticipated danger or personal disaster. A key word here is 'anticipated'. Fear can build up slowly in our minds to gnaw away at us over a long period of time. And it's something that feeds on itself. Fear begets fear. What's most damaging about fear is that it is not usually based on real dange. us a lot of unfounded worry.

When it comes to public speaking what concerns p stage fear, not stage fright. Most public speakers are their lives at risk. They probably won't even have rotten or eggs thrown at them. They're not likely to suffer p al injury at all. But they might suffer psychic damage — and this is the realm of fear.

We're born with the capacity for fright. But fear is conditioned into us through our experiences with life. Influential people in our lives, especially when we're very young, often develop fears in our minds without necessarily intending to. Misplaced humour or unthinking jokes can easily make a young person fearful of speaking in front of a group of people. And once this kind of fear develops, it can be difficult to remove.

If you had intimidating experiences in school as a child when you spoke in front of your class, your mind will store these painful memories somewhere. As an adult these memories will still have impact on your feelings (affective domain), even though they may act at a non-conscious level. In effect, fear is a form of internal programming. You can, with patience and determination, reprogramme yourself to speak without this fear.

Before you speak in front of any group make very sure that you're well prepared. When your mind is clear about what you plan to accomplish with your learners, you reduce the fear element substantially. In keeping with this, provide yourself with notes you can refer to easily while you're talking. This, as you might recall, is a key aspect of good lesson planning. And don't hesitate now and then to refer to your notes. Although you should try to keep these notes reasonably short.

Finally, in coping with stage fear, follow these suggestions:

1. Ensure that you prepare all presentations well, including finding out the learner reception levels of the people you'll be teaching.
2. Give yourself the opportunity in a variety of settings (e.g. meetings of various kinds) to speak spontaneously to develop your ability to 'think on your feet'.
3. Remind yourself from time to time of your past successes in speaking in front of groups.

4. Rehearse key parts of your teaching using a cassette recorder (sometimes just doing so in front of a mirror will help a lot).
5. Make sure you have all the notes and reference objects you need ready to hand while conducting your lessons.
6. Go over your notes shortly before conducting a lesson, but not right up to the last possible moment.
7. If you're being introduced by someone else, be sure that person has a good short biography of you to use (and make sure its language is not stiff and formal).
8. Allow yourself a couple of minutes of relaxation time just before you start the lesson — some relaxation techniques can help here — at the very least take a few deep breaths and let your muscles relax as much as possible.
9. Take a couple of sips of cool water (nothing stronger).
10. When you go to the front of classroom to start, allow yourself a little bit of setting-up time — never force yourself to start speaking the instant you're up there.
11. Once you're ready, scan your audience briefly, making eye contact here and there, being sure to project confidence (even though you might not feel it inside).
12. Start off with your opening line (and for heaven's sake don't feel obliged to say something funny), and launch quickly into describing the purpose of the lesson — also use this time to set out any procedural matters you wish to follow (e.g. when you'll accept or ask questions).
13. If you lose your train of thought, calmly give yourself some time to gather your ideas together — never engage in negative thinking when this happens — if you have to refer back to your notes, do so, and make no bones about it.
14. If a piece of audiovisual equipment lets you down, don't struggle indefinitely to make it work — move on to doing something else as quickly and smoothly as you can.
15. If an unexpected interruption occurs (e.g. someone drops a tray of dishes), don't let it throw you — if possible, work it into your presentation ('Now that we've heard from another group of customers!').

16. Don't let apparent inattentiveness or rudeness by learners intimidate you — this could just be their way of participating.
17. Always feel free to move around a bit — sometimes it helps to come out from behind different kinds of barriers. In some cases it might even work well to walk right out into the middle of your class.
18. Remind yourself now and then to remain relaxed.
19. If you start to run out of time, don't make heroic efforts to jam everything in — cover what you can of what you have left, but retain a sense of calm confidence.
20. End on a positive note of completion, being sure to leave your audience with good final thoughts and an idea of what lies ahead. Try to avoid saying little phrases such as 'thank you', or 'have a nice day' — these run the risk of suddenly trivializing everything you've said.
21. Review how each presentation you make actually goes, and make revisions in your approach accordingly — but don't drown yourself in self-recrimination. Do and learn.

Stage fear can be a very debilitating thing. It can seriously hurt the careers of people who otherwise show a lot of promise. You don't have to allow it to get the better of you. One very important point to remember is that you almost never appear as nervous to an audience as you might feel inside. They really can't see your legs or arms trembling (although it's a good idea not to hold a few loose sheets of paper in front of you if you think your arm is shaking).

Different people develop different methods for coping with stage fear. With a little experimenting you'll find you can do the same thing. One person, for instance, claims he calms himself by imagining that everyone in his audience is naked! Once he does this, he finds that his sense of fear melts away.

Work on your fear in a methodical fashion, and you'll gradually get it under control. Keep away from negative thinking or those little 'downer' comments that can arise in the mind so easily. Instead, focus on those steps you can take to make a presentation successful. By doing so, you'll find the fear just gradually fades away.

Give yourself a chance

Before the start of any session in which you'll be speaking, give yourself a chance to relax. Allow your body physically to relax in a comfortable chair. Take up all the weight of your body with the chair, not allowing any of your muscles to remain tense. While doing this, project positive and comfortable images in your mind. You can imagine yourself in a beautiful location of some kind. Close your eyes while doing this to go deeper into your projection (and don't worry about going to sleep!) You'll find that you help all of this relaxation process by breathing deeply throughout.

If you haven't tried a relaxation process before, you'll be surprised at how much calmness you can give yourself in just a few minutes. With practice, as with so many things, you'll become better and better at going through this process.

Once you've given yourself a few minutes of this seated (some people prefer to lie on their backs) relaxation, stand up and give yourself a good stretch. This will help to drain any remaining tension out of your muscles, and it will enhance the refreshment effect you'll feel.

When you go before your group, keep your body relaxed, not rigid. Remember to smile, or at least not to frown. Don't feel that you have to say something the moment you enter the room. Give yourself a chance to arrange your notes and other teaching materials. Then, when you're ready, start speaking in a calm, confident, voice (remember CALM VOICES).

During your lesson you might find yourself tensing up a little. Just remind yourself to relax. A sip of water might help too. Be sure you don't engage in self-destructive thinking while you're talking. You wouldn't be in front of the class unless someone thought you had something to offer. So remain positive about yourself and about what you have to say.

While thinking of nervousness, it's worth remembering that people generally don't see you as being as nervous as you might feel. You might think your voice is quavering or your knees are knocking, while your audience hears and sees you in rock-solid, confident form. If you doubt this, view some videos of yourself and ask for feedback from people whose opinions you trust. You'll probably be pleasantly surprised at how little, if any, of your nervousness comes through.

We all have a tendency to focus our minds on our failures, indeed many of us seem to be failure-oriented. But our failures are really few in comparison to our successes. Keep focusing on your successes. If you aren't that way already, strive to become success-oriented, not just in your speaking, but in your approach to things in general. You've got precious little to lose by doing so, and a great deal to gain.

Most of the time we tend to think people will be more critical of us than they actually are. Again, this probably has a lot to do with the way fear was programmed into our minds in the first place. However it arises, the plain fact is that the vast majority of people are far more critical of themselves than other people are. And this factor will work against you if you allow it to.

Language in learning

Language, and the way you use it, plays a fundamental role in human affairs. This role is emphasized even more when it comes to instructing. Use language well and learning can occur in solid fashion. Remember to tune your words to the minds of your learners. Keep pace with them as their understanding develops and deepens.

Permit yourself to succeed

Try to clear out the destructive pieces of language your mind harbours (Joseph Chilton Pearce, author of a number of imporant self-help books, refers to these bits of word rubbish as 'roof brain chatter'). Plant constructive thoughts instead. This sounds simplistic, but it does work. Only you have to actually do it, and believe in it. In essence, through your careful use of language, internally and externally, you permit yourself to succeed as an instructor or speaker in almost any setting.

10 Using Questions to Help Learning

You often can use questioning effectively for helping learning. Sometimes you can even build an entire training session around the use of questioning. This applies especially for more informal, learner-centred styles of instructing (more passive instructional mode).

The use of questioning as part of the teaching process is often called the Socratic teaching method, after the ancient Greek philosopher who used this method to pass on his wisdom.

By using well-selected questions you force your learners to think. You put the *pressure point* in the lesson on the learners themselves, instead of automatically taking it on your own shoulders (thereby helping to relieve some of your nervous strain).

Asking questions effectively

Good questioning stirs up learner interest. It provides a convenient and effective means of putting things from the point of view of the learner. It turns a teaching session into more of a two-way form of communication, increasing the chances of achieving a thorough understanding by the learners.

It's always worthwhile considering what role, if any, questioning might play in the design and delivery of all your training activities. When you decide that questioning makes sense, keep the following points in mind:

1. Keep the first question as straightforward as possible (without making it simplistic).
2. Make sure the first response from a learner is received and rewarded as positively as possible (you don't want people to feel like jerks for answering questions).

3. Put most of the questions into plain, specific words, keeping them relatively short.
4. In general, pose only one question at a time.
5. Don't allow anxiety to permit too short a time span for response from the learners — try to use silence as an ally for prompting thinking (a four second wait for response to a given question is not out of line at all — you can call this the use of *productive silence*).
6. If a question must be asked again, try to keep to the original wording (this helps to avoid adding confusion to the thinking of the learners).
7. Look for ways you can build on the responses received, either in additional instructor comments or with further questions.
8. When really good answers are given, note this out loud, letting the learners know clearly and definitely.
9. Inject enthusiasm. You want people to feel that responding to questions is really worth their while.
10. Make sure questions are stated clearly.
11. Be sure to acknowledge positively all responses from learners (remember the use of positive guidance).
12. Make sure you continually scan all learners while asking questions to check for possible or actual responders (you never want to leave a willing responder ignored).
13. Make sure you check your lesson plan or training design from time to time to ensure that using questions does not cause things to go off track or take up too much time.
14. In many situations, it's a good idea to summarize the responses received from learners under key categories. Sometimes you can summarize all under one heading. This technique provides an excellent means of closing some training sessions.

One of the most important things to bear in mind when using questions is that you have to make sure the learners know when questions are being asked so they will actually give responses. Many instructors have a habit of asking questions they respond to themselves. These rhetorical kinds of questions are characteristic of people using a more direct form of instructing, and they don't encourage learners to give answers.

You can use rhetorical questions, of course. They provide some variety from straightforward speech-giving. And they create some sense of learner involvement. You can make this form of question more effective too by trying to pose questions likely to relate well to learner interests. The main thing is to make sure that rhetorical questions don't get in the way of good learner responses.

At times, especially if you've used both rhetorical and learner-response questions, the learners may become unsure of which type is being used at a particular point in the learning session. To guard against this, don't answer your own questions too quickly. A four-second pause allows the learners to realize an answer is expected from them. It puts the pressure point on the learners, not you, the instructor.

Silence is a tool you can use effectively in questioning. Think of it as *productive silence*. Once you realize this form of silence exists, it makes it easier to endure silence during a given training session without undergoing the irresistible urge to speak out and break it.

Questioning is by no means a cure-all for dealing with different training sessions, but it is a valuable technique to use as a component of many types of training. And it's one many instructors ignore because their minds are set in the groove of thinking lessons are one-way forms of communication.

What if they're wrong?

One type of situation often throws people when they use questioning. This concerns dealing with answers that are wrong or not quite right. You can deal with both kinds without making the responder feel like a dunce.

In dealing with wrong answers, for instance, here are some possible responses:

'So what you're saying is ... .'

'O.K., thank you, what do the rest of you think?'

'Let's work with your answer for a bit.'

'How would you see applying that?'

'Good, now let's hear from someone else on this point.'

'I'll write your answer down here ... .'

Once you start thinking about it, you'll probably come up with numbers of good responses to wrong answers, some better than the ones on this list. The main idea is to keep the dialogue going between you and the learners, and to allow learners to sort out wrong information themselves (this includes the learner who may have come out with a wrong answer to begin with).

If you're left with no other option you may have to tell someone when they've come up with the wrong answer. When this happens make sure this process is as inoffensive and supportive as possible. You don't want to set up a 'me versus them' atmosphere in any training session.

Answers that are not quite right give you more to work with than those that are just plain wrong. They provide *stems of correctness* that you can build on. Here are some possible responses to these types of answers:

'O.K., now based on what you're saying, what about ... ?'

'So that leads us to?'

'Fine, now can someone else add to that?'

'Good, that's got us started on an important idea.'

'Then, would it be fair to say ... ?'

And on it goes. Once you allow yourself to think this way and to practise such responses, you'll find these kinds of answers can be dealt with naturally and positively. This will reflect itself in the lively activity that will occur among the learners.

What types of questions?

Many different types of questions are possible. The chart in Figure 28 gives you a good indication of four key types that are worth considering. In examining these different questioning possibilities, keep in mind the point that certain types of questions will be more useful for given training situations than others.

Here are some examples of what each of these four questions might sound like in an actual instructional situation:

Directed/Closed: 'Henry, what is the definition of the word, 'entropy'?'

Undirected/Closed: 'What is the exact latitude and longitude of Edinburgh, Scotland?'

Directed/Open: 'Adele, what do you believe will be the benefits of expanded literacy training in this area?'

Undirected/Open: 'What are some of the key considerations you should keep in mind for buying a home?'

	CLOSED	OPEN
DIRECTED	Directed at one particular learner and having just one answer.	Directed at one learner, but having more than one possible answer.
UNDIRECTED	Not directed at any one learner and having just one answer.	Not directed at any one learner and having more than one answer.

Figure 28: *The questions grid*

The *closed* forms of questions can test specific knowledge. They focus on issues that have definite answers. So they have their place. Notice, however, that they're not likely to stimulate a lot of discussion. For this reason you should keep them fairly restricted in instructing.

The *directed* types of questions serve a useful purpose when you want to bring a specific learner into a lesson. But use them sparingly. Too much use leads to a classroom atmosphere of tension as everyone starts to feel the pressure of the game: *Where will this instructor strike next?*

Some instructors love the directed types of questions. They think these keep learners on their toes. These instructors are using questions as weapons, not learning promoters. Further, they're too often teaching avoidance techniques, not genuine understanding.

Directed questions have their uses. But use them very carefully and sparingly.

Open questions, as the term suggests, help to open things up in an instructional situation.They promote thinking (as long as they concern issues of at least a little substance). When you wish to get a good discussion going, use lots of open questions.

Undirected questions help to create a comfortable and stimulating learning environment. They don't put people on the spot, yet they open up good opportunities for thinking and learner contribution.

In designing training, keep these different questioning possibilities in mind. They add a lot to any kind of learning situation.

The learner connection

Learner questions provide one of the best means of really connecting with the learners. They help to make people feel a part of the training process. They provide opportunities for clarification and confirmation. And they provide you with an invaluable means of finding out the key issues and concerns of learners in the most dynamic way possible.

But questions can be two-edged. If you don't deal with them effectively or at the right time, they might damage. In a group situation they can act like sharp knives. They can cut through a mess of confusion. But they can also draw blood. You just have to give them the respect and care they deserve. The rest almost takes care of itself.

The reluctant participant

Some people are a little shy about answering instructor questions. What to do? One temptation, of course, is to resort to directed questions and name the person concerned. Unfortunately, this can cause problems, especially if the learner has a good reason for holding back (e.g. a serious speech impediment).

If directed questions are thrown at the reluctant participant too readily, they can embarrass and hurt. And they will too easily get in the way of effective learning.

The first strategy to consider is simply to move a little closer to the reluctant participant. Then, when asking a question, you can look directly at the person (but not for too long). This puts a bit of pressure on that person, at least briefly. And this pressure might bring out a response.

If the proximity strategy doesn't work, another strategy involves talking with the participant privately at an opportune time. Here you simply ask why the person seems reluctant to give answers. Depending on the explanation given, a satisfactory solution is possible, without risk of embarrassment.

Sometimes the sheer passage of time is all that's needed to make the reluctant participant ready to take an active part.

After a reasonable length of time, if all strategies have failed, just let the person carry on in her or his own way. There are a few people whose learning styles just don't work to make them want to get into the give and take of questions and answers. They learn well in their passive modes. So there's no point in forcing them into learning modes that could prove counter-productive.

Most of the time it is possible to get reluctant participants to participate more actively. But patience and subtlety on the part of the instructor are essential qualities for accomplishing this.

Getting the timing right

When you plan to use questioning, be sure to time your questions effectively within the instructional plan. A few questions thrown in near the end of a lesson on an, 'Oh, by the way ...' basis are not likely to work well.

Questioning that starts too late often reflects poorly on the lesson, because it usually results in discussions continuing beyond the planned end time with no real summation occurring for the thrust of the lesson as a whole. People may go away with the last question or their last comment in mind, rather than the thought or action you wanted clearly to plant in their minds. You're much better off most of the time to start the use of questioning early in a lesson, rather than later.

The classroom layout pattern

The way you lay out the chairs and desks in a classroom has a lot to do with the effectiveness of using questioning, whether from yourself or from a learner. Consider the patterns illustrated in Figures 29 and 30.

In the open layout pattern (Figure 29) the lines of communication (which include the sight lines) are well set out for questioning, including questioning by learners. With this pattern the total number of participants should be relatively low for maximum questioning effectiveness. In practice, of course, this is not always possible for budgetary and other reasons.

When you are faced with smaller instructor/participant ratios (e.g. 1:12 or 1:20), try to make sure you adhere to the open layout pattern as closely as possible. You can, for instance, open out this basic semi-circle configuration to accommodate more people. Or you can try removing desks. The point is that you can still do something about helping the questioning process with the way you lay out the classroom, even though class numbers grow.

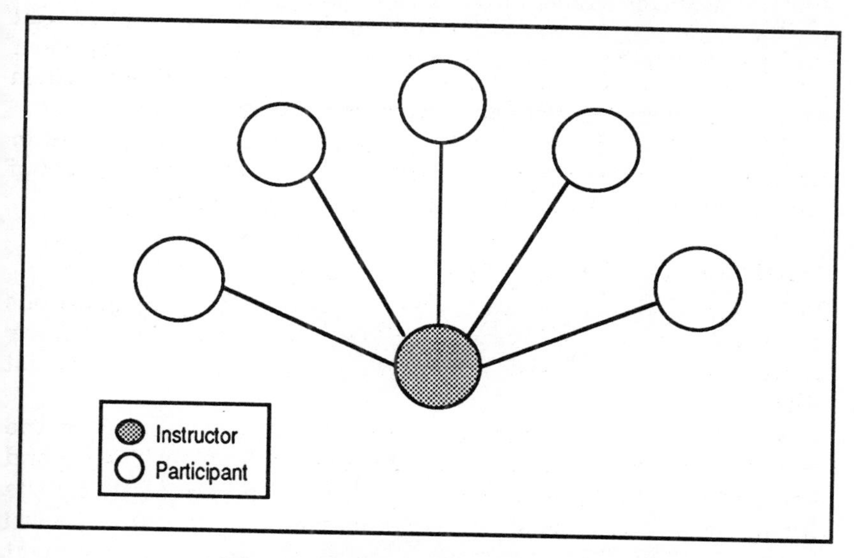

Figure 29: *Open layout pattern*

Now take a look at the obstructive pattern (Figure 30). This pattern makes things difficult for instructor/participant interaction. The people in the back row have more difficulty in establishing communicative links with you. Their links are longer than those of the people at the front. And they're subject to being cut off easily if one or more of the front people lean too far in the wrong direction.

In comparing these two figures see how the less effective pattern uses a narrower space. This shows why long, narrow training rooms hinder training.

The obstructive layout pattern looks more like the traditional seating arrangement used in the formal education system. Some people call this the 'regimental system'. Unfortunately, the tradition of using this layout pattern has had its impact too on training in business and government.

Try adding more participants using the obstructive layout pattern. Things become worse and worse as rows are added to rows.

Some people argue that the obstructed layout pattern is more efficient than the open pattern. They're thinking of efficiency in terms of stuffing bodies into a given space, rather like packing eggs into a crate. They're certainly not thinking of it in terms of learning effectiveness.

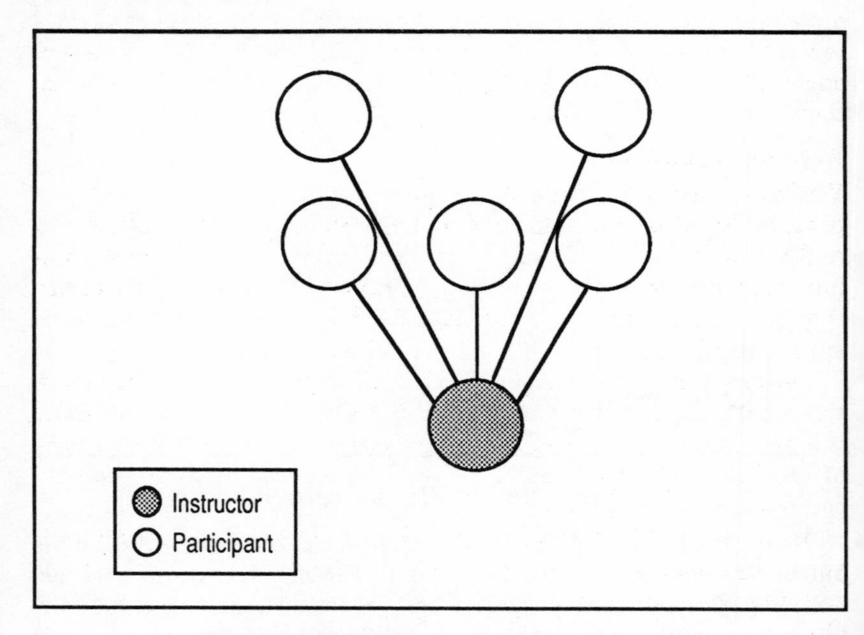

Figure 30: *Obstructive layout pattern*

The way you set things up in a training room has a lot to do with whether or not questioning will prove effective. It also has a lot to do with the effectiveness of any instructional method you use. A good lecture, for instance, should have clear communication lines between the lecturer and the members of the audience. Similarly, if you're showing a film or videotape, clear communication lines are a must for optimum viewing and listening.

Keep the layout pattern very much in mind when planning any kind of instruction. And always try to establish the pattern that is most likely to work well for the instructional approach and situation you're designing. Its impact is very important.

Dealing with learner questions

Many instructors dread the prospect of facing questions from their learners. What if I don't know the answer? What if they raise an issue I hadn't thought about before? What if they make me look foolish? What if there really isn't an answer? What if the question reveals sheer ignorance on the part of the questioner? All these questions and more can rise up to assail your peace of mind.

The game of 'what if' in any sphere of activity can reduce you to a quivering mass of jelly if you allow yourself to succumb to its terrors. The key thing is to arm yourself before any instructional encounters so you can deal with questions most effectively when they occur, as they inevitably will.

Wise anticipation

You can anticipate most of the questions learners are likely to pose. Partly this results from doing a good learner analysis. If you really know the people you'll be dealing with, you'll know their interests, and this will enable you to anticipate the subject areas they'll want to probe with questions. Naturally, you need to be sure of the responses for those kinds of questions.

Different events or unfolding situations bring their own priorities and force their own agendas. Keep yourself informed about the events and situations likely to interest the learners. This form of alertness will point out for you those issues or concerns that could attract their attention.

In working out anticipated questions play devil's advocate with yourself. What are the worst or most embarrassing questions you can imagine a learner asking? Write these out on a sheet of paper. Once you've identified all these worst-case questions, devote some time to developing answers for them.

In formulating the answers to potential questions, bear in mind that you don't necessarily have to provide a fully detailed response each time. If an area of enquiry is still under study, say so — but also try to say when you anticipate obtaining more definite answers. If an issue is confidential, say so, but in a manner that doesn't seem to belittle or put down the questioner. If you really don't know the answer, be prepared to say as much. With a little thought you can develop credible responses for the most toxic of questions.

In thinking about the kinds of questions likely to arise, remind yourself always of the *positive principle*. You want to stress the positive points in the lesson concerned, not the negative ones. When it comes to dealing with questions, this means you need to prepare yourself to pull things back on track, especially if a bout of hostile or vigorous questioning occurs. The emotional pulls of such questioning can too easily pull you away from the agenda, thereby delivering you into the agendas of those who might well be hostile to the whole learning process.

Learner questions often provide good opportunities for the instructor. 'I'm glad you raised that point,' could be a good response at times to a hard question. These words give you a little thinking time, catch the attention of the learners, and open the way for the injection of a positive commentary of some kind that you've prepared ahead of time. At times you might even get away with straining this linkage a little, provided what is said in your commentary is sufficiently attractive.

A little anticipation goes a long way in helping to cope with questions from learners. You can even apply this kind of anticipation at the very last moment just before a lesson starts. Last minute concerns or realizations might easily pop into mind. Instead of panicking, use these as additional bits of information for working out planned responses. It's surprising how much you can do here, even in a precious few minutes or seconds.

When you get into the full flow of conducting a training session of any kind, the value of having prepared well ahead of time becomes fully apparent. This preparation often results in your dealing smoothly and effectively with even the most difficult of questions, virtually automatically. And that's a truly pleasurable feeling. Prepare for it! Wise anticipation is the key.

Alert responding

Anticipation will do much to help cope with learner questions. But there are also some more general kinds of points you should bear in mind for responding to questions at any time. By committing these points to your *brain programming* you can arm yourself better for all types of training.

We'll examine a number of points dealing with the instructor's responding technique to identify and flesh out key issues worth bearing in mind at all times.

1. Keep responses positive and calm.

This can prove difficult, especially with truly obnoxious people. But you have more to lose in this situation than the questioner does. Unfortunately, some people get a lot of pleasure from putting an instructor on the spot. This seems to shore up their own needs for self-esteem. And such people really don't care about your feelings. If they can provoke you into losing your cool, they've won in their own little minds.

A lesson is usually not a debate. Arguments may arise, but you should be careful about pursuing them in this setting. This just detracts from what you have to say and loses most of the learners, even if you're right.

2. Provide instructor thinking time.

One of the reasons some instructors get into trouble with questions from learners is that they put too much pressure on themselves to answer quickly and superbly. Let's face it, you just can't be an expert in repartee each and every time. You always need to make a point of giving yourself a few seconds before actually responding. Three or four seconds of thinking time is not unreasonable.

At times you might allow yourself five seconds if the question is important enough. By following up this thinking time with some sort of standard line (e.g. 'That's an interesting point."), you extend the thinking time while actually beginning the reply. An important consideration here, of course, is that you vary the standard lines from one such response to the next. Otherwise you'll start to come across as a caricature rather than a real person.

In obtaining thinking time you might also clarify or reword what the questioner has said. This allows you to focus for a while longer on what the concern really is. It also allows the learner to use clearer terms. It can even enable the questioner to answer the question him or herself.

Often, if you remain unclear about the question being asked, you can enlist the help of other learners. Sometimes they'll be able to choose more effective words. And sometimes they'll answer the question themselves!

Keep in mind that you might be able to reword or expand the question posed. As long as this is done with the permission of the questioner, you can do quite a bit with this opportunity. At times, as long as you're careful, you can reform the question to lead logically into something you wanted to raise in the lesson anyway.

Once you start to ponder it, you can build up your own thinking time during a lesson in a number of ways. This can occur naturally, without running the risk of the learners perceiving it as fumbling or deliberate delay.

Thinking time is important. Don't let anyone steal it away. Fretting or indulging in nervous doubts simply waste precious time. Use whatever time you gain to let your brain work productively, not negatively.

3. Look for things to agree with or reinforce.

If you listen attentively, you'll often find that a questioner opens up an opportunity to pursue something you really agree with or support. Such questions help a lesson because they underscore the idea of an agenda that's shared between you and at least a few of the learners. Here you have the possibility of forging dynamic alliances with your learners.

In looking for points to support, you don't have to agree with everything a questioner may raise. Focus on those parts of the question you want to stress. This won't always avoid the issues you're not so keen on, but it will tend to place the emphasis where it's needed for the lesson. People may realize what you're doing, but if they're at all interested, they're likely to cooperate.

4. Avoid appearing defensive.

This can be tricky, as you might actually feel defensive. The trouble is that if you come across this way, the learners will tend to smell blood and start to focus on the negative aspects of what you're saying. They think they see smoke, so they'll start looking for the fire. Those people who are already negative or hostile will start to smell triumph and will redouble their efforts to pin you down or trip you up.

Even if you're not feeling all that confident inside, you must project an image of confidence and certainty. 'True confessions' can be great in some settings, but they can destroy an otherwise competently-delivered lesson. Worse, the negative reverberations can start to reflect on those points already brought out successfully.

Of course, if a particular point does have glaring weaknesses, you should not defend it to the death. Such weaknesses need to be acknowledged maturely, with promises of appropriate action, and then you must get things back on track quickly to emphasize more positive issues.

People respect confidence and poise. At the same time they reject phoniness or arrogance. If you seem defeated or outwitted, they may pity you, but they won't be admiring or see what you've said in a good light.

An air of justified and balanced confidence on an instructor's part wins friends and supporters. It associates her or him with success. And it can provide effective control of the instructional situation.

5. Remember the instructional agenda.

When the going gets hot and heavy in dealing with learners you sometimes lose track of the instructional agenda. This is deadly, as it can trap you into concentrating on the issues raised by the learners, rather than those involved in the lesson.

Good instructor notes and a careful plan of instructing will go far towards keeping you on track. Refer to these from time to time to retain the right priorities and maintain the planned direction. At times you might have to remind learners overtly through such statements as, 'Now as I was saying,' or, 'Those are worthwhile considerations, but we'll be dealing with them more fully in next Wednesday's lesson.'

If you've done a good job of introducing the lesson in the first place, learners won't generally object to the actions taken to keep the session on track. The only time this approach might cause a problem is if you seem to be using it as a means of deliberately glossing over or evading an important issue. In such cases you can still pull things back on track, but you must make some sort of commitment to deal with the issue raised in a satisfactory way (e.g. 'I'd like to pursue that point with you further at lunch,' or 'May I put that on our agenda for the next lesson?')

If you seem a little lost in the lesson or the learners lose their sense of direction, effective learning will go out the window. So it's vital not to lose your leadership of the situation.

6. Give honest recognition to the learners whenever possible.

Learners often have useful things to say or points to contribute in training sessions. Be on the lookout for these contributions and note them carefully when they occur. As a training session proceeds, find places where you can slip in positive acknowledgements of these contributions (e.g. 'As Arthur pointed out earlier ... ' 'The concerns that some of you raised a few minutes ago ... '). These little signals of recognition on your part help to solidify your relationship with learners. They also demonstrate that you are listening to what they say and making an honest effort to deal with their concerns.

At times you'll find that you can build on something raised by a question. This can be very gratifying to the person who raised the question.

The more learners you reward personally the better, as they will be that much better disposed to you and the material or skills to be learned. It brings out that your agenda is their agenda too.

7. Keep responses short.

More indirect or passive kinds of instructing make use of learner questions to lead smoothly into areas the instructors planned to deal with anyway. And for various kinds of group situations (e.g. task team building or conciliation work) this skill is invaluable. But it tends to be lost on many learners. They can too easily fail to see the shift from responding to a question to working on the instructor's agenda once again. This sometimes leads them to conclude that the instructor is becoming seriously side-tracked when this isn't the case at all.

Instructors should make some effort to clearly delineate when they've finished with a response to a given learner question. This not only shows the instructor is making an effort to keep on track, but it tells people who weren't interested in the question that they can tune back in. Many if not most people are terrible listeners, so the instructor needs to make this effort.

By concentrating on keeping your responses short (no more than a couple of minutes), instructors automatically help themselves to be clear with their learners about when they're responding and when they're continuing on with the instructional plan. This helps make the instructor seem fully in charge.

8. Don't end with questioning.

Many training plans provide for questioning at the end. This can be a trap. The end or closing of a lesson or a course is one of the more powerful communication positions. It's where final thoughts or conclusions are left in the minds of the learners. If you're hung up on someone's question at the very end of the training concerned, especially if the question is obscure or off the track, you lose much of what might earlier have been achieved with the session. And this final loss position stays in learners' minds.

When called for, set aside a time for dealing with questions by all means. But take care to reserve ahead of time the right to use the final few minutes for your own words and the instructional agenda ('I would like a few minutes at the end to summarize this lesson'). If a lot of questions still remain unanswered, make some sort of commitment to meet with people afterwards or to deal with their questions at some later point.

People judge instructors, often unfairly, by the way they handle questions, especially when the going gets a little rough. If they handle themselves positively and well, they win points, even though these points might be given grudgingly. If instructors handle themselves forcefully or in a combative fashion they'll lose support and tend to be identified as uncooperative or arrogant.

A time for questions

Differing strategies and situations may lead to questions being raised by learners at different times during a lesson. It's important to give some thought to thinking about the times that will work best for the training concerned. While thinking of this, remember that questions at the end can still form part of a lesson or training course. Don't fall into the common trap of believing that training sessions can end and then questions can be allowed.

You've simply shifted into a different mode of communication within the same learning flow.

You can tell learners to ask questions at any time. This works well in various types of freewheeling training activities. But it can backfire badly. It might lead some people to think you're not properly in charge. It can seem like an invitation to others to begin the silly season with stupid questions. It can set you up for being interrupted at inopportune times. And it raises the danger of your being pulled off the track much more readily.

If you really are in an open-ended, flexible situation, questions at any time might work well. They'll bring out the learners' agendas very fast, and enable you to address their issues that much more quickly.

If you're briefing a team or group of some sort on a new technique or procedure they're to use, questions at any time can work well. Again, though, you have to be careful that this kind of openness doesn't run the risk of causing interference with the explanation of a particularly tricky part of the training session. For longer such training sessions, you might be wiser to schedule key points where you'll deal with questions or open up discussions.

You can have question times interspersed throughout the training session. These formalize the questioning to some degree, but give you a reasonable amount of control. Such scheduling also helps to ensure that your own train of thought won't be disrupted while you're dealing with an intricate passage of information.

The main problem with question times is that people often won't take advantage of them. They don't want to appear foolish or to be the first to break the silence. In these cases you might prime the pump a little by throwing in some questions of your own, especially if these are questions learners in other situations have actually asked. This helps to show learners the types of questions they might ask and reassures them about their own concerns. If you know learners well enough to know their areas of interest and you're sure they can handle it, you might try inviting them to make specific comments or raise specific questions based on their interest areas

Whatever you do, be sure to leave enough time for learners to come up with their questions. At times you might achieve this by having them think about the questions they might ask during a scheduled break of some kind.

Once questions do start to flow, be sure to handle them effectively and positively. They add much to the impact and dynamism of any lesson.

You can save questions till the end. This is a very common strategy and, with the exception we noted earlier about retaining time for your own summation, it can work effectively. But don't do it this way as a matter of habit. Give some thought to whether or not it's the best strategy for training this time.

Questions at the end can anchor learning in people's minds, enabling them to make final connections. But they might have trouble doing this if a long time (more than twenty minutes) has elapsed before they can raise any questions. They might simply forget what they wanted to say (although you can help here by inviting people to write their questions down while you're talking so they'll have them ready for the question time). By scheduling questions at the end too, you might be tempted to fill in too much of the time with your own agenda, leaving too little time for dealing with the agendas of others.

You can invite questions in writing. This tactic often works well with large groups of learners where you can't possibly deal with everyone on a person-to-person basis. Gather together the questions and then pick a time to respond to them. If too many questions arrive this way, be sure to tell the learners, and say that you'll respond to as many as possible within the time available. If it's possible, offer to meet afterwards with those whose questions couldn't be dealt with during the training session.

In deliberately thinking about and arranging specific times for questioning, you're acting as a responsible manager of learning. You're also increasing the chances of dealing most effectively with the questions that do come up.

Fully effective training

In this chapter we've dealt with two basic kinds of questions: those posed by an instructor and those posed by a learner. Keep these two main types of questions distinct from each other. From a planning and design point of view, they should not be seen as interchangeable. Questions from the instructor should generally receive the emphasis. This helps the learning process, and works to ensure that the instructor remains in control of the learning situation.

Questioning is not suitable for all types of training sessions, but it fits most. Don't let yourself ignore this technique through lack of flexibility in your approach to instructing, or through making too many automatic assumptions. Always ask yourself if questioning will fit or enhance the type of training you're planning. When you do this faithfully and honestly, you'll find many lessons work much better.

11 A Selection of Methods

The method you use often determines the success of your instructing. And yet you may well limit your choice of method needlessly, simply because you're not familiar with the wide variety of methods that actually exist. All instructors have a tendency to use those methods they've been exposed to over the years. This tendency can build in unnecessary limitations. It can also prevent the effective use of different styles of instructing or positive guidance. Method inflexibility can cause you to fail completely to take into account learner differences and reception levels.

This chapter lays out a broad range of methods for you to consider. The range presented here is not all-inclusive by any means. But it is quite comprehensive. Remember too that you can combine different methods with the structure of a given lesson.

As far as possible, these methods are arranged in order of their flexibility for instructional use. You might consider that each method has a certain 'chaos potential'. The more flexible the method, the more chance that chaos can occur, at least in the hands of an inexperienced instructor. And yet the methods possessing higher chaos potentials are the very ones that are most likely to produce active or self-effective learners. They're the ones the instructor should use in moving from the active teaching stance to the passive one, or putting the pressure point increasingly on the learners.

1. Test

You might not normally consider this a method of instructing. Yet, when you stop to think about it, any test can and should be a learning experience. This method allows for evaluating or checking out the existing levels of skill and knowledge achieved by learners.

In many instructional circles tests are viewed with suspicion, if not outright hostility. This arises from the fact that tests don't always measure accurately those things they're supposed to measure, and they may not even be measuring the right things. In some situations the problem has been so severe that tests have been abandoned altogether. If you exercise enough care, though, you can usually design tests that are useful, at least to some degree, in most learning settings. The main thing is to make sure they really do test for those things that are relevant and important. Further, the means of testing should be consistent with or valid for the required performance application.

Tests may come in written form, or they may be structured around actual learner performance with a given piece of equipment or tool. Tests in the form of quizzes can even provide some fun as well as some learning. Whatever its form, a test provides a useful means of instructing, provided it's well conceived and fairly marked.

2. Programmed instruction

Despite its name, this method does not necessarily make use of computers. It can take the form of a carefully written work book or carefully produced audiovisual packages. The basic idea is that learners experience a process that leads them through various points about the subject in sequential order. These points reveal information in a controlled way so that learners come to understand the subject matter in a relatively painless, yet thorough manner. Various types of reinforcement for the learner are generally built in as part of the programme.

Programmed instruction can be strictly linear or it can make use of branching to allow for numbers of different responses from and to the learner. One of the strengths of computers in instructing is that they lend themselves beautifully to the branching approach, which is generally much more beneficial for the learner.

At one point, thanks in large part to the work of B.F. Skinner, programmed instruction was expected to sweep all other instructional methods aside. This has not happened, nor does it seem likely to happen in the future.

You would find this method much more useful for some subjects and some types of learners than for others. Rote learning and the learning of straightforward procedures of various types can be handled effectively with this method. Learners whose styles of learning lend themselves to learning in a patterned, continuous-progression way would use this method quite effectively.

Despite the fact that this method has not achieved all that people once believed possible, it can still produce impressive results for those subjects and learners that relate well to it.

The production of good programmed instruction demands a high level of designer or programmer skill, and it can be very time-consuming. If the result will not be subject to a great many changes over time, the planning and preparation involved will prove worthwhile.

3. Audiovisual learning package

This method employs prepared learning programmes recorded on film, videocassette, slide/sound, or other such format. This method is very popular in many settings, but the particular programme you select must offer real learning impact, and not simply exciting sounds and images.

Through careful selection of the package, you can provide effective and memorable learning with this method. Productive visual and sound impressions can impact solidly on the minds of your learners.

Top-quality audiovisual learning packages can leave life-long impressions on the mind. For this reason, programmes designed for different or poorly conceived learning objectives can cause long-lasting on-the-job problems. If you're sure the package really fits the learning need, by all means use this method.

4. Correspondence

This method has been used for learning for a long time. One of its main drawbacks involves the problem of providing sufficient motivation for learners who are remote from their teachers. Human contact and personal support of some kind are vital to the success of this method. Sometimes audiotapes, telephone communications, videotapes, various broadcast technologies (e.g. computer networking using modems) can help the correspondence learner a great deal.

If you use this method, take extra care to make sure your learners receive solid preparation and know exactly what they're expected to do in their assignments. In particular, their means of contact with you should be set out clearly along with helpful hints they can use.

Some subjects lend themselves better to this method than others. In general, theoretical subjects or subjects not requiring much human interaction can work very well with this method.

You may see this method undergo some remarkable changes in the future as the electronic technologies take hold more and more in our society. This method may well evolve in productive combinations with other methods.

In using correspondence as a teaching method, be sure to maintain careful records for individual learners. Otherwise, unfortunate and de-motivating problems for the learner can occur all too easily.

Used with the right kind of care, this method can produce some excellent results, and its cost-effectiveness can prove impressive.

5. Lecture

This method is something of a classic. Almost everyone who instructs tries to use it, and this is particularly the case for new instructors. You can be reasonably successful using the lecture if you plan your word-use well and look for involving words or illustrations to use during the lecture. But you must remember that a lecture provides instruction one-way, or in an open loop fashion, and this does have its drawbacks.

In some cases an audience question session can be used right after a lecture to provide at least some form of two-way connection. In other cases you might encourage your learners to raise their hands to pose questions at different times during your lecture. This can, of course, be disruptive. Handled well, though, it can be quite effective.

Some lecturers can have more impact on their learners through the skilled use of their voices and a variety of interesting instructional aids. A great deal depends on your ability to 'stand and deliver' in an interesting way. A good lecture can provide a good learning experience, but it requires careful work.

6. Assignment

This method, as the name implies, entails giving a specific assignment to the learner. The instructor selects the assignment for the learner, but you should involve the learner to some degree in deciding on the precise details of the assignment. The main thing is that the assignment provide solid learning for the learner.

The types of activities involved can vary considerably. They can lead to practical and usable results, or they can simply provide some useful learning. Assignments supervisors and managers can also use assignments to provide effective learning in regular work settings.

You can use this method along with several other methods, including coaching, job rotation, and field trip. Given enough guidance, especially at the outset, a learner can acquire a good deal of learning from a well-conceived assignment.

7. Computer-assisted instruction

This method of instructing, of course, requires adequate electronic equipment as well as good learning software.

Depending on the sophistication of the computer used, along with its associated software and peripherals, the learning experiences can be truly dynamic, exciting, and engrossing.

Many of the same cautions that apply to audiovisual learning packages apply here as well. In a sense, you can view a computerized learning programme as a 'souped up' audiovisual presentation. Because the 'souping up' tends to provide excitement for the learner, you have to take care that this excitement doesn't get in the way of the desired learning message. As the instructor, you should certainly have the opportunity to conduct a test run of the learning programme on your own ahead of time. During this testing you can make sure that the programme is relevant and likely to help your learners achieve the learning objectives really required.

Depending on the nature of the learning programme involved, your learners may need a certain amount of introduction and preparation before actually using the programme.

One of the advantages of a good computer-assisted instructional process is that significantly expands the activities a human instructor can engage in. You can look for and provide a variety of enrichment experiences for the learners involved. At the same time, you need to avoid the temptation to leave it all to the computer. Stay involved with your learners, at least in a general way.

8. Computer interaction

This method has many similarities to computer-assisted instruction. But it is not based on using specifically-designed instructional programs. Rather, it makes use of the regular capacities of the specific computer involved.

This method involves generalized learning that occurs simply as an automatic outgrowth of working with a computer. So a lot depends on the particular interests and inputs of the learners concerned. To some extent, you might categorize the learning that takes place with this method as simply 'computer familiarisation' or the development of increased computer literacy. These learnings themselves can lead to learning a certain form of logic or cast of mind.

This method will not always be all that rigid in its application. Newer and more powerful micro-computers could lead to it becoming one of the more flexible learning methods. Already, Apple Computer with its hypercard developments is showing newer possibilities here. As artificial intelligence research enables computers to operate in modes that more directly reflect natural intelligence, marvellous learning breakthroughs seem possible. Recent work with 'virtual reality', for instance, shows what exciting possibilities exist just around the corner. As these developments continue, the distinction between this method and computer-assisted instruction will likely blur and gradually disappear.

You can employ computer interaction conveniently as part of regular work activities. It may also lend itself well to use with other types of non-learning activities (e.g. game playing). The possibilities for the growth of this method in the future seem enormous.

9. Modelling

This method involves having the instructor or someone acting under her or his direction provide the performance model whom learners can observe carefully for later imitation. You can use this method to illustrate dynamically a complete repertoire of skills to use in given situations.

You must take great care with this method in working out the skill or skills to display. Avoiding poor examples or situations containing undue complexity is very important. Ideally, one or more rehearsals should take place ahead of time. The more important the skills, of course, the more rehearsals there should be. In some cases you might record the modelled skill or skills on film, videocassette, or audiocassette. Then it almost becomes a toss-up whether your using modelling or an audiovisual learning package method. If the learners actually know the performers, then you can say it remains modelling.

Certain skills relate well to this method. In general, skills involving a lot of repetition and limited requirements for individual decision making within relatively short time-spans lend themselves to this method. In fact, you might say that this method is almost made for teaching these types of skills.

The people who provide the modelling in this method need not possess good acting skills. They simply need to come across to people in a believable way. If the learners personally know these models, it's a definite plus. It automatically downplays the need for acting and increases the believability of the action portrayed (provided the models do possess real skill in the subject concerned!).

As work realities change, lessons using modelling must adapt. Make sure the skills involved remain up-to-date by regularly reviewing the on-the-job requirements.

10. Induction

Usually this method comes into use for training new employees in the immediate requirements and conditions of their jobs. These requirements and conditions include performing basic skills new to the employee, as well as specific points of information required by any employee within the organization (e.g. the location of the canteen).

To be fully effective this method requires more attention that it usually receives. People who are used to a particular work setting often forget how puzzling some simple things can be to a newcomer. And yet these puzzling things can cause the new employee a lot of confusion, if not embarrassment, with consequent impact on performance.

Few of us enjoy being made to feel like outsiders by a group of people, especially a group of people with whom we're supposed to work effectively. First impressions can be lasting impressions. Surely an employee's first impressions of her or his new place of work should be good ones. If they are, then the prospects are much better for the employee to develop as an excellent worker with the organization.

Induction is best carried out by the immediate supervisor of the employee concerned, not by a full-time instructor or trainer, although the latter can certainly provide useful tips and support to the supervisor.

11. On-the-job training

When someone receives training in a normal work setting, he or she receives on-the-job training. This form of training has many merits. Apprenticeships, assistantships, and some other work-linked methods of instruction use on-the-job training to a large degree. Even some apparently casual forms of learning (e.g. 'job rotations' or 'work assignments') can be termed on-the-job training.

In some situations this method is linked closely to 'job instruction training' or JIT. The use of the acronym 'JIT' in this sense has faded, though, because these initials now mainly refer to 'just in time' delivery — a management concept widely used in Japan. A suitable initialism these days would be OJT for 'on-the-job training'.

In the past many people used the term 'Four-step Method' for this instructional approach. The four steps referred to are:

1. **Prepare the learner**
2. **Present the operation**
3. **Practice**
4. **Follow-up**

These four steps were developed to a large extent during the two world wars when large numbers of unskilled people required quick training in skilled or semi-skilled factory operations. Since 1945 these steps have been incorporated into many of the training designs employed within corporations large and small, and they've not been limited to blue-collar skills training.

Because the term 'on-the-job' could refer to many different types of modern training activities, you should specify your own meaning when using this term with others. This will help to avoid confusion.

On-the-job training works well with just one learner, although various adaptations can help it apply to a number of learners at the same time. In deciding on the exact number of learners to involve with this method, bear in mind some important factors. These involve safety, equipment damage and effective learning.

Some types of skills involve significant degrees of risk to the learner, so they require close supervision by the instructor, especially in the early stages of learning. The element of risk may be so significant that you need a one-to-one instructor/learner ratio. Similar considerations apply when it comes to the potential for equipment damage.

In general, learning is more effective if the instructor monitors it carefully to ensure that the learner receives good feedback at opportune times. More involved types of skills may demand higher instructor/learner ratios (1:3 or 1:4 instead of 1:12 for example), so that better monitoring and feedback will occur. When only one or a few pieces of equipment can be spared for learning purposes, the instructor/learner ratio may have to depend on the amount of equipment actually available.

Anyone who is a supervisor should engage in a certain amount of on-the-job training simply as part of being an effective supervisor. In fact, it's quite possible that supervisors and mangers should conduct the bulk of training in modern organizations through various programmes of on-the-job training.

12. Case-study

This method entails using a description of an actual or hypothetical event or incident as the focus of study. You can write this study or display it in some form of electronic manner. Sometimes you might simply describe it using spoken language.

The Harvard Business School is famous for its use of the case method. Their cases can involve enormous amounts of work and are based on masses of data generated by actual business situations. Work on a given case can stretch over weeks, even months. But you don't have to go the lengths that Harvard does to use case-studies beneficially. Cases that last only one or two hours will often produce good results.

Learning occurs through studying and responding to the details of the case in good, analytical fashion. When the case concerns an actual situation, you can profitably compare the learners' results with those of the people actually involved in the event or incident. Much effective learning is possible in the discussions that ensue here.

In using this method be sure to lead good 'debriefing' sessions with your learners. These discussion sessions are essential to the success of this method.

A case-study can precede a variety of other methods. Role-plays, for instance, can follow case-studies. Similarly, modelling sessions could well be preceded by case-studies. It's worth playing around with the possible combinations here.

The case-study method works well in regular work sessions, often in conjunction with problem-solving activities or team-building work.

All in all, this method offers learners a useful form of 'real life' experience in a highly focused and flexible form of learning. As an instructor, you will want to exploit the usefulness of this method in a variety of ways, and you will probably find that you can design some of your own effective case-studies as well. If you feel this urge, by all means do so!

13. Laboratory work

The learner in this method works through a key learning problem within a highly controlled environment. Instruments, tools, materials and other physical aids are very important to success here.

As the name suggests, experiments of various kinds might occur effectively with this method. These experiments might replicate experiments performed by recognized past or present researchers, or they can be experiments designed specifically for the learning potentials they offer.

In using this method, ensure that your learners will have all the equipment, materials, reference sources and instructions they need to produce successful results. Make sure, also, that your learners will engage in activities that will likely be worthwhile from a learning perspective.

Learners with high levels of maturity and skill, or real self-effectiveness, could design and carry out their own experiments with excellent learning results.

Given adequate preparation and care, this method can be exciting, dynamic and revealing for everyone involved — including yourself.

14. Role-play

We all play certain roles in life, although we may not often think about them. The role-play method encourages learners to take on specific roles in a dynamic and safe group situation. One or more participants may play roles at the same time.

The resulting interactions can be most provocative, and lead to exciting and valuable learning.

You might script the roles involved to a high degree or lay them out in general terms, allowing lots of learner interpretation or spontaneity. Sometimes the learners themselves can design the required roles most effectively. The roles are always set around a given situation or scenario. This, in effect, is the central plot of the 'play' involved.

Because role-plays can easily lead to 'psychodramas' with their content of real feelings and expressions, you must use some professional discretion in employing this method. People can start to identify so closely with their roles that they lose conscious sight of the fact they're engaged in a learning process. If you don't monitor things carefully and with a good deal of sensitivity, emotional damage for one or more of the participants is possible. You always have to be ready to intervene or 'blow the whistle' if things do start to become too intense.

You can design role-plays in a similar fashion to case-studies. Partly for this reason they blend naturally and well with the case-study method. But like so many other methods, you can blend the role-play method with a good variety of other methods.

For full learning benefit for everyone concerned, the group must always debrief the role-play in a thorough fashion. Insightful questions or observations provided by you, the instructor or facilitator, will make sure that all role-play debriefings are most effective from a learning standpoint.

15. Learner presentation

The key person in this method is the learner. He or she makes a presentation to a group of people on a topic he or she chose personally, or on a topic you assigned. The range of topics possible with this method is inexhaustible.

This method has the virtue of helping learners develop their confidence in their own abilities. This gives a useful added bonus to whatever other learning may occur.

In working with this method always endeavour to provide careful and accurate feedback to the learner making the presentation. Additionally, encourage other learners to deliver objective feedback. Note here that the feedback may concern the technique of the presentation itself, the subject matter, or both.

Presentations made with this method can break new learning ground, or they can reinforce existing learnings. They can provide a very useful way of delegating teaching tasks, thus taking some load off your shoulders (dealing with the learning pressure point). At the same time, presentations by the learners can prove very motivating for those learners.

In using this method, be prepared to help learners with their presentation planning. You should always be ready to contribute further information or thoughts to the learners in discussion sessions before and after the presentation.

16. Game

For many people the concept of a game as a form of instructing is contradictory. They're used to thinking of games as frivolous, time-consuming activities designed merely to entertain people. But games of different types actually have a lot of teaching capability. They work particularly well to help people learn the fine points that occur in dynamic human interactions.

You can readily teach interpersonal skills and decision making in uncertain situations through well-designed games.

This method often has similarities to the role-play method. Players can reveal very important personal characteristics while engaged in playing games. You've likely seen this phenomenon at work in social affairs. When people play bridge or other such games, they reveal a lot about themselves. And the same thing applies to the playing of electronic games of various kinds.

When using this method, ensure that your learners have a clear idea of the basic reasons for playing the game. Similarly, everyone needs a good understanding of the rules of the game. Usually it's a good idea to have available some form of reference sheet or manual that clearly sets out all the rules, methods, and goals of play.

Some games take a long time to play. But you should always remain ready to let them go to completion if possible. Early or premature cut-offs can cause learners to react sourly to the whole process, and this would be counter-productive for the intended learning.

Clearly, as well as knowing the rules thoroughly, you must know the length of time you need to allot to a given game. Once a game is completed, conduct a complete debriefing to bring out the observations and conclusions that logically emerge.

A well-designed and well-conducted game can be one of the most effective methods of teaching and learning. But you must handle it well to make it work well.

17. Simulation

This method of instructing has a lot in common with the game method. Indeed, some instructors and training designers prefer to use the word 'simulator' when talking about or preparing a game. They feel it makes the game concept less frivolous.

The main difference is that a simulation makes use of real or mock-up equipment and instruments, rather than the more abstract devices of games, such as playing boards. The classic example of the use of a simulation is the learning process a pilot undergoes in 'flying' an aircraft using a flight simulator.

Flight simulators use electronic audiovisual effects of a very sophisticated design along with carefully-worked-out computer programs. Modern simulators can produce effects that have uncanny degrees of reality built into them. In using such simulators learners can find themselves really believing everything is happening in actuality.

The sensation of reality is, of course, the main reason for using a simulation. This method allows the closest possible approach to reality without the consequent risk of accident that applying the required skills in real situations might incur.

Simulations do not necessarily have to use sophisticated or expensive equipment. With some imagination you often can set up a simulator using quite ordinary 'props'. Given careful enough preparation, participants can quite readily use their own imaginations automatically to provide the necessary sense of reality. Simulations that use imaginative resources are very similar to games or role-plays. In fact, they often become indistinguishable.

Learners can become highly enthusiastic during simulations because they experience excitement and some degree of working reality at the same time. So if you have an idea for designing and using a simulation to meet a particular learning need, it could be well worth pursuing.

If you plan to design a good simulator from scratch, do consider involving learners themselves. Very often they will give you excellent ideas and suggestions for points to include and how to include them.

Because it is such an effective and involving method, you should always remain alert for types of learning that might lend themselves to being taught with good simulations.

18. Debate

Almost always this method requires a reasonable amount of preparation by everyone who will take part. Naturally, this includes you, the instructor. If a debate is to succeed, choose a debate topic that will provide clear lines of disagreement for the debate to explore. It's through the dynamic clash of opposite opinions that good learning occurs.

Always ensure that clear-cut supervision of the debate exists once the debate gets under way. Clear rules and clear enforcement of those rules are essential. You can act as the chair of the debate yourself, or appoint someone to fill this position. A number of copies of standard rules of parliamentary procedure, such as Robert's Rules of Order, can certainly help.

The physical arrangement of the debaters is very important. The debating people or sides must be separated from each other. The audience, if any, must remain clear of the debaters.

Timings before and after the debate require close observation. This applies particularly to the timings given to speakers for their arguments and rebuttals.

Once the debate is over, you, or someone you appoint, must provide a detailed commentary about the debate and, if appropriate, select a winner or winning side. Note that some system of scoring should be used, so participants will receive total scores for their efforts as part of the commentary or debate summation. The selection of a winner or winners might well involve members of the whole class casting of votes.

Classes being prepared for the debate method might simply be split into two opposing sides, or selected debaters can be drawn from the class on a voluntary or appointed basis. Sometimes you add an extra learning dimension of you have people support the debating position they really oppose personally.

When you use selected debaters, the bulk of the class will become members of the audience. But they should clearly understand that they have a definite role to play as audience members. Be sure to spell this role out for them.

Debates can prove highly stimulating as long as reasonable efforts are made beforehand to plan them and to thoroughly prepare everyone concerned.

19. Question and answer

Using this method you teach others by asking questions. Sometimes this is called the 'Socratic Method', because Socrates used questioning extensively with his students (although his questions were somewhat contrived, and not all that open to student interpretations or comments).

The questions you use in this method should seek out the knowledge or opinions that learners bring with them, or that they have acquired in a given learning process. Learners often don't know how much they know, or how much they may have learned without consciously recognizing the fact. Good questioning can bring this out and help learners to appreciate their own abilities. This method might even lead learners to believe they've come up with the ideas and information involved on their own. (This is really a sign of success on your part, but poorly informed observers might downgrade your work because they're not seeing you perform in an obvious way — so beware of who your observers or evaluators might be when you use this method.)

By using good questioning you stimulate thinking (often including your own) and challenge learners to probe into new areas of interest. This method should lead to good and productive interaction between you and your learners.

Other methods often use a certain amount of questioning (oral or written) to promote learning interactions. This even applies to methods such as programmed instruction or computer-assisted instruction. Nevertheless, the question and answer session with a live instructor is the prime and often the best means of achieving good interactive learning.

Question and answer classes will often swing over smoothly and naturally into lively discussions, while leaving you fundamentally in control. Learning dynamism often emerges from this method.

Because of its usefulness and flexibility, this method is one you should certainly learn to use and practise on a continuing basis.

20. Team learning

This method involves a selected group of learners working together to acquire learning over a relatively long period of time. In effect, it is much like a small group that stays active for longer than a few hours.

This approach offers a high degree of learner independence, and for this reason it can prove highly motivating. In some situations a learning team might also be called a 'quality circle'. Whatever it's called, the learning team must be built and nurtured with care.

The members of learning teams must know each other reasonably well, and they must have respect for each other as solid contributors to team efforts. Truly effective learning teams may require some time simply to help the members start getting along with each other before they can turn their attention to learning tasks.

The learning team may not have an instructor in the usual sense of the word. All members of the team, as well as being learners are also, in effect, potential or actual instructors for each other. Team learning is a very 'democratic' method of instructing.

Learning teams that stay together for a long time would be considered 'networks' by many people. Some good learning networks can last a lifetime.

Team learning requires a definite area of learning endeavour. Particularly at the start, clear objectives and goals must be laid out, either by the team itself or you.

Once a team starts working, your role becomes that of a learning consultant. You simply have to let the team know where you'll be and how they can contact you once they're clear on what they have to accomplish.

In some cases, especially in research-oriented organizations, learning teams might readily be used in regular work situations. In such situations they become project or task teams.

By using team learning, you delegate a good deal of learning responsibility to your learners. Given the right level of self-effectiveness, they will accept this delegation happily, thus increasing your own effectiveness.

Team learning provides an effective and flexible form of instructing, and definitely belongs in a complete repertoire of instructing skills.

21. Individual learning project

In this method, as the name suggests, the learner or employee is the key person. He or she identifies an activity that would involve useful personal learning. This type of activity or project can apply to any form of training or development, whether classroom-oriented or on-the-job.

One of the crucial aspects of this method involves the use of some form of definite 'learning contract'. Basically this is an agreement with the learner involving completion of a given project or projects within a certain period of time to achieve specific learning or performance objectives.

Several individual learning projects in a sequence become an 'individual learning programme' (ILP). You can tailor such programmes to the needs of individual learners by including specific projects.

This method can and should be integrated with other methods when they logically fit. The audiovisual learning package, programmed instruction, laboratory, and computer-assisted forms of learning work well with the individual learning project.

This method has a little more formality than the individual work method, with which it has much in common.

Supervisors and managers can use this method as part of their regular work assignments, thus providing a productive form of employee development.

This method often provides very cost-effective training within an organization. Because it involves real learner responsibility it is a highly-stimulating approach to learning. But individual learning projects must be well monitored by yourself and others involved in providing training. Never use this method as a form of abdicated training. It requires the professional touch.

22. Guest speaker

From time to time it may be a good idea to invite someone to address a learning group. Clearly, your guest speaker should have some worthwhile credentials and information for the learning group concerned. Additionally, the guest speaker should have a fairly good chance of making a useful and lasting impression on the group. For these reasons, you must exercise care in selecting and inviting someone to talk to a given class. The wrong choice can have disastrous results.

Any guest speaker must receive a good briefing on the type of group he or she will address. This briefing must include a good indication of the key expectations of the group. You must also find out any special support or audiovisual requirements he or she may have. If possible, your guest speaker should see the meeting room or classroom ahead of time.

During the session, you should certainly expect the guest speaker to respond at some point to questions or comments from

the group. But be sure the speaker understands this expectation
Depending on the exact type of presentation involved, you may
wish to assign a time slot for this purpose. You should also be
prepared in general to act as the chair during the session.

Guest speakers can, of course, be used for groups other than
learning groups. The same points apply to using guest speakers
for other types of groups.

As well as providing useful information from 'expert' points of
view, guest speakers can help motivation by injecting an important sense of reality to subjects that might otherwise appear
remote to learners.

23. Observation

Here you have one or more learners observe a task or a complete
work activity while it is in progress. As with so many other
instructional methods, this one requires good planning and
reasonable preparation of the learners beforehand. Additionally, a
good debriefing after the observation is a must.

The tasks or activities to be observed and the locations in
which to observe them should, if at all possible, be viewed ahead
of time. You need to check out factors such as sight lines, observation points, lighting, noise interference, dust, heat or cold, and
safety factors. Usually it's a good idea to involve a guide from the
work group concerned.

When you plan to use this method, you should be clear in your
own mind about the benefits involved for your learners.
Naturally, these should link to actual learning objectives. In your
planning you also need to take into account such factors as transportation arrangements, coordination of timings and the need for
offering food and drink to the learners.

The observation method offers some good forms of learning
particularly in its emphasis on working reality. Sometimes opportunities for observations occur on short notice. By all means take
advantage of such opportunities if you can, but do make sure you
don't end up conducting observations simply for their own sake.
They can time-consuming, and you must be able to justify the
time spent against the achievement of learning objectives.

The observation method lends itself well to being integrated
with the requirements of line supervisors and managers. It's
certainly a useful method to use when executed well.

24. Apprenticeship

This classic form of instructing has its main roots in the medieval European guild system which laid down very careful guidelines for the instruction and development of those young people who wanted to learn particular trades, crafts, or professions. This form of learning is still with us, and still has many good points.

An apprenticeship entails long-term learning, usually for about four years. It always involves some form of legal contract binding on both the apprentice and the employer. The form and technical administration of this contract comes under some type of government supervision. Nowadays this supervision is often exercised through a technical college.

When you have involvement as an instructor with this method, you must take care to provide truly useful work experiences as well as good learning for the apprentice or apprentices concerned. You can certainly use a variety of teaching methods, but avoid the temptation to use apprentices as convenient or auxiliary employees. Their prime role is to be good learners.

Because an apprentice can undergo a wide variety of classroom and work experiences over a period of years, accurate records of her or his achievements are essential. If such record-keeping seems a little lax or sloppy to you, do something to improve it. Someone's job qualifications and placement may depend on it.

As a method of learning, apprenticeship offers depth, quality, and thoroughness unique to itself. In the future it may even turn out to be a method that undergoes a significant degree of renaissance in training and education. Certainly Germany, as a pre-eminent economic power in the world, has demonstrated over and over again the virtues of well-organized and thoroughly reliable apprenticeship training.

25. Assistantship

This method is really a spin-off from the apprenticeship method with some important differences. It usually has questionable legal status as a contract, and lasts for a period of time much less than four years.

In some cases assistantship might be called *internship* or *articling*. In these special cases some forms of written agreement and legal status may well exist.

When using this method, try not to use the assistant or assistants simply as convenient personal helpers or 'go-fors'. The activities you set out for an assistant should form a legitimate part of an overall development strategy for that person as a genuine learner. They should stretch the assistant so that he or she truly learns useful things while working.

Unfortunately, this method has been used by unscrupulous employers as a means of procuring and exploiting cheap labour. If you classify someone as a learner assistant, you might decide to pay him or her less than a full-fledged employee. Even some government departments and ministries have been guilty of this. It represents training cynicism at its worst. On ethical grounds alone you should avoid acquiescing to it.

When used properly, the assistantship method can be one of the more effective ones, as it should involve a high degree of on-the-job activity.

26. Panel discussion

This a good method to use when several 'experts' are available to come together at the same time for a specific learning situation. Like guest speakers, the panellists should be selected carefully and should receive a good briefing about the learners and the learning situation.

Prepare your class for the panel ahead of time. Let them know the members and the topic areas to be covered. Specify the ground rules for the panel discussion, and be sure to spell out the role the class should fill. Rules of order are very important. You may act as the moderator of the panel or one of the panellists may agree to do this. Sometimes it's beneficial to have one of the learners act as a moderator. This is something you need to think about carefully ahead of time.

The room arrangement for a panel discussion is important. Make sure all the chairs and tables are well arranged to allow for useful exchanges among the panellists, and to allow for good visibility and hearing by the class or audience. If microphones are needed, make sure these are properly set out, plugged in and tested. When microphones are used, each panellist should have his or her own. Additionally, several microphones should be scattered among the audience for their participation at opportune times.

When your panellists arrive, introduce them properly to your class. You may wish to do this by having your panellists enter and sit down one by one, or by waiting until all are seated, then beginning. Usually it's a good idea to have well-lettered name cards set out in front of each panelist.

Before the panel discussion begins, review all the ground rules that apply. If someone else is acting as the moderator, that person should conduct this review. Then invite the first panellist to speak.

The moderator must ensure that each panel member has a fair chance to speak during the discussion. At times this will require interrupting one panel member to give the nod to another. Additionally, the moderator may need to summarize points made from time to time, particularly if these are important points for the learners' subject matter. Sometimes panel discussion can lag a little. At such times pertinent quotations, comments, or questions from the moderator will usually get things rolling again.

Questions or comments from the floor may be invited on a wide-open basis at a key moment, or they may be received in written notes submitted through the moderator.

Handled well, a panel discussion provides a useful and dynamic learning experience. But it does require good and careful management to succeed.

27. Discussion

In this method everyone in a class or learning group, including you, the instructor, works together verbally to examine and flesh out a given topic or topics. The discussion can be quite freewheeling, but it may need some astute and subtle guidance on your part to keep it from degenerating into a 'bull session', a 'gripe session', or a noisy general argument in which participants simply 'share their ignorances' volubly.

Effective discussions build the knowledge and skills of all participants. The dynamism of the process forces people to think about their positions and to justify or expand on them. This, in turn, deepens the thinking that must occur.

The very dynamism of this method makes it all the more important that you provide good leadership for its conduct. You can do this with effective questions and comments, and by introducing various resources at key points if these suggest themselves. Additionally, you must do what you can to ensure that each learner has a fair chance to participate. Some people may need a bit of quietening down at times, while others will need a good deal of coaxing and encouragement.

In general, discussions should help participants to speak up and give their opinions, even if they think others will disagree with them. Productive disagreement can form the main strength of this method of instructing. Indeed, discussions can become quite noisy and chaotic while remaining productive from a learning standpoint.

One of the most important keys to controlling discussion is a good lesson plan or agenda, particularly if this is focused on key objectives. This can provide the reference track for guiding and assessing the discussion as it goes on.

The discussion method is an excellent all-round method. All it requires is careful and perceptive management by the instructor.

28. Field trip

This method simply involves taking learner or a group of learners on a trip to one or more specific locations. It has many similarities to the observation method. In fact, observation is very likely to form part of a field trip.

The main idea of the trip is to provide useful information to your learners. It's not really meant to be a holiday excursion, although it can provide a lot of fun, and prove memorable to everyone involved.

When you plan a field trip make sure you consider all the specific points of information you want people to take in. You can highlight these as part of delivering a presentation to your audience before the trip begins or just as it's getting under way. Pre and post briefings for a field trip, by the way, are an excellent idea.

Careful attention to the details is important for a good field trip. You might have to consider such details as the type or types of transportation used, providing meals, the location and timing of rest stops, back-up arrangements and, possibly, accommodations. All these details and more are important. When they're looked after well, few people notice. But when something goes wrong with one or more of these details, look out!

This method offers you a good means of introducing learners to the realities of specific forms of work under reasonably-controlled conditions. Here it overlaps with the observation method. Usually a field trip is much longer and larger in scope than an observation. Also, a field trip may be organized as a complete training process in itself.

The field trip helps to integrate classroom learning with the outside world. It gives learners a general grounding in a given activity or about a certain location. Because it's useful for orienting or familiarisation activities, line supervisors and managers may wish to use it as well as instructors.

While the field trip has a lot to recommend it from a learning point of view, it does require care in planning and execution, particularly to achieve worthwhile learning objectives. It can be an expensive form of training, so you should be able to justify its costs against tangible learning gains.

29. Individual work

In some ways this method is similar to small group work. The key difference is that it involves only one person instead of a small group of people.

Individual work usually takes place in a location other than a classroom. To be most effective as a learning method, you must make clear provision for the learner to get in touch with you if necessary while carrying out the work involved.

In some cases individual work may occur in the context of an assignment given by you, the instructor. In other cases it will take place on the initiative of the learner. The difference from the individual learning project is that this method involves more general types of learning over much shorter time spans.

In theory there is no limit to the types of subjects or kinds of activities individual work could encompass. Modern educational research shows that almost everyone can work well as individual learners in those areas where they genuinely wish to learn. Modern technology will probably open up more and more possibilities for using this method.

30. Small group work

A small group consists of three to five people. Using this method a small group works in a cooperative fashion on a given project. This project might be one that you assign, or one decided on by the group itself. One member of the group usually acts as the group's leader. Similarly, members of a small group may also be assigned as recording secretaries or speakers for the group.

You will find that small groups can provide effective vehicles for learning. They usually work well in settings other than formal classrooms or standard work locations, but the locations in which they do get together should be fairly quiet and secluded.

Small groups will probably require resources such as flip charts or other audiovisual equipment. They may also require books, manuals, or instruction sheets. You should also plan on visiting each of your small groups regularly to provide help if needed, and generally to monitor their progress.

Small groups encourage individual learners to open up more than they would in larger gatherings. So they can explore things more effectively. But the points to be explored should be clearly laid out by you or the groups. Also, small groups may require some assistance simply in learning how to work effectively as small groups.

One of the attractions of the small group method is that it allows a large class to be sub-divided into more manageable groups without the necessity of involving more instructors.

Small groups generally work on the same problem or case in their separate locations. Then their results are compared with those of all the groups in full session. This procedure adds an element of surprise and competition to the learning process that helps learner motivation. A variation on this approach is to have each group work on different aspects of the same problem. With this variation the full class session that follows becomes a building or cooperative process made up of the contributions of the different groups.

You can use small groups in conjunction with almost any other method or combination of methods. For full effectiveness, you must carefully plan the use of small groups ahead of time.

In some cases small groups might become learning teams. This would occur when an issue arises that the group plans to work on over a long period of time, or when the members of a group find that they can work so well together that they do not wish to lose their new network.

Of all the methods available to you, the small group is probably the most flexible. The possibilities for its use are virtually unlimited. At the same time it's an effective method from the learning perspective.

31. Coaching

In this method you provide careful coaching or guidance to a learner who is involved in learning a given skill or job. The learner should operate freely while under your guidance. Trial-

and-error or problem-solving techniques might well come into use as part of this method.

Before the learner begins working under this method, he or she will require some careful preparation. Important tasks and key learning activities should be clearly identified. And the process for consulting with you or remaining in touch must be quite clear.

Coaching can come into use easily in a regular work setting. The coach can be a supervisor or manager instead of an instructor. In long-term work situations coaching can shift naturally into mentoring.

Coaching offers all the advantages of one-on-one instructing, while putting a lot, if not most, of the learning responsibility on the shoulders of the learner. You can, of course, coach several learners during a given time period. But it is important to meet with them individually from time to time to go over their progress and to provide them with detailed feedback.

You can provide coaching on a close supervision basis or in a looser fashion. Decide about which type of supervision to use based on the learner's self-effectiveness and the nature of the skill to be learned. In effect, this decision forms part of your training strategy for this particular situation.

The types of skills you can teach using this method vary widely. They range from the skill of operating a piece of equipment to the skills required in carrying out a given administrative function. The choice is up to you as the instructor or supervisor.

For full success, this method requires a good relationship between the coach and the learner. A good level of trust is essential. Sensitivity and receptivity on the part of the coach are also vital.

32. Problem solving

This method focuses learning activities on solving hypothetical or actual problems. It has many similarities to the game, simulation, and case study methods.

Before entering into a problem-solving session, ensure that the participants receive good pointers and guidelines for effective problem solving. Various types of hand-outs as well as practice problem-solving drills can be useful here.

During the actual conduct of a problem-solving session, group dynamics must come into play strongly. This makes the application and maintenance of sound rules for conducting problem solving most important. Different problem-solving techniques are available. Make sure the groups involved know which one or which combination they should be using.

Most problem-solving techniques involve these stages in one way or another:

1. **Defining the problem**
2. **Identifying the factors involved**
3. **Working out potential courses of action**
4. **Selecting a solution**

In your monitoring activities during this process ensure that the rules for the problem-solving technique in use are applied consistently and objectively. Be prepared to step in if you find that a group is not doing this. It's especially important that the key stages of problem-solving approach are applied deliberately and carefully by the group. Inexperienced problem solvers often have a tendency to 'short circuit' some of these stages.

Careful and observable records of the ideas or points brought out in this type of session must be maintained. A chalk-board or a flip chart can provide a good medium for displaying this information. It's essential that any solutions or preferred courses of action that develop from a problem-solving session are clearly laid out for all to see and agree with.

This method can readily take place in a normal work setting, so it lends itself well to use by line supervisors and managers as well as instructors.

During regular training sessions instructors can use this method to help learners help themselves to understand and apply the points brought out in a wide variety of activities within the session.

Problem solving can give learners a unique sense of reality and practicality in their learning. It can even lead to new discoveries. The challenge is real and the results are demonstrable.

33. Job rotation

This method often comes into use as a means of training employees within a regular work situation. This method is another one that supervisors and managers should use as a regular part of their supervisory activities.

Trainers and instructors should recommend specific job rotation activities from time to time to supervisors when they believe such activities could yield significant learning results.

As with most methods, care in planning and preparation is important for job rotation. The learner or learners involved need clear ideas about the reasons for given job rotations. These ideas should be related to their own development in the organization concerned. They should also know the length of time the job rotation will likely last and the performance standards expected of them.

When job rotations are being handled on a multiple basis with different individuals going to different jobs, you must use even more care in your planning. Some form of charting (e.g. PERT or GANTT charts) should be used for laying out and controlling multiple job rotations.

Job rotations should always be aimed at employee development, and should not occur simply as a convenient means of having employees switch around through various jobs for production needs. Ideally, of course, job rotations should benefit both the organization and the learner.

This method offers excellent training opportunities without the need to provide such training facilities as classrooms or various types of instructing aids.

34. Job relief

This method comes into play as a means of providing replacements for employees who are on holiday, ill, or away from their regular jobs for any other reason. Job relief may need to occur at unexpected times and on short notice. For this reason, you should probably maintain a record of different people who might provide relief to others on sudden notice. This will save a lot of fluster and confusion when you find out someone is needed for a specific job.

In using this method, try to ensure that learners are called upon to perform jobs with reasonable learning potential. Good training and development records will assist you very much here. Encourage supervisors or managers to maintain such records.

Sometimes job relief will blend in naturally with job rotation. And previous job rotations can certainly help to provide a pool of people available for job relief.

This method will often provide good learning experiences, and it will lead to a more diversified workforce.

Expanding your range

From the selection of different methods given in this chapter you can see that your choice of instructional methods is by no means limited. If you find that you seem to use one method all the time or a great deal of the time, take a look at possible alternatives. By expanding your range of methods you expand your capabilities as an instructor, and you become that much more professional into the bargain.

While thirty-four methods are described here, they by no means represent all the methods possible. Others might well come into use in a wide variety of settings. No matter what the method, however, it will almost certainly employ the instructional and learning elements outlined in this set of methods. Additionally, many other variations emerge automatically from the various combinations of methods given here.

Master your methods

A key part of the education and development of a training professional involves becoming competent in actually using most of these methods. Human learning involves far more than the instructional methods used to achieve it, of course. But these methods provide a powerful support structure for enhancing that learning under different conditions and in different organizations.

Master most of these methods and you provide yourself with flexibility and confidence for meeting many different training challenges. And you establish yourself as a worthy enhancer of human learning in its varied and multiple forms.

12 Survival Tips for the Instructor

Many little incidents can occur to plague you as an instructor. Some of these incidents are trivial. Some are very serious. And some can simply seem serious at the time, allowing you to laugh about them afterwards.

How you respond to a particular incident often determines how serious the incident will turn out to be. It helps if you keep cool when others become frantic. You help yourself remain cool by having at least some idea of how to cope, or simply being prepared to cope in whatever way you can.

The tips outlined in this chapter are not comprehensive. The potential number of incidents is too enormous to take them all into account. But these tips do cover a reasonable number of points. They also help to illustrate how you can sometimes think your way out of apparently hopeless situations.

1. **Question:** What items should you always carry with you in your instructor's case?

Answer

Writing paper, chalk, felt tip marker pen, overhead projector pen, white board marker pen, several pencils, pencil sharpener, an eraser, a couple of ball point pens, blank acetate sheets, several small magnets, a small pair of scissors, a ruler, some thumb tacks, a roll of masking tape, sellotape, several paper clips, a small dictionary, a bottle of correction fluid, a couple of sheets of carbon paper, a small stapler with spare staples, a small pointer for the overhead projector, some sheets of facial tissue, a small sewing kit, a small bottle of water, an empty file folder, several name cards, a small screwdriver, a small torch, a small container of aspirins. In addition you may wish to include some materials related to your own subject area. These are all little things, but they can make a big difference to your effectiveness.

2. Question: Where should you place your lesson plan while conducting a class?

Answer

Place it in as inconspicuous a location as you can find, but make sure you'll still be able to refer to it during your lesson. Sometimes you can place it near a board or overhead projector. Or you might place it on the seat of a handy chair. Low tables can also prove useful for this. You may even find, at times, that you can simply place your lesson plan on the floor near where you'll be. No matter where you place your lesson plan, do check that you'll be able to see it properly even if you're moving around during the lesson. And try to make sure you'll be able to refer to it without being too obvious about it.

3. Question: When and how should you give out handouts?

Answer

Try to give out all your handouts or reference materials as close to the learning they concern as possible. Do be careful about giving them out too soon. People have a tendency to look over things the moment you put them in their hands. And this natural tendency could interfere with the continuity of your lesson (media conflict). If you have a lot of handouts, you might be wise to give them all out at the start of your training session. In this case you might consider setting up a manual complete with table of contents.

4. Question: What should you do if a participant asks you a question and you don't know the answer?

Answer

Whatever you do, don't try to bluff or evade the issue, unless you think you have a compelling reason to do so. Try turning the question back to the learner or to the class as a whole. Of course you can only do this a few times before it may start to irritate people. Sometimes it's best just to say you don't know the answer, then ask if anyone in the class does. This approach will often heighten learner motivation, especially for the ones who might actually know the answer. Another approach is to turn the question into a learning project. Invite everyone to try to find the answer for your next meeting. Be sure to say that you'll be looking too, but don't automatically take on the entire responsibility for finding out. Make the situation a genuine learning opportunity for everyone.

5. Question: What should you do about the smoking issue in your classroom?

Answer

Increasingly, this is a non-issue, as various institutions and businesses simply ban smoking on the premises completely. But when the issue does come up, you must be clear and unequivocal from the start. Otherwise you'll have to contend with the thin edge of the smoking wedge becoming an overwhelming cloud. Declare that there will be no smoking in your classroom. If no public sign exists to this effect, and you think it's needed, make one of your own to post prominently. If designated smoking areas exist in the building, let people know where these are.

Something to be on the lookout for too, especially in hotel settings, is hotel staff quietly coming around at different times to place ashtrays. Many smokers take the presence of ashtrays as a cue to smoke. Remove all ashtrays as quickly as possible to remove misunderstanding and temptation.

6. Question: What can you do if you've arrived in your classroom and suddenly realize you've forgotten your lesson notes?

Answer

Above all don't panic. Check first to see if you still have time to obtain them from wherever you may have left them. If not, find a quiet spot to sit down to work out a plan. Relax and give yourself a chance to think. Take a blank sheet of paper and write out key headings for your planned lesson at random all over the page. You'll be amazed at how much you can recall this way. Think too of the resources other people might provide. A colleague may have some useful material. One of your learners might have some notes you can refer to. Think of a learning project that your class might now be able to embark on instead of going through with your original lesson. This might include working with a film, videotape, or game of some kind. If you give yourself a chance, you'll probably surprise yourself with how well you can cope in this situation.

7. Question: How can you use the overhead projector that's available to you if you have no transparencies to use on it?

Answer

Make sure you have a damp paper towel or facial tissue handy first. Then, using water-soluble overhead projector pens, write directly on the glass top of the projector's illuminating surface. You can also use grease pencils or dry-ink marker pens (white board pens) for this. In the case of grease pencils, however, you may find a little rubbing alcohol (isopropyl alcohol) handy for erasing. Remember too that some types of solid objects project themselves well from the top of an overhead projector. You may find also that some glass or plastic sheets of transparent material are available that you can cut into substitute transparency sheets.

8. Question: What should you do about remembering the names of your participants?

Answer

You know that many memory systems are available these days. You may have tried one or several of them. But here's a system that's straightforward. First, if you can, be sure to use name cards from the start. These should generally be the 'tent' type, and might be supplemented with stick-on name tags. Next, give yourself some time to attach faces to the names. At this point the use of special markers could help ('Robert the Red', 'Freckled Farrah', 'Yawning Joan', etc.). Create an informal seating plan for your own use. Simply draw circles to show the approximate positions of the different people and write in the correct name for each. If you forget someone's name and see no name card or other record of that person's name, listen carefully for someone else to use her or his name. This may require a little discreet eavesdropping. Or you might be able to spy out the person's name by casually looking for a name on the covers of books or notes she or he is using. Deliberate effort and practice can yield excellent results in dealing with this often frustrating question.

9. Question: What should you do if the class has achieved the planned learning objective(s) and there's still a reasonable amount of time left?

Answer

A lot depends here on the type of subject matter you're dealing with. For less technical or more open-ended subjects, you might simply carry on into the next logical issue. Or you might simply expand on one of the issues already covered. An alternative approach, especially for more technical subjects, is to congratulate your class on its good work at the point of achievement. Tell them they've achieved the objective(s). Then ask them what they'd like to deal with in the time remaining. Try to be flexible in your responses to their suggestions. If they want to leave early, this might be a good thing to do. Of course, organizational realities may dictate to some extent what can be done here. The main thing is to avoid inadvertently punishing a group of learners for their success.

10. Question: What can you do when several people in your class know as much or almost as much about the subject concerned as you do?

Answer

Relax! Who says the instructor has to be all-knowing anyhow? That's God's job. At the first good opportunity acknowledge these experts in your class in a good, adult fashion. Invite them to make their contributions to class learning from time to time. In a sense, you might use them as assistant instructors. Don't worry about the fact that you may receive pay for instructing and they don't. More than likely they'll appreciate your recognition and respond in supportive fashion. You want them as allies, not enemies. Treat them as good resources, not threats.

A caution does apply here. Don't go overboard in using these people as assistant instructors. This could build resentment in other members of your class. It could also lead to your agenda becoming side-tracked. A danger exists too that these knowledgeable people turn out to know less about the subject area than you first thought.

11. Question: What's the maximum number of people you can instruct using an interactive or informal approach?

Answer

First of all, don't use any arbitrary upper limit. Depending on the exact situation and the technology available, you might be able to deal interactively with hundreds if not thousands of people. Just think of the radio talk show format to remind yourself of what might be done. Most of the time you probably won't have to worry about class sizes of more than one hundred, at least on a face-to-face basis. With the larger classes you may need to arrange for microphones in key locations around the room, including one or two located well for your own use. Even with the larger classes, you can still ask a few questions. You just have to be sure you have some rules of procedure for the group to observe. You might also solicit answers to your questions indirectly through small note replies, replies written on questionnaires, or on a community communication board (a designated board of some type or simply a blank stretch of wall where people leave stick-on notes), or replies given by groups after small group discussions.

The main thing here is to be sure to let your mind look for ways to interact, regardless of the class size. Don't automatically conclude that you have to turn a large class situation into a complete lecture.

12. Question: What should you do if you're in the middle of conducting a lesson and you find that it isn't working the way you'd planned?

Answer

Try to give yourself a small break to sort out your thinking. Make a note of any significant incidents or comments that might give you clues about what's going on. Whether or not you have a chance for a short break, set up a discussion with your class about the problem. Let them know frankly that the session doesn't seem to be working. Tell them you'd appreciate their advice on putting some zest back into the learning process. Explain to them your reasons for feeling that things aren't working well. It may be a good idea to split them off into small groups to develop their observations and responses to the situation. When the small groups meet, develop some ideas and suggestions of your own.

Then, when the full discussion takes place, let it be open and honest, even if you find some of it a little painful. Remember, you'll be a better instructor for the experience.

You may be surprised at the misconceptions people have, or the misinformation they've received. At times too you may find that they've already gone over everything you're dealing with, or think they have. When this sort of problem arises, it's very important to avoid the temptation simply to barge ahead. And most of the time your learners will appreciate your honesty with them.

13. Question: What should you do if you've prepared transparencies for use on the overhead projector during your lesson and you find that you can't have an overhead projector?

Answer

Don't panic! If you're sure you have sufficient time, enlist others to help you transfer the information on your transparencies to flip chart sheets or a large writing surface of some kind. Free-hand reproductions of diagrams are better than no diagrams at all. You may find that latent artistic talents in yourself or your learners emerge to produce quite good results in copying. Something else you can do is to put your most important transparencies on a light-coloured wall or on an outside window to create a picture gallery of information. This will allow you to group your learners near your gallery at a key point in your lesson to go over the displayed information. Another route you can try is simply to distribute your transparencies among the participants in your class for individual viewing. Up to three people at a time can usually view one transparency comfortably. When doing this, you might tape blank sheets of paper to the transparencies to make their information stand out better. Once people have viewed the transparencies, they can pass them along to others. If photocopying equipment is available, you can have some or all of your transparencies copied to produce handouts. Finally, you might simply incorporate a few or all of your transparencies into the pages of your lesson plan for use as teaching references.

14. Question: What should you do if one of your participants says something to the effect: 'What you've just said is a load of crap!"?

Answer

Take care not to lose your cool, or to appear to lose your cool. This could be just what the person wanted to provoke. Instead, stop what you're saying or doing and politely ask this learner to clarify the comment in more specific terms. Do this calmly and with confidence. Invite other participants to join in the discussion to add their viewpoints. This should produce a healthy exchange of information. It will also give you a chance to delve into the perceptions of your learners to discover fine points of information that you may have missed, or that you might be able to clarify for your learners. As the discussion proceeds, work on turning it more and more into a good learning experience for everyone. This will improve everyone's feelings. If the interrupter remains intransigent, he or she will gradually become isolated in the group. This will tend to have a quietening effect on him or her. Later on you may be able to discuss things further with this person in private.

In this kind of delicate situation you have to open yourself up as honestly as possible. This may prove uncomfortable for you, especially if you come to realize that the interrupting participant was correct! In this case strive to be enough of a teacher to admit your own failings or errors. Most people will admire you for doing so.

15. Question: One or two of your participants tend to dominate all the class discussions. How can you deal with them?

Answer

This can be a tricky one. You don't want to turn these people off, but you do want to encourage other participants to talk more. Consider the feedback factor. Basically you want to encourage the non-talkers to speak up. Concentrate on this idea rather than looking for ways to discourage your talkers from speaking. You can do this using direct eye-contact with non-speakers or by positioning yourself physically near them. While doing this, avoid direct eye-contact with your talkers. Sometimes too you can pose questions directly to non-talkers. Take care in doing this, though. You don't want to leave people feeling they're on the spot. When a non-talker finally does say something, try as hard as you can to find ways of rewarding her or him for doing so. If the more subtle approaches don't seem to work, tell the class that you would like to get more people actively involved in the discussion. If the talkers are particularly active and continue to drown out any possibility of response from your non-talkers, you may have to discuss it with them directly at a convenient break time. Above all, don't stop trying to even out the discussions.

16. Question: What can you do if you planned on using a white board and it turns out that you won't have one for your lesson?

Answer

You could, of course, revert to using a flip chart or chalkboard. If you have a dry-ink marker pen with you, another smooth surface in the room might serve as a substitute white board. A sheet of glass with white paper backing would work. Similarly, some smooth metal surfaces work quite well. Take care, though, if they've been painted over with a flat paint of some type. If this is the case you might not be able to erase the dry-ink markings! In general, non-porous, smooth surfaces can be written on with surprisingly good results. So, use your creativity, and try to set up some form of substitute white board (or whatever colour you find).

17. Question: You planned on using a flip chart during your lesson. But you arrive in the classroom to find that none is available to you. What can you do?

Answer

Again this calls for some creativity. First off, see if any pads of flip chart paper are available in or near the room. If you have at least one pad, then your problem becomes one of propping up or suspending this pad by some means. Nails, hooks, cords and so forth could allow you to put the flip chart pad up on a convenient wall. The back of a door, an up-ended table, or a flat board could all serve as substitute flip chart stands.

If you don't have any flip chart paper available, you have a tougher problem. But there might still be some solutions. Look around for substitute paper you might use instead of flip chart paper. Brown wrapping paper could work well, as could wrapping paper of a variety of other colours. Similarly, some institutions now have paper tablecloths on hand. These could work nicely for you too. If you're really stuck, you might try making your own flip chart paper by taking a number of ordinary, blank, notebook papers and sticking them together with masking tape, transparent tape, glue, or even staples. This can be time-consuming, but you might be able to get people to help you. If you're working with a small class, you might set up a ring-binder notebook to serve as a mini flip chart. Do this by setting the notebook on its cover edges to form a tent with the rings at the apex. You'll probably need to secure the cover edges with weights or by taping them in place. Write on the blank pages in this notebook arrangement just as you would on a normal flip chart, using normal flip chart pens. Ignore the lines if you're using lined paper. This type of set-up can be seen quite well from up to three or so metres away.

18. Question: What should you do if an outsider suddenly walks into your classroom and proceeds to talk intensely with one of your participants?

Answer

This is a very annoying situation to say the least. It usually indicates ignorance, arrogance, or plain rudeness on the part of the outsider. Unfortunately, this type of behaviour is widespread in our business and academic worlds. You have to take charge. After all, you're the manager of the learning environment, and in this type of situation that environment has been contaminated. Sometimes this contamination will interfere seriously with the learning process.

As calmly and unobtrusively as possible, move closer to the outsider. Sometimes this action alone will cause him or her to realize that he or she is contaminating things. The person may then try to explain, or may simply retreat. If the intruder isn't sensitive enough to pick up on things this way, you'll have to resort to more direct action. Ask if you can be of assistance. This forces the person to make some sort of response to you and to the situation that has occurred. This may elicit an apology for interrupting with an explanation. You can then suggest a remedy. You might, for instance, simply ask that he or she talk with the participant elsewhere at a convenient break time, unless some type of emergency really does exist. Most of the time this suggestion should work all right. In cases of supreme ignorance (or arrogance?), the intruder may not apologize or back off in any way. If this happens you have little choice but to ask that he or she leave.

In making this request you may have to spell out for him or her the damage caused to the learning process by this type of interruption. It may prove a valuable lesson for the intruder in the future.

19. Question: You're rapidly running out of time for your lesson, and you're still not even half-way completed. What should you do?

Answer

Well, plainly and simply you've got to do something. Find some plausible reason to declare a brief pause in the lesson. During this pause review your lesson plan to identify the key elements you still need to deal with. Plan to concentrate only on these elements during the remaining time. Make a note to yourself to deal with the other elements at some other point or in some other fashion. Estimate your time for the key elements carefully and accurately. Sometimes you may have to put off dealing with at least a few of them. One thing you should not do in this situation is to try to speed up your lesson. This could prove detrimental to learning. It also runs the risk of leaving learners with some sense of misplaced emphasis in the way they see or understand things. If written exams or tests are involved for the learners, a speeding-up approach on your part could be most unfair, because it could put them on the wrong track in their studies. Instructors in this type of situation are always tempted to speed up. But do try to train yourself not to give in to this particular temptation.

20. Question: How can you handle things if one or more of your learners are showing increasing signs of boredom or restlessness?

Answer

Once again you have to do something as the manager of the learning setting. Consider the possibilities. Is it time for a break? Is the room too hot or stuffy? Is it too soon after a meal? Are you being repetitious? Are you trying to cover too much material. Are you talking too much? Is the material itself boring? Have your learners lost touch with the relevance to them of the subject matter? Be open in your thinking, and you might identify the cause of the problem. You might even ask the participants themselves. They should be able to give you some idea! Your solution could simply be to declare an exercise break. If the weather allows it, a walk outside to get fresh air could be just the thing. Sometimes a change in your method of instructing will work. And sometimes you need to proceed in the same way as in the answer to question 12. The main thing is you need to do something.

21. Question: Your classroom is equipped with a flip chart, but it lacks a solid backing plate or board, and a firm backing of some kind doesn't seem to be available. How can you cope?

Answer

One approach could simply be to forget about the flip chart stand and proceed as in question 17. Another approach is to look for a substitute backing of some kind. This could take the form of several sheets of unused poster board. If you can't find substitutes, try the 'webbing' approach. This entails forming a support on the flip chart frame by interweaving masking tape, string, or rope. Remember the way many lawn chairs use wide ribbons of material to provide good support by their interweaving? By keeping that model in mind, you can achieve the same kind of support on the flip chart frame.

22. Question: A noisy piece of equipment starts up nearby, or someone begins making a lot of noise with hammering or some other action. What can you do?

Answer

Depending on the point you've reached in your lesson, you might simply be able to continue briefly, especially if the noise is not completely overwhelming. If the noise continues, however, you must do something more. Perhaps it's time to declare a break. In this case you might go ahead with the break and hope the noise disappears during this time. But you probably should take advantage of the break to investigate what's going on. Find the noise-maker or noise-makers, and then inquire politely about how long they're likely to make the noise. You could explain to them that the noise is disturbing a class in session. If this approach doesn't work, take some time to look for another location for your class. Depending on the type of organization you're working in, you might clear such a move with an authority of some kind.

One thing you should not do in this type of situation is to carry on regardless. This could irritate everyone, including yourself, as a lot of shouting would occur instead of straightforward talking. Stress levels would rise. And the quality of learning would certainly suffer.

23. Question: You plan to use a flip chart during your lesson, and a properly equipped flip chart is available. But the room is a little too dark for the participants to see what you will have to show them during the lesson. What do you do now?

Answer

The first thing to do is to look around for some sort of light source in the classroom. Perhaps there's a doorway that's better lit from an outside source. If so, you could move the flip chart so the outside light falls on it. You may find a floor lamp or a table lamp somewhere you could position to light the flip chart. Even a large torch might lend itself to use as a temporary spotlight. In fact, if could even add an extra little 'gimmicky' flair to your training session. In some cases you may find that you can replace light bulbs with ones that have higher wattage. If you look closely, you might discover that the darkness of the room stems from a lack of light bulbs in some sockets. Finally, if you have an overhead projector available, you can use it as a temporary spotlight. Position it so that its light will fall neatly on your flip chart, and you will have solved your lighting problem. You will also have created an excellent attention-focusing system for your lesson.

24. Question: What should you do if one of your audiovisual set-ups, such as a flip chart or a poster, suddenly crashes to the floor right in the middle of one of your lessons?

Answer

As with so many instructing problems, the first thing is to remain calm. Then, if the situation allows for it, try to turn the incident into a joke ('Obviously that's pretty heavy information!'). You might make light of it at your own expense ('I knew I should have nailed those points down better!'). Or whatever you can think of at the time. The key thing is not to let the incident interfere with your lesson more than it absolutely needs to. And this means you must not become unduly flustered or annoyed. Very often you'll find that participants will rush to help you. If there's damage or spillage, do what's required to repair things or clean them up as soon as seems necessary. Make note of anything that's likely to require future action by someone in connection with the mishap. Never return damaged equipment or materials to any type of media centre without letting them know what's happened. In coping with this type of problem your central theme should be 'The show must go on!'

25. Question: How do you handle a situation in which one of your participants suddenly exhibits disturbing symptoms of some sort of physical or emotional problem?

Answer

Many possibilities exist here. Avoid jumping to the conclusion that the learner is 'fooling around' in some way. Treat all occurrences of this kind very seriously, unless you have definite information that indicates you should do otherwise. The person involved could be suffering an embarrassing personal problem. If this is the case, the last thing needed is for you to add to the sense of embarrassment. If another participant seems to be helping the person in an effective way, and they want to leave the room, let them leave as discreetly as possible. But know where they're going, and take steps to ensure that things turn out all right. If it looks as though you need outside help, such as medical or rescue people, by all means call for it. Delay could prove fatal. Many sudden emergencies can arise. The person could be suffering an epileptic seizure, a stroke, a heart attack, a diabetic seizure, choking, or some other form of sudden attack. Whatever the situation, keep yourself calm, remain confidently in charge, and get help — fast. If one or more of the participants knows how to apply first aid, enlist the help. The action you take in this type of situation could well be vital to another human being's life. Once the problem has been handled successfully, get your class back to normal as quickly as possible. In some serious cases, you may have to dismiss the class altogether for a reasonable period of time.

If the occurrence is serious enough, be sure to record all the relevant details such as time, place, specific symptoms, names, actions taken, people contacted, and so on for producing an appropriate report for the authorities.

Keep your wits about you

The preceding questions and their answers cover a wide range of upsetting problems. But the range of possible problems is really much greater than can be covered here. You have to use your own wit and imagination to deal with whatever issues actually face you. Just remember that you can work your way through most of the instructing problems you're likely to encounter if you keep yourself calm and allow yourself to find a solution. If you panic or become emotionally frazzled, then any unexpected situation could prove disastrous for you. The secret is to remain calm, cool and confident while looking for the solution most likely to work for the dilemma you face.

You might not be able to meet every terrible instructional situation confidently and successfully, but you can increase your chances of doing so to a marked degree. Believe there's a solution and look faithfully for it. You'll be surprised how often you'll find one.

13 Keeping the Records

Various types of records are important to training and education. They have many purposes, and often prove invaluable over longer periods of time. Good records document learner progress, flesh out research, and give access to a wide range of human resource information. They clearly establish learner accomplishments and help managers to make decisions about transfers or promotions. Records also form the basis of organizational certificates. These kinds of certificates will often be useful outside the organization granting them.

Good records don't just happen. They require careful setting - up and maintenance. A very important person in making sure this is done well is you, the instructor.

Training and education records can take the form of:

1. Achievement records
2. Learner evaluations
3. Experience logs
4. Programme evaluations
5. Information sources
6. Research notes
7. Training and education schedules
8. Evolving programme designs
9. Management intentions

We'll now take a look at each of these types of records in turn.

Achievement records

These important records detail the specific achievements people have earned through their learning work. These achievements could include mastering new skills, earning diplomas or degrees, completing important tasks or assignments, and other notable learning milestones.

As well as the actual achievements themselves, achievement records must note the dates and organizations involved. Each entry in an achievement record should be signed or initialled by a responsible person, such as an instructor or teacher, and this person's name should be typed out for complete clarity.

In many respects a person's learning achievement record is like a medical record. It's meant to document significant learnings in order to develop an in-depth profile of the individual concerned. This profile becomes invaluable for deciding on additional learning experiences that should be considered in the future. It can also become a critical element in managerial decisions about assignments, job placements, or promotions.

An achievement record requires careful and confidential handling at all times. Its contents can have legal significance in a variety of situations (including formal accident inquiries). These types of records must be assigned due importance and receive a high level of care and attention. This care and attention is one of the marks of a truly professional training or educational system.

Learner evaluations

As the term suggests, these are evaluations of the learners themselves. They may take a variety of forms and should be as objective as possible. The main thrust of these evaluations should be to show learner progress in performance terms as measured against standard criteria. Good use of learning objectives within the learning sessions concerned will sharpen the details involved here.

Learner evaluations should mark the progress of individual learners towards the kinds of learning achievements that should be detailed in the learner's achievement record.

While learner evaluations should concentrate on demonstrated performance, some degree of anecdotal or impressionistic judgment by an experienced instructor can usefully flesh out the strictly factual information. Insights and predictions offered by informed professionals have their uses. But they generally should not outweigh solid demonstrations of competent learner performance.

In some organizations the anecdotal and impressionistic judgments of instructors have been the mainstay of learner evaluations. Such organizations can find this approach attractive because it's easy to apply and cheap. But this form of economy is false, although its consequences might not damage the organization's productivity for some years.

A number of organizations use self-evaluations produced by the learners themselves. Some managerial minds find this form of evaluation hard to swallow, yet it can be very effective if applied with intelligence and care. These evaluations work especially well when they involve interview sessions in which learners set out their evaluations of themselves with their instructors. If evaluations of this type are used, they too should be included in the learner evaluation records.

When organizations carry out learner evaluations with a high degree of care and attention to detail, they treat their learners with respect and honour. What's more, they treat themselves well also. Organizations that take care to use fair learner evaluations are more likely to use fair employee evaluations. This kind of square dealing with their own people is a factor of real importance to organizational success.

Experience logs

These are record books maintained for individual learners to document their work experiences. The idea here is to highlight particular kinds of experiences or jobs that enhance the learner's skill competence. This is a form of achievement record focused primarily on the work setting.

While specific experiences are important ingredients for this type of record, more routine forms of experience should be recorded also, simply to reflect the period of time during which an employee/learner held a particular job or carried out a particular function.

When specific experiences will be recognized for the granting of certificates, diplomas, or degrees, standard criteria should come into use for detailing the experiences in the most meaningful manner. Well-designed performance objectives will help render this type of information much more professional.

As with achievement records, dates and signatures are important. Each entry should have a date, and should be supported by the signature or initials of the instructor, supervisor, or manager directly involved.

Experience logs might also contain evaluative information. This could take the form of comments by the authority figure concerned about the employee/learner's quality of performance and general suitability for the work involved. This type of impressionistic information should be kept within the same kind of objective perspective as should be used for learner evaluations.

Experience logs play an invaluable role in continuing types of training programmes, apprenticeships being a prime example. The information contained in this type of record should be combined with that contained in learner evaluations for the recognition of specific learning achievement points.

Again, because of their relevance to employee development and competence, experience logs deserve serious and well-organized support by the organization concerned.

Programme evaluations

These types of records contain evaluation information about specific training or education programmes. This information can include learner comments and feedback, but this should certainly not be the only type of evaluation information used.

The comments from the instructors involved in the delivery of a given programme can be relevant and important. And the information provided by the co-workers, supervisors, or managers of the learners involved is invaluable, particularly when it is focused on evidence of improved on-the-job performance.

Performance objectives provide effective instruments for attesting to the effectiveness of learning programmes. For this reason they should always be used, if at all possible, for producing this type of evaluation.

As noted in earlier chapters, performance objectives should provide the base information for designing effective learning objectives. So the analysis information becomes the design information which then becomes the evaluation information. Here we have the closed-loop structure for effective training.

While performance analysis and its resulting performance objectives are fundamental to programme evaluation, some attention should still be given to the intangibles that anecdotal or impressionistic information can give. The influence of differing philosophies of management or the cultures of specific work groups can definitely affect human performance on the job. So too can such factors as organizational regulations, equipment or machine peculiarities, physical work conditions, distorted communications, and so forth. You can't measure these factors in mathematically discrete terms, but you can develop a practical and useful idea of their impact through the comments of experienced and competent employees, supervisors, or managers.

Programme evaluations require care, depth and performance honesty for true value. Never base them on mere whims or the hasty judgment calls of inexperienced or incompetent people. Shoddy or glib programme evaluations build in long-term flaws for the overall quality of continuing training activities.

Well-managed and well-conceived programme evaluations can and should be central to on-going training and education excellence.

Information sources

The sources of information related to training and education planning and delivery vary. They might include books, manuals, journals, handouts, or extensive electronic databases. They might also include handwritten notes concerning useful technical or procedural points. Additionally, the names of key people within and outside the organization should be maintained in convenient reference form. Similarly, the locations of particular tools, pieces of equipment, displays, structures, or information centres such as libraries should also be available.

Information sources may require cross-referencing with research records, as these records often form important source material for training. Also consider cross-referencing with other types of records. Wherever it exists, pin-point information for your potential use.

Research notes

These records consist of accumulated information taken from a wide variety of sources. As an instructor you can contribute a great deal to research by producing notes now and then concerning the relative degrees of success of different teaching methods and materials, and also by passing on comments from participants in courses related to the relevance of certain subject material. Participants are a good source of research information about training needs or organizational shortcomings. This kind of information is so invaluable that you should regularly be encouraged to pass it on.

One good way of passing on information is to conduct some sort of debriefing shortly after a given training session. This could be done with other people such as training managers, or it could consist of writing notes in some form of journal to capture the flavour and experience of delivering the course concerned. A desktop computer would be useful for this. Over time an accumulation of such debriefings would provide impressive and insightful research notes about training that could have many useful applications.

Research notes may contain information from informal or formal types of research. These notes should also contain information from research conducted by other organizations, especially research groups, government bodies, or universities and colleges.

Extensive research notes demand good storage and retrieval systems. These can be manual systems of organized and indexed files, or they can be well-conceived databases. Increasingly, computerization should allow trainers and teachers to make relatively easy use of good research data on a continuing basis for training design and delivery.

Training and education schedules

These schedules show the details of training courses including their dates, subjects and planned instructors. Usually some form of wall chart is useful for displaying this information. This type of information is so obviously important that it may seem a little simplistic to highlight it. Unfortunately, numbers of different organizations still handle this form of record in far too casual a manner.

When only a few courses are involved, a casual approach to training and education schedules may be fine. But this kind of approach quickly falls apart when a substantial number of courses are planned. As few as six courses of two or three days' length each could benefit from being recorded in chart display form.

Details of subjects, instructor names, nomination closing dates, clients involved, numbers of registrants, training locations and special requirements (including the need for a guest speaker) can all be included on a wall chart of schedules.

Well-maintained schedules reveal such potential problems as lack of classrooms, lack of instructors, insufficient planning time, or possible shortages of training materials and equipment. With the effective use of colour coding, such charts are a boon to training planning and organization from a coordinator or manager perspective. They can yield a lot of important information in one sweep. The use of magnetic or erasing chart boards also allows a fair degree of flexibility in arranging or changing different training sessions.

Nowadays, of course, computers can play a more useful role here. Detailed schedules can be produced on various types of computer programs and then printed up for distribution as needed.

Evolving programme designs

Good training programmes are generally not put together in one sitting. They require the application of thought over a good period of time. A week may be reasonable, or a couple of years may be necessary. Whatever the length of design time, a good record of the basic sketch design and continuing modifications is important.

This type of record can be maintained in a manual file or displayed on a convenient wall to allow several people to participate in the design process at the same time. Naturally, evolving designs might also be stored electronically. If computer networks or mainframe systems are involved, different people can call up the design at its latest point of evolution as they wish.

When an evolving training design is displayed well, it encourages openness and brainstorming by the designers. It also enables people who are not the designers, but who have some stake or interest in the design, to review its evolution from time to time and to make suggestions.

Management plans

Interestingly, management plans that could have a direct impact on particular training courses sometimes remain obscure or hidden until suddenly they are revealed to those training people immediately involved with the course or courses that will be affected, sometimes drastically.

Sudden revelations of this type can be destructive to training, and they can result in a lot of hard work going down the drain. Unfortunately, many managers don't recognize the importance of eeping trainers and teachers informed as they develop their lans. Given the importance of training to the success of many nanagement plans, this lack of effective liaison is, to say the east, curious. In fact, managers ideally should be involved lirectly with all aspects of training on a continuing basis.

If managers don't routinely provide useful planning informaion, you need to develop your own ways of connecting with nanagement thinking in every way possible. This includes ttending meetings, maintaining contacts with a good network of ine people in the organization, visiting key locations, keeping up o date on in-house newsletters, public announcements and hanges in key management personnel. If you can link with mangers who may be privy to important planning information, so nuch the better.

Information gathered about management thinking and intenions should be recorded on its own for referencing on a regular asis. In effect, this information becomes a form of 'organizational ntelligence'.

As with other kinds of record keeping, instructors may not fully ppreciate the need for keeping an eye on management intenions. Such tasks as training design and classroom teaching may ecome so engrossing and interesting that instructors may be eluctant to spend the time to remain alert to management thinkng. Yet, for this very reason, they must remain alert. Otherwise, hey run the risk of putting a lot of time and hard effort into pecial areas of interest that later turn out to be irrelevant.

Jsing forms

pecific forms for the different types of information you may equire will often help. They set out definite categories and hunks of data in set locations on the page, thus helping the etrieval process.

One thing you must guard against with forms is the temptation o design your own the moment you think you see a need for one.)ften you may discover that a good form already exists but, for ome reason, hasn't been properly distributed. Make some nquiries to find out if this might be the case.

If the design and use of forms is not controlled, organizations vill often become overwhelmed by a monstrous blizzard of differnt types of forms following inconsistent patterns and providing neven types and qualities of information. If this happens, the sefulness of forms goes right out the window.

When forms are being designed, all potential users must be involved in some way. They must agree to the contents and layout. Then the form must be tested with some form of sample group to ensure that people understand it and use it as intended. Without the right design care and attention to detail, forms will not come out well, and they will become more trouble than they're worth.

Well-designed forms more than pay for themselves. They help to ensure that the right information is brought out for the right purposes. They help to set up consistent information bases. And they provide an excellent resource for meeting a wide variety of training and education needs.

Writing tips

When you keep records you must write, whether on paper or on computer. The cardinal rule here is 'keep it short', otherwise known as the KISS principle (the second 'S' represents the word 'sweet').

The field of education and training holds many temptations for high-flown phrases or various types of jargon. But don't yield to any temptations you may feel to employ psychological terms just because you like the sound of them. For instance, don't write: 'The individuals involved engaged in a productive interactive process to elicit multi-faceted verbal contributions', when all you really meant was, 'Everyone discussed the issue and came up with some good ideas'.

In writing records favour short words. If a one-syllable word will do the trick, use it. Never allow yourself to use longer words because you think they'll sound more important. Short words used correctly have an impressive power and directness all their own.

Keep your sentences short — in general, no longer than eighteen words. When point-form lists will set out information effectively, use them. The idea is to enable readers to retrieve important facts effectively when they need them.

Continuing maintenance

Training and education records can cover a wide field. And they require a lot of conscientious work to keep them in good shape. If they are kept in good shape, you'll find them a blessing. If they go out of date or become disorganized, they become a curse, and learning suffers.

Some organizations downplay the need for good training records. They see this area as a low-priority, clerical one, without real impact on training programmes. This type of thinking, however, is short-sighted and wrong-headed. Even the best-designed training programmes packaged in the glossiest of covers become badly out-dated over time. Some means of continuous up-dating is essential.

Well-maintained training records contain a considerable amount of good information. This information is important to the planning and conduct of good training and education programmes. To be most useful, all this information must be set up to permit ready access by users.

Security

If training records are good, they will often contain sensitive information. This information could concern organizational plans or issues. It could also include personal information, such as performance evaluations and career recommendations.

Given the nature of the information involved, access to these records must be effectively controlled. Otherwise damaging leaks of information will occur that could hurt productivity or embarrass individual people. Keep in mind that many training records deserve the same protection as legal or medical records. In this connection, poorly protected training records could at some point lead to legal repercussions for the organization that failed to look after them properly.

Proper controls should include locations that are not readily accessible to casual observers. If the information is confidential, it should be kept under lock and key. On computer systems it should be protected by secure access codes.

When training or education systems are not seen to look after their information in a professional way, people will tend to distrust them. They will not be as forthcoming with their comments or suggestions. People won't be so ready to volunteer information for the record. Learners will hold back on self-evaluations or on providing experience information. Teachers will refrain from being so detailed in their comments about learners or training designs. And managers and employees in general will be guarded in their cooperation with training people.

While security is important, guard against going overboard. In some cases you want information to go out to a wide audience.

Just be sure you know which type of information needs the security treatment, and which should be publicized.

Records security must never be given a low priority. It's a responsible process designed to secure important and privileged information. Never treat it lightly.

The record-keeping system

The actual system of record-keeping can be simple or complex, manual or electronic. Small notebooks with index tabs can be useful for keeping records, at least at the operating or teaching level. Larger record books or files can be useful for maintaining more extensive records. And, of course, full-fledged databases for specific types of training and education records may be maintained in computerized systems.

In one sense trainers and teachers always maintain records. They do so simply by remembering certain details about learners, materials, equipment, locations, or situations. This is an informal level of record-keeping, and it's subject to all the human frailties of perception and memory. More formalized record-keeping helps to maintain a certain measure of objectivity. It also underscores the point that training and education is an important activity, worthy of long-term consideration and care.

Advantages

Good record-keeping will help to avoid repeating the errors of the past. It provides a resource base for the continuous up-dating of training. It highlights organizational trends. It helps to identify the full measure of an organization's culture. It provides a useful base for launching various forms of research, including performance analysis studies. It's invaluable to human resource planning. And it helps to ensure the long-term excellence of training in the organization.

Significant recognition

Keeping the records in training is not beneath the dignity of professional people. It is an important and essential part of the training operation seen as a whole. Record-keeping requires attention to detail, and it requires a significant level of recognition in its own right. Training based on good records will have depth, relevance, polish and power. And such well-based training will demonstrate the quality and effectiveness of the trainers involved.

Professionalism

In a world that puts increasing emphasis on employee rights and human rights, the records concerning people at work have assumed more and more importance. In some cases, such records are subject to seizure and examination by the courts. So the records must be accurate and fair.

By concerning yourself with good record-keeping of all types, you round out your professional role as a practitioner of human resource development. And you deepen your role as an important contributor to the education and development of the human beings you deal with.

Record-keeping may not be glamorous or exciting in itself, but it is essential. It provides for the long-term future. It builds the base for continuing training and education success. And it generally enhances the productivity of all concerned.

14 Audiovisual Tips

Your audiovisual aids can be vital to your training effectiveness. Yet many instructors have a tendency to ignore the little details that are so important to using them well. And this can prove embarrassing or downright disastrous to your training efforts.

Most of us know that we should check audiovisual equipment ahead of time. Yet, when we faithfully do this checking, how careful are we? And how far ahead of actual lesson time should we do this checking?

It's quite possible to check out equipment thoroughly the night before a training session, and then discover that things don't work quite right once you start the lesson. Bulbs can burn out. Electrical connections can short. Portable screens can suddenly collapse. Or overhead lights can fail to work. When it comes to modern electrical aids, 'gremlins' can intervene at any time.

When you really want to be sure of your media support, check it out completely as close as possible to the time when you actually plan to use it. This will increase the chances that glitches will not occur at key moments.

When you think back on your experience with instructing, how often have you encountered problems with your audiovisual equipment? Have you ever expected to have a particular piece of equipment available to you, and then discovered that it was nowhere in sight when you needed it? Have you had a chalkboard available for your use, but no chalk? A film projector, but no take-up reel? A videocassette recorder, but no blank cassettes, or cassettes of the wrong type?

Experiences such as these can prove quite disheartening. And they can hurt your image with learners, despite that fact that you might not be to blame. People tend to judge an instructor by immediate events, rather than by overall or general results. And images built in this short-term way can be lasting, even if they are really unfair.

For your own sake you have to be very careful about relying on others to have your equipment where you want it, when you want it, and in proper working order. You just can't rely on hotels, for instance, to look after audiovisual requirements properly, even though their staffs give you the most sincere of assurances. Similarly, audiovisual suppliers can prove frustratingly unreliable at times. Even the audiovisual departments of polytechnics or universities frequently fail to deliver properly.

One way of helping to guard against support media foul-ups is to use a good checklist. This will help you to decide on what media equipment you really need, and to identify the related requirements that you may have. Use of such a checklist will enable you to plan for the use of specific media resources in a highly professional manner.

Here and on the following pages is a checklist that may help to make things easier for you:

Audiovisual Checklist

Medium	Related Equipment	Key Tips
Chalkboard	❒ Chalk (colours)	– Look for smooth board surface and solid backing
Whiteboard	❒ Marker pens (dry, erasable)	– Try not to leave written work on too long (it'll be harder to erase)
Flip chart	❒ Blank pad(s) ❒ Marker pens	– Ensure that the easel is a solid one – Try not to accept a poster stand as a flip chart – Have grease pencils available for back up

Lectern	❒ Built-in microphone ❒ Built-in light ❒ Storage compartment	– Make certain that the lectern is a solid one that won't 'travel' or shake
Flannel board	❒ Cardboard shapes	– Ensure the flannel is taut – Test the cardboard shapes on the flannel ahead of time to make sure they adhere
Poster board	❒ Posters ❒ Drawing pins ❒ Stapler	– Ensure that the location won't readily allow passers by to brush against it
Magnetic board	❒ Magnets ❒ Magnetized display plates	– Ensure that your magnets are large enough to hold any papers or cardboard that you may wish them to hold
Hand-outs	❒ Required number ❒ Storage box or file ❒ Binders ❒ File folders	– If you have a lot, make up a table of contents for them and package them in binders (this will often get you started on producing a training manual)
Pens, pencils	❒ Pencil sharpener	– Test the pens ahead of time if possible

Name cards	❒ Marker pens ❒ Plastic holders or stick-ons (as applicable)	– Make sure standing name cards are stiff enough to remain standing on their own – 5" x 8" file index cards work well as name cards
Overhead projector	❒ Pens (water soluble ❒ Pens (permanent) ❒ Spare bulb ❒ Screen (tilting type) ❒ Paper towels ❒ Small bottle of water	– Remember to focus the projector before you actually use it – Ensure that all glass and plastic surfaces are dust and smear free – Make sure cooling fan works properly
Slide projector	❒ Slides ❒ Slide tray (carousel?) ❒ Spare bulb ❒ Remote control	– Check that all slides are inserted properly – If sound is involved, ensure compatibility of available sound equipment
Filmstrip projector	❒ Filmstrip(s)	– Check whether filmstrips are in cartridges, and ensure that the projector is compatible

Audiocassette recorder	❒ Cassettes ❒ Microphone ❒ Batteries	– Check that the microphone will rest on a solid surface free from immediate noise sources
Videocassette recorder	❒ Video-cassettes ❒ Monitor ❒ Microphone (omnidi-rectional?) ❒ Camera tripod ❒ Remote control for play backs	– Check the micro-phone as for audio-cassette recorder – Extra lighting?
Film projector	❒ Film(s) ❒ Take-up reel ❒ Spare bulb ❒ Screen	– Switch the sound system on a little ahead of time
Desktop computer	❒ Blank Disks ❒ Correct software ❒ Mouse ❒ Hard disk ❒ Printer ❒ Modem	– Ensure that comput-ers are set up for comfortable use by all students – Have appropriate user manual(s) available – Ensure that master screens are comfort-able for viewing at a distance

Given the large array of audiovisual equipment available nowadays, this checklist is by no means complete. As you come to use different types of equipment that aren't on this list, simply add them in using the same basic format set out here. This way you'll keep yourself and your list fully up to date.

The following checklist is a general one that you should apply for using most types of audiovisual aids:

General Pre-course Checklist

Paper punch (3-hole, metric?)	❒	Electrical extension cord(s)	❒
Photocopier(s)	❒	Projector stand(s) (low or high?)	❒
Availability of electrical outlets	❒	Batteries (types?)	❒
Blackout arrangements	❒	Extra speaker(s)	❒
Ventilation quality	❒	Special screen requirements	❒
Temperature control	❒	Pointer(s) (electronic?)	❒
Lighting level(s)	❒	Masking tape	❒
Acoustic quality	❒	Sellotape	❒
Special materials	❒	Stapler (and staples?)	❒
Isopropyl alcohol	❒		

Control your media

Many of the items in these checklists may seem trivial or 'obvious'. In a sense they are. But what seems trivial when you're just thinking about it may well turn out to be supremely important when you actually need to use it.

The audiovisual aids or support media you use for instructing activities must be controlled in some manner, or they will end up controlling you. And when your media are not properly under control, learning definitely starts to suffer. If you retain good control, learner can be enhanced markedly. Well orchestrated learning accompanied by top notch media support produces the ultimate in modern instructing. It's yours to plan, and yours to provide.

Selected Readings

The following references give you a selection of additional books you might wish to consult in furthering your own understanding of the field of instructing others.

Aranguren, J.L. (1967) *Human Communications*. New York and Toronto: World University Library: McGraw-Hill.

Borger, Robert and Seaborne, A.E.M. (1971) *The Psychology of Learning*. Harmondsworth: Penguin.

Bradford, Leland P. (ed.) (1978) *Group Development*. San Diego: University Associates.

Broadwell, Martin M. (1975) *The Supervisor and On-the-Job Training*. Reading, Massachusetts: Addison-Wesley.

Buckley, Roger and Caple, Jim (1990) *The Theory and Practice of Training*. London: Kogan Page.

Callahan, Raymond E. (1962) *Education and the Cult of Efficiency*. Chicago and London: University of Chicago Press.

Drucker, Peter F. (1980) *Managing in Turbulent Times*. New York: Harper & Row.

Friesen, Paul A. (1971) *Designing Instruction*. Ottawa: Friesen, Kaye & Associates.

Heron, John (1989) *The Facilitators' Handbook*. London: Kogan Page.

Hersey, Paul and Blanchard, Kenneth H. (1977) *Management of Organizational Behavior*. Englewood Cliffs: Prentice-Hall.

Highet, Gilbert (1950) *The Art of Teaching*. New York: Random House.

Hunt, Morton (1982) *The Universe Within*. New York: Simon and Schuster.

Ingalls, John D. (1973) *A Trainer's Guide to Andragogy*. Washington, D.C.: U.S. Department of Health, Education, and Welfare.

Jaques, David (1991) *Learning in Groups*. London: Kogan Page.

Jastrow, Robert (1981) *Mind in the Universe.* New York: Simon & Schuster.

Jaynes, Julian (1978) *The Origin of Consciousness in the Breakdown of the Bicameral Mind.* Toronto: University of Toronto Press.

Kenney, J.P.J. and Donnelly, E.L. (1972) *Manpower Training and Development.* London: George G. Harrap.

Kidd, J.R. (1960) *How Adults Learn.* New York: Association Press.

Knowles, Malcolm (1975) *Self-directed Learning.* Chicago: Follett.

Lankton, Steve (1980) *Practical Magic.* Cupertino, California: Meta Publications.

Laver, John and Hutcheson, Sandy (eds.) (1972) *Communication in Face to Face Interaction.* Harmondsworth: Penguin.

Leigh, David (1991) *A Practical Approach to Group Training.* London: Kogan Page.

Loftus, Elizabeth (1980) *Memory.* Reading, Massachusetts: Addison-Wesley.

Mager, Robert F. (1990) *Developing Attitude Toward Learning.* London: Kogan Page.

Mager, Robert F. (1990) *Making Instruction Work.* London: Kogan Page.

Mager, Robert F. (1990) *Measuring Instructional Results.* London: Kogan Page.

Mager, Robert F. (1990) *Preparing Instructional Objectives.* London: Kogan Page.

Mager, Robert F. and Beach, Kenneth M. (1967) *Developing Vocational Instruction.* Belmont, California: Lake Publishing.

Mager, Robert F. and Pipe, Peter (1990) *Analysing Performance Problems.* London: Kogan Page.

Naisbitt, John and Aburdene, Patricia (1985) *Re-inventing the Corporation.* New York: Warner Books, Inc.

Napier, John (1980) *Hands.* New York: Pantheon Books.

Olmstead, Michael S. (1968) *The Small Group.* New York: Random House.

Ostrander, Sheila and Schroeder, Lynn (1979) *Super-learning.* New York: Delta.

Parnes, Sidney (1981) *The Magic of Your Mind*. Buffalo: Creative Education Foundation and Bearly.

Pascale, Richard Tanner and Athos, Anthony G. (1981) *The Art of Japanese Management*. New York: Simon and Schuster.

Pearce, Joseph Chilton (1976) *The Crack in the Cosmic Egg*. New York: Pocket Books.

Peters, Thomas J. and Waterman, Robert H. (1982) *In Search of Excellence*. New York: Harper & Row.

Rogers, Carl R. (1969) *Freedom to Learn*. Columbus: Charles E. Merrill.

Rogers, Jennifer (1973) *Adults Learning*. Harmondsworth: Penguin.

Segalowitz, Sid J. (1983) *Two Sides of the Brain*. Englewood Cliffs: Prentice-Hall.

Sexton-Lanning, Linda (1988) *Teaching Computers*. Winnipeg: Learning Publications.

Skinner, B.F. (1968) *The Technology of Teaching*. New York: Appleton-Century-Crofts.

Stammers, Robert and Patrick, John (1975) *The Psychology of Training*. London: Methuen.

Suessmuth, Patrick (1986) *Training Ideas Found Useful Part 3*. Winnipeg: Paracan Publications.

Taylor, Gordon Rattray (1979) *The Natural History of the Mind*. New York: E.P. Dutton.

Toffler, Alvin (1990) *Power Shift*. New York: Bantam Books.

Toffler, Alvin (1980) *The Third Wave*. New York: William Morrow.

Tyler, Ralph W. (1949) *Basic Principles of Curriculum and Instruction*. Chicago: University of Chicago.

Wittrock, M.C (ed.) (1977) *The Human Brain*. Englewood Cliffs: Prentice-Hall.

Wolfe, Jeremy M. (ed.) (1986) *The Mind's Eye. Readings from Scientific American*. New York: W.H. Freeman and Company.

Young, J.Z. (1978) *Programs of the Brain*. Oxford: Oxford University Press.

Index